IN CHRIST, I

IN CHRIST, IN COLOSSAE

Sociological Perspectives on Colossians

Derek J. Tidball

17 16 15 14 13 12 11   7 6 5 4 3 2 1

First published 2011 by Paternoster
Paternoster is an imprint of Authentic Media Limited
Presley Way, Crownhill, Milton Keynes, MK8 0ES
www.authenticmedia.co.uk

British Library Cataloguing in Publication Data

A catalogue record for this book is available from the
British Library

ISBN 978-1-84227-736-2

Cover design by David McNeill
Printed and bound in Great Britain by Bell and Bain, Glasgow

Contents

Preface   ix
Abbreviations   xi
Map 1. Asia Minor: Major Trade Routes   xiii
Map 2. Lycus Valley   xiii

1 **Why Sociological Perspectives on Colossians?**
   Introduction and Orientation   **1**
   Getting Our Bearings   1
   Previous Studies on the Sociology of Colossians   4
       Margaret MacDonald   5
       Clinton Arnold   8
       Colossians Remixed   10
   The Authorship and Dating of Colossians   11
   Conclusion   12

2 **Colossae: Its History, People and Church**   **13**
   Colossae and the Lycus Valley   13
   Colossae and Its History   14
   Colossae and Its People   16
       General orientation   16
       Jewish population   19
       Named individuals in the church   20
       The barbarians and Scythians   24
       Other factors   25
   Conclusion   26

3 **Conversion: How and Why People Became**
   Christians in Colossae   **28**
   The Religious Milieu in Colossae   28

Sociological Understanding of Conversion in the
   New Testament Period   31
   Recent sociological discussions about the nature of
     conversion   31
   The value of structuration theory   33
Application to Colossians   36
   'This you learned from Epaphras' (1:7)   36
   'He has rescued us . . . transferred us' (1:13)   37
   'As you therefore have received Christ Jesus the
     Lord' (2:6)   40
   'Put to death . . . clothe yourself with' (3:5,12)   41
Why Did Christianity Prove Attractive to Converts?   43
Conclusion   47

**4 Identity: The Construction of Personal and Social
   Identity**   **48**
The Construction of Identity in Contemporary
   Sociological Thought   49
Application to New Testament Studies   52
Social Identity in the Greco-Roman World   56
Colossian Christian Identity: Unimportant Factors   58
Colossian Christian Identity: Important Factors   60
   The problem and the strategy   60
   The only category that matters: 'in Christ'   61
   A different perspective: the proposal of Van
     Broekhoven   64
Conclusion   66

5 Theology: The Social Construction of Belief   **68**
The Sociological Perspective   68
The Social Construction of Belief   69
Initial Application to the Apostolic Gospel   73
Application to Colossians   75
   The maintenance mechanisms of Colossian theology   76
   The construction of Colossian theology   80
Conclusion   91

6 Institutionalization: From Charisma to Institution   **92**
From Max Weber to Bengt Holmberg   92
   Max Weber   92

Peter Berger and Thomas Luckmann 95
Thomas O'Dea 96
Bengt Holmberg 99
Institutionalization in the Pauline Churches: The work
of Margaret MacDonald 102
Application to Colossians 108
Charisma 108
Sect 110
Ritual 112
Doctrine 114
Ethics 115
Conclusion 116

7 **Household: Its Significance for Ethics, Mission**
and Organization 118
The Significance of the Household in the Greco-
Roman World 118
Households in the New Testament and at Colossae 119
The Colossian Household Ethical Code 121
Its originality 121
Regressive or progressive? 123
The Social and Missionary Implications of the
Household in Early Christianity 127
Implications for mission 127
Implications for conversion 129
Implications for social integration 130
Implications for leadership 131
Conclusion 134

8 **Culture: Values and Arrangements** 135
Honour and Shame 136
Patrons, Brokers and Clients 139
Social roles in the early Mediterranean world 139
Application to Colossians 140
The Body: Physical and Symbolic 143
Purity: Clean and Unclean 146
Limited Good 148
Reading 149
Conclusion 152

9 Concluding Comments   **154**

Bibliography   159
Endnotes   172

Preface

As I write a younger brother has just been unexpectedly and controversially elected to lead the British Labour Party, when it was widely anticipated that his older brother would assume the role. Colossians and Ephesians strike me as brothers, and until recently Colossians has been comparatively neglected in favour of what is often considered to be the more theologically mature (though not chronologically older) letter to Ephesians. But younger brothers have a way of capturing attention and recently Colossians has been well served by commentators, and rightly so. Colossians contains some of the richest theological concepts and practical insights to be found in the New Testament.

Most commentators, however, live almost exclusively in the realm of ideas and are content endlessly to discuss the philosophic background to the so-called problem that is addressed in Colossians and that of the high theology that the letter adopts. Many lose sight of the fact that this letter was written to farmers and traders in wool who would have had no formal education and many of whom would have been illiterate. The readers were ordinary people – not post-Enlightenment theological graduates – eking out an existence in a precarious world. They did not read it in a vacuum but as people who had been shaped by the realities of their social lives and moulded by the social forces and currents at work in their culture. There is room, then, to shed light on the letter by reading it through sociological eyes and that is what I seek to do in this book.

Rather than writing a sociological commentary, my aim has been to explore, from a critical standpoint, a number of sociological themes, models and perspectives that are relevant to

Colossians. Since the discipline of sociology is still a largely unknown field among New Testament scholars, although better known that it was, little prior sociological knowledge is assumed and I have made the deliberate choice to introduce the various perspectives in some detail before applying them to Colossians. I hope this fulfils the general aim of whetting the appetite and showing the relevance of reading the New Testament sociologically, as well as the particular aim of illuminating Colossians. Because I have adopted a thematic approach and sought to make each chapter stand alone, there is some overlap on occasions even though I have sought to keep this to a minimum.

The book has been gestating for some time. It was probably supervising Jonathan Green's MA dissertation in 2002 that put it on my agenda. It was only after writing my manuscript that I looked again at his dissertation and realized what a subconscious influence it must have exercised on my thinking. Thank you, Jonathan! I owe a debt of gratitude to Mike Lowe who produced the maps with great efficiency. I am grateful for the use of the libraries at Spurgeon's College, St John's College, Nottingham, and London School of Theology and also, once more, to Jenny Aston for her detailed eye on my script. My other debts are numerous but I have tried to acknowledge my scholarly debts where I was conscious of them and apologize for any that I have inadvertently missed. In spite of those debts, the responsibility for what is written, as authors now customarily say, is mine.

Derek Tidball, Leicester, September 2010

Abbreviations

ABD	*Anchor Bible Dictionary*, 6 vols, ed. D.N. Freedman (New York: Doubleday, 1992)
ASR	*American Sociological Review*
BibInt	*Biblical Interpretation*
BNTC	Black's New Testament Commentaries
BTB	*Biblical Theology Bulletin*
DNTB	*Dictionary of New Testament Background*, ed. C.A. Evans and S.E. Porter (Downers Grove: Inter-Varsity Press, 2000)
DPL	*Dictionary of Paul and His Letters*, ed. G.F. Hawthorne, R.P. Martin and D.G. Reid (Downers Grove: Inter-Varsity Press, 1993)
ICC	International Critical Commentary
Int	*Interpretation*
JAAR	*Journal of the American Academy of Religion*
JBL	*Journal of Biblical Literature*
JSNT	*Journal for the Study of the New Testament*
JSNTSup	Journal for the Study of New Testament: Supplement Series
JSOT Press	Journal for the Study of Old Testament Press
JSOTSup	Journal for the Study of Old Testament: Supplement
JSSR	*Journal for the Scientific Study of Religion*
LNTS	Library of New Testament Studies
NICNT	New International Commentary on the New Testament
NIGTC	New International Greek Testament Commentary
NovT	*Novum Testamentum*
NTS	*New Testament Studies*

PNTC	Pillar New Testament Commentary
SBL	Society for Biblical Literature
SBLDS	Society for Biblical Literature: Dissertation Series
SBLMS	Society for Biblical Literature: Monograph Series
SJLA	Studies in Judaism in Late Antiquity
SNTS MS	Society of New Testament Studies: Monograph Series
SNTW	Studies of the New Testament and its World
SP	Sacred Pagina Commentary Series
TNIV	Today's New International Version
TNTC	Tyndale New Testament Commentaries
WBC	World Biblical Commentary

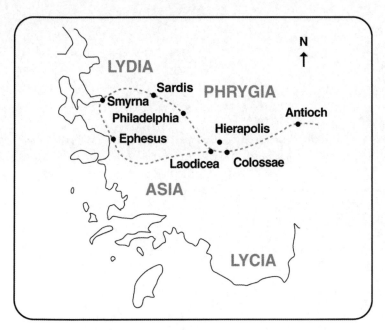

Asia Minor: Major Trade Routes

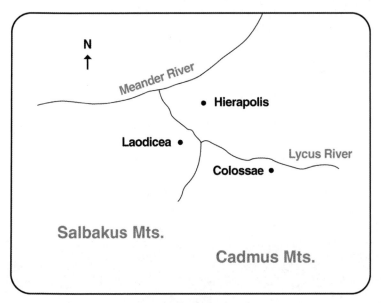

Lycus Valley

1

Why Sociological Perspectives on Colossians? Introduction and Orientation

Getting Our Bearings

'Colossians could fairly be described as the most intriguing of the Pauline letters.'[1] This verdict by James Dunn would be shared by many for several reasons. First, the short letter to the Colossians sets out some of the most developed theology in New Testament literature. Its exposition of the person of Christ as a cosmic ruler and of the Christian believer as being already 'raised with Christ' (3:1) advance Christian understanding beyond its previous limits and anticipate the even grander claims of its companion letter to the Ephesians. Second, it is written to warn its readers that their belief in 'the gospel' (1:23) is in danger of being corrupted by false teaching, though it presents us with only a tantalizing glimpse of the nature of the threat which they face, with the result that much ink has been spilled trying to identify those who would destabilize the Colossians' faith. Throw into the mix, third, the thought that the style and vocabulary of Colossians[2] have suggested to some that it is not written by the apostle Paul but originates after his time, and it is easy to see why it has been subject to a great deal of interest among scholars.[3]

For all the intrigue, however, attempts to interpret Colossians often seem to suffer from a two-fold failure. First, there is what might be called the 'ideational fallacy' whereby ideas are seen to have a life of their own and come into being as a result of intellectual discussion and then become determinative of belief.[4] Stephen Barton has rightly pointed out that this is a reductionist approach to theology which leaves our understanding deficient.[5] The theology of Colossians did not emerge as a result of pure intellectual debate but developed, as did all the other New Testament letters, as a result of the apostles grappling on the front line of missionary advance with the urgent pastoral questions thrown up by the churches they planted.

Second, and not unrelatedly, many scholars fail to bear in mind the original readership of the letter and convey the impression that its recipients were high-flying students in the theological faculties of the world's best universities. They see the readers as if they were made in their own image. In doing so they commit what has been called the 'docetic fallacy' and strip the readers of their real humanity, show little understanding of the social context or of ways in which the social norms, the community's needs and real-life conflicts are managed.[6]

One of the most intriguing aspects of Colossians is that its highly developed theology was addressed to people who were farmers, shepherds, wool dyers and market traders – ordinary men and women, concerned to make a living (probably it would be correct to say, 'scrape a living') so they could survive in a very precarious world.[7] This is not to say that they were unintelligent. Some of the most intelligent people I have known were not formally educated but self-taught coalminers who developed a thirst for learning as a result of their Methodist roots. It is rather to comment on the sort of intelligence they would have had and the nature of the world in which they lived. It was a practical intelligence. The grand ideas with which they would have wrestled in the church in Colossae would have involved a thoroughly 'down-to-earth'[8] approach to the practical issues of everyday living. Unless we take the readers and their circumstances into account our interpretation is liable to miss the significance of what is being said.

Sociologists are quite as capable of committing both the ideational and docetic fallacies as other academics, and of losing sight of real people in their discussion of explanations, in their proposing of models and their development of theories. But, given that the *raison d'être* of sociology is to seek to understand social relationships and to explain their common patterns and changing nature over time, they, at least in principle, stand a better chance than those who are immersed solely in the realm of ideas of not losing sight of 'real' people in their discussions.

Most commentaries on Colossians helpfully begin by describing the town and its history (ground which we will cover in the next chapter) but then do not connect the subsequent exposition of the letter to what has been said in the introduction. By using the tools of sociological analysis we hope to illuminate the text itself and shed light on both what lies behind it and how it functions, always keeping its readers and their situation in focus.

Sociology offers no single perspective in interpreting social relationships but offers a variety of methods, models and theories to explain social behaviour. In recent years a growing volume of literature has applied various sociological approaches to the New Testament with varying degrees of success.[9] Most valuable, perhaps, has been the work of the 'Social Context Group' who, using chiefly the tools of anthropology, have advanced our understanding of early Mediterranean people and their culture, although even this has been not without controversy.[10] They have made a special contribution in challenging the individualistic assumptions we late moderns bring to our interpretations of the text. Yet, the application of some present-day models, such as class, status, or organizational theory, has sometimes proved problematic and needs to be used with care. Social historians have been particularly sceptical, and rightly so, about reading back contemporary patterns to the ancient world and prefer to deal in the particulars of events rather than generalizations. But generalizations have their place. There is value in the close-up photograph presented by the social historian, but there is also value in the more distant, wide-angled photograph presented by sociologists. The latter must be consistent with the former but is not in competition or conflict with it.

No single perspective is ever adequate to explain human behaviour because all human behaviour is complex and multi-layered.

Max Weber, the greatest of the founding fathers of sociology, was surely right in seeing that 'every generalisation was a precarious victory over the infinite complexity of the facts'.[11] Generalizations should be treated with a certain amount of caution and no single generalization is ever sufficient. Nonetheless, they have their place and give us a true, if partial, insight into reality. Human behaviour manifestly demonstrates recurring arrangements as well as unique circumstances, common patterns as well as singular actions.

Consequently, the approach taken in this book is to view the letter to the Colossians through various sociological lenses to bring its teaching into focus. They act as filters through which we may interpret its meaning. It uses more than one lens because no single lens provides us with a comprehensive picture. Various models or perspectives are called into play in order that we might gain a variety of insights and a fuller understanding of the church there. Some lenses will provide a sharper picture than others and we may therefore conclude that some are more useful than others.

Previous Studies on the Sociology of Colossians

By the start of the twenty-first century, a variety of sociological theories and models had been applied to the books of the New Testament. Some, like 1 Corinthians, have provoked a wealth of sociological comment and analysis, starting, in this case, with Gerd Theissen's seminal work, *The Social Setting of Pauline Christianity*, which first appeared in English in 1982,[12] up to and beyond David Horrell's more recent, *The Social Ethos of the Corinthians Correspondence: Interest and Ideology from 1 Corinthians to 1 Clement*,[13] with numerous journal articles in between and since. The same could be said of most New Testament books, although Colossians has been less well served than others. As yet, for example, although social-science commentaries have been published on most of the New Testament, including Revelation, a commentary on Colossians and Ephesians, and the General Epistles, is still awaited.[14]

There are probably several reasons for the relative neglect of Colossians.

1. Paul never visited Colossae and was not directly involved in the founding of the church there, and so it lacks the immediacy and even the wider dimension of relationships of some of his other writings.
2. Colossians yields less sociological data than other letters, especially when compared to the Corinthians Correspondence or Philemon.
3. Colossae declined in importance as a city after it experienced an earthquake in 61 AD[15] and no longer played the significant role that other cities, such as nearby Ephesus or Laodicea, did.
4. Unlike Ephesus and many other New Testament sites, Colossae has only recently begun to be excavated and little has been learned so far from archaeological evidence. We have to rely on evidence from the surrounding area, which almost certainly applies to Colossae as well, but the absence of actual local evidence inevitably creates hesitancy in the claims that can be made.
5. The uncertainty over the date and authorship of the letter means we can be less confident about the relevance of some sociological approaches than we can be in other contexts.

The relative neglect of this intriguing letter is nonetheless somewhat surprising since what has been published in the area demonstrates the fruitfulness of the field. Two scholars who have contributed significant works for any sociological understanding of Colossians are Margaret Y. MacDonald and Clinton Arnold. Both have laid good foundations for further research.

Margaret MacDonald

Margaret MacDonald published her doctoral thesis in 1988 in which she employed sociological tools to understand the process of transformation that the early church underwent from its formation in the middle of the first century into the second.[16] The theory she chose as her primary perspective was that of institutionalization. MacDonald builds on the work of Berger and Luckmann, who in turn were building on the work of Max Weber.[17] The theory proposes that what begins as a free and unstructured movement, led by a charismatic leader, soon settles into more of a routine and develops structure, as actions are repeated and become typical, in contrast to one-off actions, and as habits (or habituated behaviour) begin to emerge. The questions any such movement faces are not asked *de novo* each time but, after a time, are met by ready-made answers. The process of institutionalization is advanced by the challenges thrown up when the original charismatic leader either passes from the scene, or merely becomes weary and less active. As this process unfolds, the movement becomes less flexible, less open to novel directions, and more fixed in its structures, customs and patterns of behaviour. This process of a movement 'ageing' is known as institutionalization.

The process of institutionalization has implications not only for the ways things are done but also for the attitudes and motivations of those involved. The founding generation are usually very focused and indifferent to personal reward. Those who join later are typically less single-minded and more concerned about rewards and their rights. As time passes questions are also raised about why things are done in a certain way and the rightness of views that are held, leading to a discussion of what is termed 'legitimation'.

The Pauline churches make an ideal case for a study of institutionalization, especially if you believe, as MacDonald does, that Colossians was written by a disciple of Paul, either just before or just after his death, and that Ephesians and the Pastoral Letters were definitely post-Pauline.

MacDonald divides the Pauline letters into three groups that reflect an early, middle or late phase in the early churches' life. MacDonald calls the first, which relates to those letters of Paul that all agree to be genuine, the community-building phase; the second, which involves Colossians and Ephesians, is called the community-stabilizing phase; and, the third, which refers to the Pastoral Letters, is called the community-protecting phase of institutionalization. She then examines each phase from the viewpoint of what it says about attitudes to the world/ethics; ministry; ritual and belief. The result is an insightful study with many implications for the study of Colossians, even if it suffers perhaps from being occasionally contrived to fit the scheme of institutionalization.

Subsequently, MacDonald applied her skills to a full-length commentary on Colossians and Philemon, which is distinctive in its approach from other commentaries in that it capitalizes on a sociological interpretation of the letters. She situates this commentary in the context of her earlier study of institutionalization and aims particularly to investigate the changes and development that the letter reveals in the second phase of the life of the Pauline churches. 'Insights from Weberian sociology,' she writes, 'are employed to help us comprehend the challenges faced by the Pauline circle in the face of the imprisonment and death of its central leader.'[18] In fact, a plethora of sociological tools is brought to bear on the text, even if institutionalization remains of primary interest throughout. So in this commentary we encounter concepts of charisma, legitimacy, sectarianism, in-group and out-group, boundaries, rituals, social construction of theology, liminality, symbolism, initiation rites and social roles, alongside a discussion of the social values of patronage, purity, honour and gender.

Given MacDonald's excellent work, why is another book on the sociology of Colossians necessary? Three reasons might be offered by way of defence. First, given the nature of a commentary much of the sociological insight MacDonald offers is scattered throughout her text and embedded in the midst of other comments. There is a place for a work that makes sociological perspectives explicit, draws them together, and brings them to the front of the stage rather than their being merely one actor, however important, among a somewhat crowded caste of theological tools. Second, by being primarily concerned to view Colossians from the perspective of institutionalization, MacDonald underrates, or even omits, some other sociological perspectives which can prove illuminating. Third, MacDonald's work, however seminal, is in need of critical wider discussion. Ben Witherington III, who has made an industry out of writing 'socio-rhetorical commentaries' and thus might be expected to be favourably disposed to MacDonald, suggests she 'relies too heavily on B. Malina and later cultural anthropological concepts and too little on actual social history tied to the period'.[19] Regardless of this, her work is stimulating for and of primary significance to any who want to read Colossians through sociological spectacles.

Clinton Arnold

Clinton Arnold's work is of a somewhat different kind. It is not essentially a sociological work but has major implications for the sociology of Colossians. His monograph, *The Colossian Syncretism*, is aimed at 'reconstructing the situation' that lay behind the false teaching that was making inroads among the believers in Colossae.[20] Initially focusing on the much-debated meaning of 'worship of angels', in Colossians 2:18, Arnold argues that angels were regularly called upon by the Jews of the Dispersion to provide protection. They were supplicated by name, as the various recovered papyri and amulets show. While in pure Judaism direct appeal may have been made exclusively to God, Arnold believes the evidence demonstrates that 'Many Jews were increasingly inclined to appeal to angels rather than to God for deliverance and for the provision of their needs. Angels were becoming mediators in a manner like the *angeloi* and *paredroi*[21] in pagan religion and magic'.[22]

Arnold sets out a huge amount of evidence that demonstrates that the existence of a cult of angels in Asia Minor was not confined to pagans but had infiltrated Jewish and Christian[23] worship as well. Unfortunately, the evidence is almost wholly from the surrounding area, including Ephesus and Laodicea, rather than Colossae itself,[24] and some of it from a later date. Even so, he contends that Colossian Christians would be subject to the same influences in their context and hence by the practices of folk religion we know about from nearby places later on. Then he writes:

> The history of the church at Colossae, not far from Laodicea, points to a special place the Christians there accorded one angelic mediator, the archangel Michael. Michael was believe to have saved the population of Colossae from inundation by the Lycus river by making a new opening in the bank that diverted the waters from the city. This is the legend behind the origin of the great church of Michael the Archistratēgos at Colossae. There was also a miraculous spring, made effective by Michael located between Colossae and Hierapolis at Chaeretopa. Allegedly, the spring healed all who called upon the name of the Father, Son and Spirit in the name of the archangel.[25]

Using this background and other evidence that exists about the nature of pagan worship, mystery religions (on which he bases a lot), wisdom philosophy and Judaism, Arnold then investigates in depth the wider description of the Colossian false teaching and concludes that the problem from which they are suffering is not that they have accepted wrong ideas, so much as they have been seduced into practising a folk religious version of their faith. They have mixed a pure worship and confession of Christ with all sorts of other less worthy beliefs and practices. 'Because we are in the domain of folk religion', he rightly understands, 'there is a significant overlap in the practices of these people coming from different backgrounds.'[26]

The appealing aspect of his exposition is that he demonstrates a realism about the way ordinary people practise their religion. Few people have a faith which is 'pure' and totally free from the contamination of other religious practices and beliefs in the culture that surrounds them. Most are syncretistic to one degree or another.[27] Even in the most doctrinally well taught and evangelical of churches, members mix popular superstition with what they think of as faith in Christ alone. Colossians, then, is addressed to Christians who are influenced by folk religion and contends for a purer understanding of Christ, his achievements on the cross and the implications for creation and for their lives. Their problem was that they had not yet realized the full and practical implications of the apostolic gospel.

Arnold's views have not commended themselves to all. Ben Witherington III says Arnold's case 'rests on some very questionable assumptions' and that he bases his conclusions on too little evidence.[28] Witherington believes that the description given in Colossians of the false teaching leads to understanding it as 'some sort of esoteric and mystical Jewish philosophy, perhaps lightly influenced by Greek philosophy'.[29] There are, of course, other explanations of the much-debated issue of the origin of the Colossians threat. DeMaris groups these explanations under the headings of Jewish Gnosticism, Gnostic Judaism and Hellenistic syncretism, in addition to Arnold's syncretism and Witherington's mystical Judaism.[30] Notwithstanding Witherington's criticisms, which point to the absence of precise confirming evidence rather than to the inherent weakness of Arnold's case, Arnold has the feel of entering under the skin of the original readers and of living in their world, rather than in the more rarefied air of cleaner academic debate whose atmosphere is chiefly composed of ideas. Arnold's research helps situate the flesh-and-blood readers of Colossians in the real world of their day and that is not an insignificant factor in judging whether an interpretation is credible or not.

Our intention here has not been to offer a thorough critique of the work of either MacDonald or Arnold but rather to introduce their work as making a major contribution to our task as we come at a sociology of Colossians from a different angle than they have done.

Colossians Remixed

Attention might be drawn, more briefly, to one other work that provides fresh sociological insight into Colossians. In *Colossians Remixed*,[31] Brian Walsh and Sylvia Keesmaat offer a rereading of Colossians for a post-modern culture. Their fresh reading of the text accomplishes two things. It provides a new interpretation of Colossians that sets it firmly in the context of living in the Roman Empire and then crosses the cultural divide to apply it to believers living in the context of contemporary power structures and idolatry. Second, it provides a model of apologetics and teaching for a post-modern generation in which being taught by an 'authority' is not as acceptable as it was in the age of modernity.

Their work is original and immensely stimulating. It highlights the radical nature of the teaching in Colossians. Whether the Roman Empire is as present in the thinking of the writer as Walsh and Keesmaat claim is a moot point. Various statements in the letter that they take as a reference to 'the Empire' may be as adequately interpreted as referring to the Jewish Scriptures alone.[32] And the unseen spirits may well be better understood as unseen malevolent spiritual powers, rather than 'rulers and authorities' being a way of speaking about the embodied and seen power structures of the empire.[33]

Colossians Remixed in some respects provides an example of a sociological take on Colossians but any sociology in it is implicit rather than explicit[34] and its interpretation is more political than sociological. It is, therefore, perhaps one step removed from our concerns in this book.

The Authorship and Dating of Colossians

It is reasonable to expect that a chapter of introduction and orientation will contain a comment on the authorship and dating of Colossians. The arguments for and against Pauline authorship are rehearsed in most standard commentaries, to which the reader is referred for the details. Colossians clearly is distinctive in its theology and language, but this does necessarily lead to the conclusion that Paul could not be its author. Language and styles change over time and the expression of theology varies according to the situation addressed. It is self-evidently written late in Paul's ministry, but probably before 61 AD when Colossae was most likely destroyed by an earthquake. Furthermore, it may have been actually penned by Timothy, who is mentioned in the opening greetings (1:1) under Paul's direction rather than in Paul's own hand (see 4:18). This could partly explain some of the differences in style and vocabulary, although not in thought. In the light of what we know of Paul's latter years, it was probably written from Rome. The associated letter of Philemon, which is usually considered genuinely Pauline, was certainly written from there.

Given this, although I recognize the date and authorship are matters of unresolved dispute, I shall call the author of the letter 'Paul' throughout, rather than 'the writer'. To refer to 'the writer' may be more inclusive of those who hold other interpretations but is somewhat stilted and impersonal. In doing this, I shall be reversing the advice given by Andrew Lincoln, who believes it to be pseudonymous and who therefore does use the term 'the writer'. He wrote, 'For those who disagree with such a stance on authorship, all that is necessary in most of what follows, is, of course, to make the mental substitution of "Paul" or "Timothy" or both for "the writer".'[35] This invitation is offered again, in reverse: all that is necessary is to make a mental substitution of 'the writer' for 'Paul' if your conclusion on authorship is different from mine.

Whatever one thinks of authorship, all are agreed that the letter must have been written within a narrow window towards the end, or just after the end, of Paul's life. In that regard, there is little difference to be taken into consideration in interpreting the letter through sociological eyes, although the genuineness of the authorship may have implications for the canonical authority of the letter.

Conclusion

In what follows we will first situate the letter of Colossians in what we know of the history of Colossae and its population. Then we will try out the various sociological lenses that are currently available to see if we can find a clear picture of the real people and the challenges to their faith they were facing.

2

Colossae: Its History, People and Church

The church at Colossae was a second-generation church. It was not founded by an apostle but by one of Paul's co-workers, Epaphras (1:7), whose home was there (4:12). The founding of the church, and those of nearby Laodicea and Hierapolis, would seem to be the result of the 'wide door for effective work' (1 Cor. 16:9) Paul mentioned while he was in Ephesus.[1] The name Epaphras, a shortened form of Epaphroditus,[2] was associated with the goddess Aphrodite, which suggests that his parents were not followers of Jesus Christ, at least when he was born.[3] We do not know how Epaphras became a believer but it is often assumed he was converted during Paul's time in Ephesus. Whether converted then or earlier, he became a member of Paul's missionary network and took the gospel with him when he returned home to a place which the apostles themselves would never personally reach with the good news.

Colossae and the Lycus Valley

By the time the letter was written, Colossae was a small and not very important town. On the western border of the region of Phrygia, in the west-central part of Asia Minor, it was situated 120 miles east of Ephesus, on what, for many years, had been a significant crossroads. The road connecting the western coast to the interior of Asia and the River Euphrates intersected at Colossae with the north-south road from Pergamon and Sardis to the Mediterranean coast. The main arterial road from Ephesus or Sardis to the east followed the Meander River. Approximately a hundred miles from its mouth on the western coast of Asia, this river was joined by one of its main tributaries, the Lycus River. Colossae lay on the south bank of the Lycus River, forming a triangle of cities with Laodicea and Hierapolis, which were located either side of the river ten miles or so downstream to the north west.

Standing at the head of a gorge, the valley in which Colossae was located was fertile and well irrigated. A stream divided the city into two, with brooks flowing to its west and east, both of which ran into the Lycus. So, 'the fertility of the district was and is unusually great'.[4] This made for rich pastures on which to graze large flocks of sheep and resulted in the production of wool of a superior quality that was particularly soft. Lightfoot points out how the rich minerals in the streams assisted in producing fabrics of a very fine quality. The three cities were known for the vibrancy of the colours of their cloth: scarlet and purple at Hierapolis; 'probably a glossy black' at Laodicea; and a particular shade of purple at Colossae.[5] According to Pliny, wool dyed purple was known as 'Colossian wool'.[6] In 401 BC, Colossae had been described as 'a prosperous and large'[7] city which had grown rich through the manufacture and trading of its specially dyed wool.

Lying at the foot of what is now known as Mount Honag Dagi, the city is now buried beneath a large mound. The remains of a theatre can be seen to the east, minus its rows of seats, together with a burial site to the north, and a few pillars which would have formed a processional route out of the city. Otherwise, as yet, few archaeological treasures have been unearthed in what Michael Trainor describes as this 'magnificently unspectacular' site.[8]

Colossae and Its History

The history of Colossae is rehearsed in most commentaries on the letter. From ancient times it had been an important city; more important in fact than Laodicea and Hierapolis which were eventually to eclipse it. When Xerxes' army marched down the road to the interior in 481 BC, Heroditus spoke of it as 'a great city of Phrygia'.[9] Xenophon made a similar comment about it in 401 BC.[10]

Four or five centuries later it was a very different story. Although Pliny the Elder spoke of it in his *Natural History*, which was completed in 77 AD, as among the famous cities, this is probably a reference to what it had been, rather than what it still was when he was writing.[11] By Paul's time the town had declined in size, prosperity and significance. Several decades before the Pauline mission in Asia, Strabo had referred to it in his *Geography* as 'a small town'.[12] Although the reference is disputed, it probably correctly indicates the size and significance of Colossae at the time.

The decline is accounted for by the rerouting of the east-west arterial road, which was moved to the west of Colossae. Consequently the fortunes of Laodicea prospered, at the expense of Colossae which became more isolated. Rome smiled on Laodicea, enhancing its significance further by designating it as the seat of government and finance for the district.[13] By the time the letter to the Colossians was written, then, it was a town of somewhat faded glory.

A further factor is important for our understanding of the letter. The district was subject to earthquakes.[14] Tacitus records that in 60–61 AD an earthquake destroyed Laodicea, and although Colossae is not specifically mentioned it is more than likely that it too suffered significant damage at the time.[15] Eusebius recorded that earthquakes destroyed Laodicea, Hierapolis and Colossae in 63–4 AD.[16] It is generally believed, however, that this refers to the same episode which Tacitius records rather than a different one. The significance of this for any understanding of the sociology of Colossians lies in the sense of insecurity and the fear of being subject to malevolent powers that the citizens of Colossians may have felt.

There is evidence from inscriptions and coins that Colossae continued to exist for some time after this period. But, whereas 'Laodicea was soon restored without any outside assistance from Nero or the Romans . . . Colossae never regained its place of prominence.'[17] Some centuries after the New Testament era, Colossae relocated, because of continuing earthquake activity, to nearby Chonae (Honza).

J.B. Lightfoot's endearing verdict has commended itself widely: 'Without doubt Colossae was the least important church to which any epistle of St Paul was addressed.'[18]

Colossae and Its People

General orientation

Care must be taken in referring to Colossae as a city. It was, but it was not like the places we call cities today. It was a pre-industrial city and far less complex than contemporary cities both in its social organization and its infrastructure. Like most cities, Colossae would have been connected to the surrounding countryside and villages, rather than being sharply cut off from them, and served as something of a centre for them. Some cities, such as Rome, were 'consumer cities' but Colossae was a 'producer city', one of the many which would have supplied the 'consumer cities' with their needs. The vast majority of its population would have served a very small elite who would have lived centrally. The poor and average people, on the other hand, lived on the periphery and did not benefit from the prosperity they produced in any sense in proportion to the effort they expended.[19]

Sufficient has been said to recognize that the population of Colossae was composed of ordinary men and women who earned their living by farming crops, looking after sheep, shearing, dyeing and in other ways processing their wool, and selling it and the textiles produced from it in the marketplace. Literacy is likely to have been as low as 10–15 per cent of the population since farmers had no reason for reading.[20] It was essentially an oral culture. Laodicea could boast its civic status. Hierapolis could boast its hot springs, which were much sought after for medicinal purposes, and also that it was the home of Epictetus, the renowned Stoic philosopher and moralist, who was born there in 55 AD. Colossae could make no such boasts. We know of no renowned educational, philosophical, medical or administrative claim to fame around the time when the letter to Colossians was written. It was distinguished by its ordinariness.

What more can be said about the citizens? While little is known specifically about Colossae, there is no reason to assume that it would differ much in its social make-up from most communities of the Roman era.[21] The vast majority of the population would have been 'low born' (*humiliories*) and ranked low among the social strata. In the empire generally the upper stratum was composed of a very tiny minority, usually estimated as between 1 per cent and 3 per cent of a city's population. Status related to birth rather than to wealth. In Colossae, there would have been local magistrates and councillors who formed the lowest rung of the ladder of privilege in Roman society (the Order of Decurions) whose membership and role were clearly defined and whose privileges were protected by law. But they would have been very few in number. The Order of Decurions had only 100,000 members throughout the empire.

The rest formed the great bulk of the peasant society of the day, whether freeborn men and women, merchants, traders, artisans, day labourers or slaves. Slaves would have probably made up a third of the population of the city.[22] They worked alongside a smaller number of people whose occupations required intelligence and skill, such as those in medicine or education, but were not greatly distinguished from them socially. Obviously some owned the land which was farmed and would employ others, but care must be taken not to mistake these for the middle classes of contemporary times. Great wealth was not required to employ at least one slave to help in the household. The picture of slave-owning households in the first century should not be confused with the plantation owners who subjected multitudes to slavery in the eighteenth and nineteenth centuries. The bottom of the social pile was mostly made up of 'degraded' people whose occupations or lifestyle made them subject to suspicion and marginalization. Beneath even them were a few whose lives were considered expendable.

All are agreed that the status and economic systems of the time were designed to be deliberately static. Although there was inevitably some fluidity, the social system was essentially rigid. Your place in society was fixed.

Estimates vary as to the significance of this, depending on whether people are primarily talking about social status or economic experience. Some interpret the lot of the majority as 'in the middle levels'. Recently a consensus has developed that the early church was much more socially mixed and included a good number from the middle strata and so was less like the slave movement that it was once commonly believed to be.[23] Osiek and Balch, for example, speak for many when they write: 'It is in the middle levels (but not the middle class), between the elites and those of no status at all, that most early Christians are to be located; urban artisans, merchants, traders, slaves, freedmen and freedwomen, most of whom would fall into the categories of *inferiors* and *humiliories*, though with some members and families of distinction, and probably also some statusless persons.'[24]

Justin Meggitt does not essentially disagree with the assessment of the type of person or their occupation that composed the early Christian churches. They may well have reflected the normal social mix of the towns and cities in which they dwelt. But such arguments, he believes, can lead to a very distorted picture of the world of Paul's time, of the lot of the early Christians and, specifically, of Paul himself.[25] Viewing their lives from the economic perspective, rather than that of status, the above picture is far too idealistic.

The economy of the Greco-Roman world was pre-industrial and underdeveloped.[26] It created enormous disparities of wealth but the overwhelming majority of people, such as those mentioned in the occupations above, lived lives 'dominated by work and the struggle to exist'. They repeatedly experienced toil, hardship and hunger. 'Over 99% of the Empire's population', Meggitt concludes, 'could expect little more from life than abject poverty.'[27] Nearly 90 per cent lived off agriculture, and agriculture was primitive, inefficient and undeveloped. Any manufacturing was undertaken by independent artisans running their own very modest outfits. 'The skilled artisans were the most wealthy among the *plebs urbana*, yet their trades seem to have only allowed them to live at, or slightly above, subsistence level.'[28] Semi-skilled or unskilled workers faced even greater hardship and insecurity. Unemployment was an ever-present threat. The market was not a free market but a politically controlled market, with those in power determining prices, taxes and wages. Clothes were expensive, and housing anything but plentiful with many living in slum conditions. Meggitt summarizes the position like this: 'The under-developed, pre-industrial economy of the Greco-Roman world created enormous disparities of wealth, and with this inequitable, rigid system the non-elite of the cities lived brutal and frugal lives, characterised by struggle and impover-ishment.'[29]

Meggitt's work is helpful in setting the discussion of the social level of the early Christians in its economic context and not just the status context of the day. If we fail to do this, our discussions of social stratification become free-floating and ultimately devoid of much meaning. His work confronts us with the harsh real-ities of life for the majority in the Roman Empire. Discussions of the early churches as having a base in relatively 'wealthy' house-holds may lead us to imagine a level of comfort which did not exist. Yet, in assessing what confidence can be based in his research and conclusions, Meggitt himself becomes somewhat diffident. 'To speak,' he writes, 'of a "conclusion" to our quest is a little premature. I certainly believe in the fundamental veracity of my thesis.'[30] He acknowledges that economic factors are not the only factors determinative of the reality of life but they do play a prominent role in shaping life. His work, which is based on persuasive evidence, offers a necessary corrective to earlier studies which, by their failure to take the economic context into account, can lead to too rosy a picture of life in the Greco-Roman world.

Jewish population

Colossae had a significant Jewish population. Antiochus III had settled two thousand Jewish families in the area of Phrygia and its neighbour Lydia in 213 BC as a means of overcoming local sedition.[31] It would be surprising if Colossae had not received some of these families and, as Lightfoot remarked: 'A Jewish set-tlement once established, the influx of their fellow-countrymen would be rapid and continuous.'[32] By Roman times the Jews were there in large numbers. Based on the confiscated temple tax that the Jews had hoped to send to Jerusalem in 62–61 BC, it is esti-mated that there were 11,000, or even 14,000, Jewish men (exclud-ing women and children) in the district of Laodicea.[33] Whatever the size of the population of Colossae at the time, 'that would make Colossian Jews a substantial and possibly influential ethnic minority'.[34]

Evidence suggests that 'the presence of local Jewish communities was often a real factor in the life of the early Christian churches in Asia Minor' generally. They maintained their identity by paying the annual temple tax and honouring the Torah. Other key practices included observance of the Sabbath, of food laws and of 'ancestral traditions'.[36] These customs, and others, are all reflected in the teaching that Paul's opponents were advocating according to Colossians.

Named individuals in the church

Even if there are no sure or explicit guides to the population of Colossae outside the New Testament, there are indicators of a few of its residents embedded in the letter to Colossians itself, of which the first to receive attention must be Epaphras.

Epaphras is mentioned in 1:7 and 4:12–13 where he is spoken of as 'one of you'. His name, as we have already indicated, suggests a Gentile, whose family were happy to associate their child with the worship of Aphrodite. It was a common name and belonged to people who engaged in a wide range of occupations, 'from servile to elite',[37] with the result that it is impossible to locate Epaphras in the social hierarchy of his day with any certainty. In spite of this, Trainor advances several reasons why Epaphras was likely to have been a slave.[38]

1. The name was frequently associated with slaves.
2. Slaves 'were integral to the domestic landscape and presumed to have been members of Jesus households'. Trainor thinks that the listing of Epaphras as the first to send greetings to Philemon, in Philemon 23, confirms this. One of Philemon's trusted slaves was likely to be mentioned before others in any such list.
3. The extended discussion of slavery in the household code (3:22–5) – an issue to which we will return – and the mention of Epaphras shortly afterwards lends further support, in Trainor's view, to his interpretation.

Truth to tell, none of this evidence is very strong and all that we can honestly say is that Epaphras could have been a slave, but it must remain a matter of conjecture.

Whatever Epaphras' social background, we know that he was a close associate of Paul and warmly spoken of by the apostle (4:12–13), who uses a couple of *syn* words to speak of him. Epaphras is Paul's 'fellow-servant' (*syndoulos*) (1:7) and 'fellow-prisoner' (*synaichmalōtos*) (Phlm. 23), and is probably even included in the expression 'co-worker' (*synergos*) (Col. 4:11).[39] The sharing of Paul's imprisonment was likely to have been a voluntary act of companionship rather than an involuntary act resulting from a criminal conviction. It is unlikely that the term is being used metaphorically to indicate that Epaphras (and Aristarchus) was a fellow captive of Christ. Given the importance of the value of honour in Paul's world, the voluntary sharing of Paul's shame would indicate a very close relationship between them.[40]

Since Epaphras came from Colossae he was obviously enmeshed in a variety of local social networks, ranging from that of his family to that of the wider community, so he was in an ideal position to spread the gospel. Given that he was also closely committed to Paul, Trainor justifiably concludes that he 'became the guarantor of the authenticity of Paul's teaching, the faithful interpreter of his teaching for the next generation of Jesus groups, and the tangible link back to Paul and the apostolic tradition founded on the experience of Jesus Christ'.[41] Though based in Colossae, it would seem from 4:13 that his ministry extended to Laodicea and Hierapolis as well.

The other names Paul mentions as being associated with Colossae, as opposed to those to whom he sends them greetings, are Onesimus (4:9), Nympha (4:15), Philemon and Archippus (4:16). Of these Onesimus is the most straightforward. We know from the companion letter to Philemon[42] that Onesimus was a slave who ran away from his master and became a Christian through Paul's influence in Rome (Phlm. 10). He became Paul's servant there and instead of being labelled 'a runaway slave', had, in Paul's thinking, now earned the title of 'faithful and beloved brother'. The useless one had been transformed by the gospel and become 'useful', which is the literal meaning of his name (Phlm. 11). The time came, however, for Paul to send him back to Philemon, his master, to face the music, but Paul appeals to Philemon to receive him back not as a fugitive slave but as a brother in Christ (Phlm. 16). Onesimus is described in Colossians 4:9 as 'one of you'. The phrase carries more freight than merely being a reference to his place of origin. Rather it suggests that Onesimus belonged to the people there as never before.

It is evident from this that Philemon's household was located at Colossae. Dunn portrays him as 'well-to-do' with a house large enough to host the church, provide a guest room, and to be the owner of more than one slave, since if Onesimus had been his only slave that would have been reflected in the letter to Philemon. Dunn also infers, on the basis of Philemon 17–18, that he was 'probably a successful businessman' who travelled a good deal. After his conversion (probably through Paul)[43] he became an active partner in Paul's missionary enterprise and provided hospitality for the church in Colossae. All of this seems a reasonable portrait to draw from the evidence, providing one bears in mind Meggitt's strictures and understands that his business activities, size of house, ownership of slaves and ability to travel were indicators of relative wealth rather than anything necessarily substantial.

The puzzle is why Philemon is not mentioned in the letter to the Colossians, as one would expect, especially since the church met in his house and was under his patronage (Phlm. 2). He and Apphia, who was probably his wife, were obviously generous in using their resources for their fellow believers. The silence regarding Philemon is compounded by the fact that Nympha, the hostess of the church down the road in Laodicea, is addressed in Colossians (4:15).

The most straightforward answer is that the letter to Colossians accompanied the note to Philemon so there was no need for him to be addressed again in the general letter to the church. The traditional view was that the letter to Philemon was an appendix to Colossians, so any reference to Philemon would be redundant. Whether this is so, or not, depends on one's view of the dating of the two letters and the solving of a couple of other problems.[44] Where Paul does address a householder in a letter to a congregation, as he does Stephanus in 1 Corinthians 16:15, it is because there was a particular need to encourage the believers to respect their leadership. No such need existed in Colossae where it would seem that Philemon's leadership was appreciated (Phlm. 4–7).

Many are dissatisfied with such an answer and piece it together with the other uncertainties that surround Colossians 4:15–16 in an attempt to find a solution to the question. John Knox,[45] for example, has suggested that Philemon lived in Laodicea and that the letter Paul addressed to him was the letter mentioned in 4:16 as 'the letter from Laodicea'. But this is highly improbable in view of what is said of Onesimus in 4:9.[46] Others, who assume Colossians to be written by one of Paul's later disciples, rather than the apostle himself, explain it in terms of the writer saying enough to lead people to think Paul wrote the letter but providing a clue, in this omission, that someone else was truly the author. The genuine Paul, they argue, would never have made such an omission.

We simply do not know why Philemon is not addressed personally in Colossians, but the absence of such a greeting does nothing to undermine the picture of Philemon as a relatively wealthy householder who hosted the church, or at least one gathering of it, in his house.[47]

The other person who is identified with Colossae is Archippus. He is generally assumed to be the son of Philemon on the basis of the reference to him alongside Philemon and Apphia in Philemon 2. There is no strong reason to doubt this assumption, which was held by some of the early church fathers although, because it is not explicitly stated, some suggest that Apphia may have been Philemon's sister and Archippus his brother rather than wife and son respectively. Still others think Archippus was merely a friend of Philemon's family.[48] Archippus is described in Philemon 2 as Paul's 'fellow-soldier' (*synstratiōtes*) and, like Epaphras, was evidently one of Paul's missionary agents.

Enigmatically, Archippus is told to 'complete the task that you have received in the Lord'. We can only speculate what that means. Was Archippus timid, youthful, lacking in courage, or liable to be distracted from ministry? Was there an urgent task which Paul had committed to him? Was it a general comment of encouragement, or did it relate to something specific? We simply cannot say. But the command clearly indicates that Archippus has a ministry in the church. The word used for his role is the word *diakonia*, which some take as evidence of him occupying the office of deacon. A few have even seen the grander offices of presbyter or bishop in the term. But to read such a formal office into the term which clearly indicates 'the service' rather than 'the diaconate' is not warranted by the text and is an anachronism.[49] Because Archippus is mentioned immediately after the reference to the letter to the Laodiceans, Lightfoot, among others, conjectured that Archippus' ministry was exercised in Laodicea rather than Colossae.[50] But this is an unnecessary inference. It is more likely that he had joined with Epaphras and his mother and father in forwarding the work of the gospel first in Colossae and then in the surrounding district.

The barbarians and the Scythians

Interesting changes occur between Paul's statement in Galatians 3:28 of equality before God and the version of the statement that occurs in Colossians 3:11. Both say there is no longer 'Jew or Greek', although in Colossians their order is reversed, which may suggest that the complexion of the church was predominantly Gentile rather than Jewish, and that the problem encountered in Colossae did not arise exclusively from the Judaism of the time, as it did in Galatia. The inclusion in Colossians of 'circumcised and uncircumcised' seems merely to parallel 'Greek and Jew' by way of explaining the great divide of the ancient world from a religious viewpoint, although they too occur in reverse order. Both say there was neither 'slave [n]or free' in Christ. The gender distinction mentioned in Galatians is omitted from Colossians. Why this should be so is only a matter of speculation but perhaps the legitimacy of women having an equal role alongside men in the church was not an issue in Colossae as it was in Galatia. The mention of Nympha and the lesser stress on traditional Jewish customs and its mindset in Colossians, when compared with Galatians, would support this.

The most interesting modification of the saying in Colossians is the inclusion of the terms 'barbarian, Scythian'. Schweizer describes their inclusion as 'remarkable'.[51] Barbarians were non-Greeks who spoke neither the language nor appreciated the culture of the Greek world. Scythians were the lowest kind of barbarian. Inhabitants of the northern coast of the Black Sea, they were considered to be especially savage and barbaric, in fact 'little better than wild beasts'.[52] Both the groups named were uncivilized, only the Scythians more so. The terms 'barbarian' and 'Scythian' are immediately followed by the terms 'slave' and 'free'. If the writer is following the same pattern as he adopted in the first part of the verse where 'Greeks and Jews' were paralleled chiastically (in reverse) by 'circumcised and uncircumcised', it would mean the barbarians were free while the Scythians were slaves.[53] R.McL. Wilson queries whether people 'would be aware of free barbarians dwelling beyond the frontier of the empire to the north, in contrast to Scythian slaves living in their own vicinity'. He therefore concludes they were most likely to be slaves in Colossae.[54] It is possible that the writer is writing hypothetically and referring to people at a distance of whom the Colossians would have no first-hand experience. But it is surely more reasonable to assume, with R.McL. Wilson, that their inclusion has some local relevance and perhaps some from both of these despised groups were to be found among the Colossians Christians. If so, the gospel of Jesus Christ had certainly embraced the lowest of the low in social terms and given them a place among God's chosen ones who were 'holy and beloved' (3:12). Those who from the viewpoint of Greek civilization were non-entities had a place of equal standing with those Jews and cultured Gentiles who had turned to Christ.

Paul's point is abundantly clear. Social divisions continue to exist; they are not obliterated in the church. But they are of no significance. 'Only Christ should count', not social markers of any description. 'He is the measure by which everything is defined.'[55]

Other factors

There are several incidental references in Colossians which might be relevant to assessing the social level of the members of the church there. The implications of each of them, however, are somewhat ambiguous and they do not clarify the picture beyond question.

In 2:6–7 Paul uses three metaphors to encourage the growth and stability of the young converts in Colossae. The first is an agricultural metaphor ('rooted'); the second an architectural one ('built up'); and the third is a commercial one ('established'). Dunn explains: '*Bebaios* and *Benaioō* were commonly used to denote the formal or legal guarantee required in the transfer of property or goods.'[56] Another business or legal allusion occurs in 2:14 where Paul speaks of 'the record that stood against us with its legal demands'. The word *cheirograpson* is 'a signed certificate of debt in which the signature legalized the debt (cf. Phlm. 18–19), a promissory note signed by the debtor'.[57] Wayne Meeks judiciously concludes about 2:14, although the same point holds for 2:6–7: 'By themselves these passages would prove nothing about the occupation and wealth of Christians, but they may add one small increment to the cumulative impression that many were artisans and merchants with a modest income.'[58]

The second area of interest is the disproportionate amount of space given to instructing slaves in the household code of 3:18 – 4:1. Some have argued that the extended treatment given to slaves indicates that the church was largely composed of slaves but this is not necessarily so. Andrew Lincoln believes that the amount of attention given can be explained on other grounds, namely that 'the writer sees the slave/master relationship as paradigmatic for the motivation of all members of the household'. This is seen in that the 'warrants and motivations (given for behaviour) contain five references to Christ as Lord'.[59] So little can be concluded about the social composition of Colossians from the extended reference to slavery in the household code.

Even less support is found for Crouch's argument that the extended reference is provoked by unrest among Christian slaves who, taking Galatians 3:28, or the similar teaching, to its logical conclusion, enthusiastically and disruptively sought their freedom.[60] There is, however, no evidence of unrest among slaves during this period and no hint elsewhere in the letter of any unrest between members. The theory, then, remains highly unlikely.

Conclusion

The cumulative evidence is that Colossae was a socially mixed town whose population included a significant number of Jews as well as a majority of Gentiles. Their occupations placed them, along with the overwhelming mass of the Roman Empire, at the lower end of the social strata. Their lives would have been precarious for economic and other reasons and characterized by relative poverty.

What we can tell of the church suggests that in most respects it reflected the community in which it was situated. The description of the false teaching that the letter opposes shows that there was a significant Jewish element within the church while much of the rest of the letter, including the discussion of slavery and the names of those who are mentioned, suggests the majority were Gentile. Philemon was among the relatively wealthy, wealthy enough not only to own slaves but also to entertain the church in his house. There may have been one or two others in that category and the church might have met in more than one house, as we deduce it did elsewhere.[61] But in Colossae only Philemon is mentioned. The majority would have been involved in farming and its associated trades, and consequently less prosperous.

Based on his examination of the language of ruler, authorities and powers (to which we shall return), Wesley Carr thought that there was no evidence that they feared mighty forces that were hostile to them and from which they sought relief in the first century AD.[62] His position, as we shall see, is probably not a viable one. But even if we were to grant it, and deny that fear of supernatural forces is reflected in the 'power' language which Paul uses, it remains true that the people of Colossae would still have felt their lives to be precarious. For all the benefits of the *Pax Romana*, the physical, economic and social context of Colossae and its church reminded them daily of the uncertainty and severity of their ordinary lives.

3

Conversion: How and Why People Became Christians in Colossae

Why did people become followers of Christ Jesus in Colossae? A huge range of religious options were available to its citizens by the time Epaphras brought 'the word of the truth, the gospel' (1:5) to his home-town. Worshippers would have been enmeshed in the family relationships and social networks that were associated with the worship of particular deities. It would have been a brave move to jeopardize these by worshipping a new deity and would have required a powerful incentive for people to convert. So, what was the attraction of the message about Jesus Christ?

The Religious Milieu in Colossae[1]

The religious milieu in Colossae, like that of the rest of Asia, and even Rome, was essentially conservative and calm during the mid-first century, if Wesley Carr is correct.[2] It was only toward the end of the century, and particularly in the second century, that stirrings took place that led to religious creativity. Assuming Colossians is written at least towards the end of Paul's life, some breaking up of the settled religious period might well have been evident in Colossae even if it did not reach its full flowering until later.[3] In any case, even if the letter is situated in that mid-first-century period, it is evident that a group of people broke free from their previous religious allegiances and became followers of Jesus Christ. So what sort of a spiritual background did these converts have?

Given the numbers of Jews we estimate to have lived in Colossae, the local Jewish synagogue must have been a thriving institution. For Jews to belong to the synagogue was as much about their ethnic identity as their religious convictions, and to leave it would have been to commit social suicide as well as religious treason. The synagogue was the place where they belonged to each other as much as where they prayed to God, and where travellers could readily find a welcome and a temporary home. The monotheism of Judaism and its high moral standards attracted some Gentile adherents who showed varying degrees of commitment up to as full a conversion as it was possible for a Gentile to undergo. Judaism in Colossae, as elsewhere in the Dispersion, was almost certainly less than 'pure' and a number of syncretistic elements had infiltrated it, including a fear of demons and the worship of angels (2:18) as a means of warding off evil.[4] The folk variety of its worship and practices is what would have made it comfortable to its adherents.

The Asia to which Colossae belonged was strongly devoted to the imperial cult.[5] Evidence of the cult was manifest everywhere. Imperial priests and shrines were common and the annual celebration of the emperor's birthday was a major civic festival which involved feasts, athletic contests, music festivals, processions and, of course, the offering of incense before the emperor's statue. It was difficult for anyone to avoid contact, although 'participation in such cultic activity was not generally obligatory'.[6] All the business, social and political networks were intertwined with it.[7]

For the Gentiles, there was also a complex medley of gods and goddesses on offer in addition. Clinton Arnold has listed twenty-two goddesses and thirty-eight gods who had devotees in this area of Asia Minor generally.[8] In Colossae, more specifically, the evidence which has been provided by the discovery of coins leads him to conclude that the goddesses and gods who were most frequently worshipped were 'the Ephesian Artemis and the Laodicean Zeus, but also . . . Artemis (the huntress), Men, Selene, Demeter, Hygenia, Helios, Athena, Tyche, Voule, as well as the Egyptian deities Isis and Serapis'.[9] Elsewhere he gives a fuller list and adds Asclepios, Leto, Selene, Dionysius, Nike, Boule and the flood gods of the Lycus.[10]

Since Colossae has not yet been excavated it is impossible to tell how many of these deities would have been honoured with a temple but local cults were evidently prolific and smaller shrines would have been common, as well as its citizens having personal shrines at home. Individuals expressed their allegiance by devoting time and money to the cult and participating in the meals which drew the cult members together. Gentile converts to Christ would have participated in these before their conversion and a great deal of social and business life would have revolved around them.

Farmers would have been accustomed to looking to the skies to gain a forecast of the weather. This did not mean they had a belief in astrology but there was a growing acceptance of fatalistic astrology during the relevant period in Rome,[11] and it was an interest which would have long permeated Colossae from the east through Persian religion.

The smorgasbord of cults included Roman and Greek deities such as Zeus, the supreme god, the god of the sky and lord of thunder, and Artemis, or Diana of Ephesus, the mother goddess of fertility. It included goddesses of the underworld such as Hekate, the goddess of the crossroads who held power over earth, sea and heaven,[12] who was associated with Artemis, the huntress, and Selene, the moon goddess, who needed to be placated through spells, prayers and hymns, in order that they might afford protection against the occurrence of evil. There were variously angels who protected people and demons who harmed them. As with the long-standing mystery religions of Egypt that were practised in Colossae, some cults offered people secret initiation in order to access revelations and knowledge only available to the insider and to gain ongoing success, good fortune and salvation.[13] There are some similarities between these initiation rites and Christian baptism although, sadly, by the nature of the case, we know all too little about them. There are also some differences.[14] The mystery cults did not require exclusive allegiance from their adherents and participation in them did not affect one's social standing, since observance of the cults was perfectly socially acceptable. They also had 'a limited impact upon morality'.[15]

The various religions were different from each other but nonetheless formed an embedded conglomerate which was shaped by syncretism, which demonstrated tolerance of each other; they were not seen as exclusive.[16] The religious milieu into which Christianity came was a dualistic one in which cosmic powers ruled, including many hostile forces that needed to be subdued through various rites if the fragile lives of the citizens of Colossae were to be made a degree less precarious that they would otherwise have been.[17]

As E. Schillebeeckx puts it, the people of this region 'were aware of a cosmic fault, a kind of catastrophe in the universe, a gulf between the higher (heavenly) and the lower (earthly) world. The problem of meaning and meaninglessness is experienced in cosmic terms and is expressed in a longing for salvation which will consist in the restoration of the unity of the cosmos.'[18]

Wedderburn, who cites Schillebeeckx, rightly adds that the conflict may not be between heaven and earth so much as 'between the warring elements that make up the entire cosmos', leading to the 'dislocation and disruption' of the harmonious creation which the Creator brought into being.[19]

In Lightfoot's words, 'cosmological speculation, mystic theosophy, religious fanaticism, all had their home here'.[20] Even Judaism, it would seem, had been infected by this world-view with the result that it had adapted its worship to include the worship of angels, whose good influences would be sought through prayer to bring some control over people's lives and in the quest for initiation into an extraordinary level of revelation and visionary experiences (2:18).[21]

Sociological Understanding of Conversion in the New Testament Period

Recent sociological discussions about the nature of conversion

Sociologists have shown a great deal of interest in religious conversion in recent decades because of the growth of contemporary new religious movements and 'cults'. The popular view, much encouraged by sensational journalism, is that people 'convert' as a result of intense psychological pressure or 'brainwashing'. Sociologists have studied what really goes on when someone becomes a convert and this has led to a revision of understanding in three important respects. First, greater attention is given to the process of conversion, rather than the assumption that it is a dramatic, unprepared or sudden experience. Second, greater recognition is given to the fact that converts play an active role in their conversion and are not simply passive 'victims'. Third, the context in which the conversion takes place is taken more seriously, rather than approaching conversion as if it takes place in a vacuum. Rather than being an individual and isolated act, the social dimension and the social consequences of conversion are now seen of great importance.

Although the details of schemes vary, Lewis Rambo[22] speaks for many in identifying a number of stages in the process of conversion:

Stage 1 is context, cultural, social, religious and personal.
Stage 2 is crisis, a crisis in a person's life which provokes the next stage.
Stage 3 is quest, a searching for an answer to the crisis.
Stage 4 is encounter, meeting those who offer a religious answer.
Stage 5 is interaction, when the potential convert continues with the contact.
Stage 6 is commitment, when the decision to make the change is made.
Stage 7 is consequences, which usually involves a new set of relationships and the adoption of a new lifestyle.[23]

The conversion process acts as a funnel that narrows as it continues, with people choosing to exit the process at each stage. Therefore, only a minority of those who begin the process become full converts.[24]

Debates about the definition of conversion abound among sociologists. In a desire to find a meaning that covers a wide range of conversion experiences, the definitions often seem remote from what is understood as conversion in Christianity. In essence, conversion involves a change of identity and world-view and results in the re-socialization of the convert. Converts not only see themselves but also their world as well in a new light and they adjust not only their beliefs but also their relationships and lifestyles accordingly. People who were once significant now recede into the background and others become significant. The practices, customs, values and ethics that belong to the newly adopted religion are taken up and former practices and ethical stances are dropped. The change is often marked by the undergoing of an initiation rite, such as baptism, and other visible changes such as the acquiring of a new name or a new dress code may well follow.

Just as important as initial conversion, if not more so, is ongoing commitment, especially if the movement a convert joins is to survive and thrive. As Peter Berger and Thomas Luckmann claim, 'To have a conversion experience is nothing much. The real thing is to be able to keep on taking it seriously; to retain a sense of its plausibility.'[25] Rosabeth Kanter[26] has examined the process in contemporary religious groups by which converts become increasingly committed and concludes that commitment involves three dimensions with each dimension having a positive and negative aspect.

Instrumental commitment is about commitment to the organization. Commitment is made firm positively through a convert's investment in it, for example, through tithing, and negatively through sacrifice, for example, through self-denial.

Affective commitment is about commitment to persons in the group and emotional bonding. Here, involvement and communion with the new group positively enhances commitment, while detachment and even renunciation of former relationships serve as the negative aspect that makes for strong commitment.

Moral commitment is about commitment to the customs, norms and values of the group. Positively this is strengthened by what Kanter calls transcendence, that is, the discovery of truth, hope and meaning through the group. Negatively, it involves mortification as converts humble themselves and feel their past 'selves' or identity to have been worthless. It may be accompanied by some act of mortification but essentially is about the probing and humbling of the inner self.

The value of structuration theory

Sociologists use models to explain common patterns of behaviour which, in turn, are informed by a theoretical approach. In place of the models which arise from theories of functionalism[27] and sociology of knowledge,[28] two scholars have recently turned to find a 'sensitizing device' in the structuration theory of Antony Giddens.[29] David Horrell has been followed by Stephen Chester in applying structuration theory to the Corinthian church; Chester particularly to the question of conversion.[30] They argue the value of Gidden's approach lies in his overcoming the dualism between action and structure and thus his catering both for change and continuity more adequately than previous theories. Horrell quotes a key element of Giddens' approach: 'Every act which contributes to the reproduction of a structure is also an act of production, a novel enterprise, and as such may initiate change by altering the structure at the same time as it reproduces it.'[31] Stability and transformation thus go hand in hand.

Christianity does not exist as a reified entity, which has an external existence of its own ('facticity' is a favourite word of Berger and Luckmann). Rather it may be viewed as 'a symbolic order embodied in communities'.[32] When people are converted, then, they not only join a pre-existing group who are committed to a particular tradition of interpretation of the world, with all the constraints and limitations which that entails, but they also make an impact on it and change it. As one example, Stephen Chester remarks that 'Even those advocates of conversion whose endeavours meet with success discover that their ability to control the process is limited. Converts bring their existing cultural resources to the task of interpreting the new faith, and the degree to which this interpretation matches that of the advocates varies.'[33] We may find that comment of particular relevance to the church in Colossae.

Chester makes plain that he is not seeking to ask the usual question which preoccupies social historians and sociologists,[34] about why people were converted, but rather to use the text to demonstrate how conversion took place, and even more about its consequences.[35] He separates his investigation of the conversion of Gentiles from that of Jews.

He bases his discussion of Gentile conversion on two passages: 1 Corinthians 14:20–25, which describes the event of an individual's conversion, and 6:9–11, which describes the before and after position of converts collectively. The former[36] makes unrecognized sin that is revealed in the worship service by a prophet central to conversion. It leads to a sensitizing of the convert's practical consciousness, a rejection of the convert's former value system, presumably that of the dominant values of Greco-Roman society, and reorientation to the values of the believing community.

So 1 Corinthians 6:9–11 brings 'the social and communal issues' to the fore.[37] Using a traditional formula to speak of what would have been known as particularly Gentile vices, Paul contrasts them strongly with the way the converts now live. There is a sharp distinction drawn between past and present and their moral identities are now being reconstructed. What might have been formerly approved was now considered incompatible with being 'washed . . . sanctified . . . [and] justified in the name of the Lord Jesus Christ and in the Spirit of our God' (1 Cor. 6:11).

Drawing these two texts together leads Chester to conclude that 'Gentile conversion is not the resolution of a pre-existing crisis, but is itself both crisis and resolution. The convert moves from false consciousness to crisis and security in Christ.'[38] The crisis is provoked by the revealing of unrecognized sin and leads to the transformation of the convert's identity and their reconstruction of identity in Christ and through the believing community.

Jewish conversion[39] is examined through the lens of 1 Corinthians 4:1–5, which Chester is careful to set in the wider context of Paul's attitude to Judaism as shown in Galatians 1, Philippians 3 and Romans 7. The advantage of having a Jewish background was seen in the cultivation of a conscience that had been moulded by the law. This meant that, in contrast to Gentiles, the lives of Jewish converts stood 'in little need of reconstruction'.[40] But conscience was not a perfect guide and Jews needed to show a measure of distrust towards it as unrecognized sin and false desires were revealed. In Paul's own case, he only came to recognize his persecution of Christians as a sin after his conversion. It was possible for a Jew to live in a state of 'false consciousness' and consider himself blameless when he was not. This being so, Jews, no less than Gentiles, can be appropriately spoken of as converts when they are called by God through grace to become righteous.

The value of Chester's work is four-fold. First, it lies in recognizing conversion as a dynamic process in which converts actively join the new community of Christ's followers and then inevitably change it, as structuration theory proposes. Second, it gives serious attention to the relevant texts, as opposed to a surface reading of the texts that imposes on, or assumes the relevance of, some sociological model regardless of what the text says. Third, as mentioned earlier, Chester relates the Corinthian understanding of conversion to the related practices of other groups in the Greco-Roman world. Fourth, it reaffirms our initial understanding of conversion as a change of a person's identity and world-view which leads to a re-socialization of the convert within a new community. It calls into question, however, whether conversion is a way of resolving a personal crisis or whether it provokes a crisis where there was none, before resolving it.

Application to Colossians

What does Colossians reveal, if anything, about the nature of conversion? Several texts are relevant, namely 1:6–7,13; 2:6,8 and 3:18 onwards.

'This you learned from Epaphras' (1:7)

The Colossian converts were said to have 'learned' (*emathete*)[41] their new faith from Epaphras. The interest of the commentators is usually fixed on the identity of Epaphras and his connection with Paul, so the verb 'learned' is often passed over without comment. But perhaps 'learned' contains more than is usually recognized. It means that they received instruction and that they were taught the gospel, as the use of 'taught' (*edidachthete*)[42] in 2:7 underlines. Paul could have used a simpler word such as 'heard' ('You *heard* the gospel from Epaphras'); 'learned' is somewhat unusual and suggests rather more than mere hearing. Dunn diffidently writes that the verb 'may imply that Epaphras had seen his task in Colossae not simply as winning them to faith but as instructing them in the traditions and parenesis without which they would have no guidelines in translating their faith into daily living (cf. Rom. 16:17; 1 Cor. 4:6; Phil. 4:9; see also 2:6)'.[43] Peter O'Brien is more direct: 'The term "learned" . . . probably indicates that Epaphras had given them systematic instruction in the gospel rather than some flimsy outline and that these Colossians had committed themselves as disciples to that teaching (cf. 2:6,7).'[44]

The word almost certainly implies that conversions were not sudden, dramatic experiences so much as a process in which Epaphras unfolded the new teaching about Jesus Christ and the implications of becoming his disciples, and that during this process people would have come to a point of commitment to Christ and of decision to leave their previous religious faith and practice. Conversion, then, may be fairly said to have involved an education, or a re-education, not only in belief about God but also in a new world-view and lifestyle. The conversion would have been sealed in baptism, which, while only mentioned in 2:12, is thought to be implicit in so much of the letter.[45]

'He has rescued us . . . transferred us' (1:13)

Colossians 1:13 describes conversion as being transferred from one realm, that of 'the power of darkness', into a different one, that of 'the kingdom of his beloved Son'. The language is the language of salvation. The Colossian converts have been 'rescued'. No implications as to the form of the rescue can be read into the text at this stage. It is not implied that it was a dramatic rescue, planned and executed in daring fashion by special, elite forces, as distinct from a gradual loosening of the hold of a corrupt regime and its replacement by another. Colossians 2:15 might suggest, however, that the event that made their deliverance possible was dramatic, even full of guile. But the way in which the converts came to appropriate the benefits of Christ's victory is not implied in 1:13 and may have been either dramatic or gradual.

The language is also the language of governance and, from this standpoint, the text does say something about the nature of their conversion. While the reference to release from tyranny and removal to another home might seem to be an obvious reference to the exodus, and is rich in Old Testament allusion, in using the word 'transfer' (*methistēmi*) Paul is using the word for the removal of people from one area and their 'wholesale transportation' to another, 'of which the history of oriental monarchs supplied so many examples'.[46] R.McL. Wilson suggests that it was probably not a particular allusion to the relocation and resettlement of Jews under Antiochus the Great in the area of Colossae, but a more general reference, given the majority Gentile composition of the Colossian church.[47]

Christians had been subject to the tyranny of darkness but had now been released from that life-draining power and become subjects of another Lord, that of God's Son. There has been a clear transfer of allegiance from one government to another. The decisive event of the cross broke the power of those who previously controlled their lives and has permitted the converts to experience release and freedom. But conversion is not a one-sided act but a two-sided act. They have been rescued, not so that that they can live autonomously – for, given their flawed human natures, that would simply result in a new form of bondage – but so that they can come under the authority of a new Lord, under whose rule they would experience the freedom, love, security and harmony the Creator intended.

History and personal stories demonstrate, however, that the fact of a regime change does not mean those who have undoubtedly experienced it automatically work through the implications of it easily or fully. The old con, used to a structured life inside prison, sometimes finds it very difficult to live in conditions of freedom once released. The implications of Lincoln's Emancipation Proclamation in 1862 took a considerable time to work through after it had been announced, especially in the lives of some of the slaves! Some who lived under the Communist regimes of Eastern Europe have taken a long time to enjoy life under the new forms of government, in spite of the undoubted collapse of Communism in 1989. The transfer from one governing authority to another is the basis on which lives begin a process of reconstruction.

Consistent with our definition of conversion, what happened in Colossae was that converts to Jesus Christ assumed a new identity and its accompanying world-view, rejected their old identities and the symbolic universes which shaped them, and began a period of re-socialization where the implications of their new belonging were worked through. The language is not inherently the language of crisis. But the language is inherently about the escape from living a life of perpetual crisis, where evil powers enslave and where they might strike catastrophically at any moment. The resolution of the ongoing crisis is justifiably described as 'redemption' (1:14), that is, releasing someone from slavery by the payment of a price.

The perpetual crisis from which people are released is, however, not simply from external tyrannical forces but from inner personal powers that can be equally 'dark', namely, 'sins' (1:14). As in Corinth, potential converts from a Gentile background might not have been particularly aware of their own faults and contribution to the disharmony of the cosmos. The absence of a conscience schooled in the Jewish law might have led them to believe that the sinful behaviour they exhibited was merely conventional and acceptable behaviour in their Gentile context. Part of the gospel teaching, then, must have involved making the converts aware that the way in which they lived, described in some detail in 3:5–10, merited the accusation of the law (2:13–14)[48] and provoked God's wrath (3:6) against them.

Chester's interpretation of Gentile conversion in Corinth, then, is echoed in part in Colossae. In Colossae there was a crisis which potential converts wanted to resolve, that of the 'cosmic fault', 'the catastrophe of the universe' which was all too apparent to them. But converts had to become aware of another dimension to that crisis before a true resolution could be experienced: the crisis concerning sin had to be provoked before the gospel could resolve it. There is no mention here of prophecy as the means by which they became aware of their sin, as there was in Corinthians. It is most likely that it was Epaphras' instruction that made them aware of it.

It will be recalled that Rambo's scheme spoke of 'a crisis' as the second step on the road to conversion. Wayne Meeks hinted that many became converts because they found their conversion to be a way of resolving the tension of status inconsistency whereby they rated high on some measures of status but low on others.[49] The idea has been much criticized, because of doubts about both its historical validity and its causal significance.[50] But there is no need to resort to an explanation of status inconsistency as generating a personal crisis when the evidence is that many in Colossae lived in perpetual external crisis mode and, furthermore, had another crisis – that of the need for forgiveness – revealed to them. Here were two genuine crises that the gospel of Jesus the Messiah and Lord could resolve.

'As you therefore have received Christ Jesus the Lord' (2:6)

Many contemporary Christians speak of 'receiving Christ' but do not mean by it what 'receive' in 2:6 means. Contemporary use of the word, in line with the subjective and individualistic culture of the modern world, means having some form of existential experience by which Christ is 'received' into one's life as one might invite, 'receive' and host a guest for supper.[51] But that is a modern misunderstanding of the concept involved. 'Received' (*paralambanete*) in 2:6 'is more or less a technical term for receiving a tradition'.[52] In this case the tradition does not go back to the prophets, still less the rabbis, or even just to the apostles, but beyond them to Jesus Christ himself (1 Cor. 11:23).[53]

The 'tradition' which they have accepted is summarized in the phrase, 'Christ Jesus the Lord'. The new believers in Colossae had accepted the proclamation that Jesus was the Christ, God's anointed agent or Messiah, who would inaugurate the new age which was to replace the age in which sin and evil were destructive of creation and its peoples, and that Jesus was Lord, that is the supreme ruler of the cosmos.[54] The christological hymn of Colossians 1:15–20 both defined who Christians believed this Jesus to be, that is, in his true nature, and what kind of rule he would exercise. New believers were not free to devise and propagate their own understanding of Christ Jesus, for they were taking their stand on an already existing tradition, which had been brought to them by Epaphras (1:7,23) and in which they needed to persevere faithfully. In confessing Jesus of Nazareth to be Lord they stood in solidarity with others who affirmed the earliest Christian confession that 'Jesus is Lord'.[55]

The use of the word 'receiving' should not be taken to imply the recipient is passive. In line with what we know of conversion generally, 'receiving' involves an active choice as converts choose to accept for themselves the tradition that is being passed on.[56] Since the Christian confession was a minority and deviant belief, with attendant costs, no one was going to fall into or accept it passively.[57]

It would have been a brave and conscious choice to identify with the proclamation about Christ. Spoken of this way, conversion is primarily a matter of identifying with a group and endorsing a set of teaching rather than of having an individual, spiritual, existential experience, which may or may not be present.[58] This interpretation makes sense of what Paul says in the following verses. Having identified with this tradition, in 2:6 Paul encourages his readers to 'continue' in their stance and to strengthen and develop it. Furthermore, in verse 8, he contrasts the tradition about Christ with the 'human tradition' that lies behind the 'philosophy and empty deceit' which some of them were beginning to find attractive. The confession they had made then was evidently not a one-off statement but a life stance and one which would require the convert to undergo closer and closer identification with the Christian community and greater and greater re-education in the way of living as a Christian, in contrast to living as others who owed allegiance to other gods or religions.

'Put to death . . . clothe yourselves with' (3:5,12)

From 3:5 onwards the concern of Paul's letter concentrates more and more on what it means to live as a Christian, first in terms of ethics and morality (3:5–12); second, in terms of relationships with others in the church (3:13–17); third, in terms of behaviour in the household (3:18 – 4:1); and, finally, in terms of those outside the church (4:5–6). Here are Katner's instrumental, effective and moral dimensions of commitment at work, expressed in the form of character, ethics and relationships.

The moral dimension is explored first, with Paul's instruction to new believers to 'put to death' their former way of life and 'clothe yourselves' with the new way of living which was compatible with 'the Lord'. The language is transparently the language of 'mortification' as their former way of life is condemned and 'stripped off' (3:9), and of 'transcendence' as the new way of behaving which is consistent with God's 'chosen ones, holy and beloved' (3:12) is adopted.

The moral dimension is revisited in 3:18 – 4:1 as Paul details his version of the household code. While the framework of the moral advice given here may be similar to conventional Hellenistic moral teaching,[59] it is transformed by the frequent inclusion of references to 'the Lord'.[60] Relationships between Christians did not involve the abolition of their social position but it did transform its nature and their behaviour toward each other. Their relationships were now governed by the greater reality of their being 'in the Lord' rather than the reality of their social position. For example, slaves remained slaves but were also now brothers to their masters and servants of the Lord, not just of their earthly masters. Slave owners remained masters, but were also themselves slaves of Christ and subject to a heavenly master. This could not but introduce an entirely new dynamic into their relationships, as well as a new code of conduct.

The affective dimension of Katner's commitment theory is clearly implicated in what is taught about morality. It is explicitly addressed in 3:13–17 where encouragement is given to the closest of bonding with other believers. Relationships within the fellowship were to be governed by the practice of compassion, forbearance, forgiveness, mutual admonition, love and peace. The new believers are not encouraged to distance themselves from unbelievers, except in terms of their attitudes and behaviour but, on the basis of 4:5, the separation was already a reality.

The instrumental dimension of Katner's theory is perhaps the one which is least evident in Colossians, although not elsewhere in the New Testament. The explicit reference to baptism in 2:12 and the fact that baptism is what lies behind the 'put to death . . . clothe yourselves' metaphor of 3:5–12, as baptismal candidates would strip for baptism and then reclothe themselves, suggests the instrumental dimension is assumed rather than explicit. Since the purpose of the letter is to challenge those who argue that certain ascetic practices are essential if one is truly to encounter God (2:8–23), it is not surprising that the negative element of instrumental commitment finds no place in Colossians.

Conversion, then, may justifiably be seen as an active choice by converts to resolve the tension or crisis under which they lived. It involved a change of social identity and world-view, rather than a subjective, psychological or mystical experience, which leads to their re-socialization in and by the new community with which they have identified. The process of re-socialization is one in which the converts strengthen their commitment to their new faith and transform their attitudes, behaviour and lifestyle.

Why Did Christianity Prove Attractive to Converts?

The question about conversion may be reframed to ask not why an individual and his household converted to Christianity but why Christianity generally proved successful in growing and attracting so many converts. Sociologists who seek to answer this question usually approach it from the discipline of social history.[61]

One of the earliest studies in this area was by A.D. Nock. He defined conversion as 'the reorientation of the soul of an individual', involving the rejection of their old piety as wrong and the acceptance of their new piety as right.[62] The success of the cults in the first century, he argued, was largely due to their continuity with what had gone on before and their ability to illuminate old understandings in new ways.[63] In line with this, Christianity spread initially because it was not seen as a new religion until the time of Nero but a reinvigoration of the Jewish faith.[64] Even when it was distinguished from Judaism, Nock concludes its growth was due, neither to the attractiveness of Jesus, nor to its having an effective missionary strategy, but because it matched the philosophy of the time, satisfied the inquiring mind, answered the desire for the escape from Fate, provided security, and met people's social needs and gave them a way to escape loneliness. Unlike other cults, 'it made uncompromising demands on those who would continue to live in the brotherhood, but to those who did not fail, it offered an equally uncompromising assurance'.[65] The severe demands it made on its converts, even to the point of martyrdom, proved an effective means of attracting others to believe. While its real novelty may have lain in 'the motive which it supplied for good conduct and the abhorrence of past conduct which it demanded', its strength lay not only in supplying the motive but also in supplying the power by which to live this new life.[66] Its success in recruiting those of lower as well as the intellectual classes, and of those who were not the children of existing Christians, bred yet more success.[67]

Ramsey MacMullen rejected the black-and-white distinctions of Nock, and questioned whether the soil in which Christianity grew was as hospitable as Nock had argued, but agreed with him in much else, especially in his individualism and belief that the early Christians lacked a missionary strategy.[68] Unlike Nock, he differentiates between intellectuals who were converted as a result of a journey of enquiry and converts in the lower classes.[69] Those in the lower classes were often converted as a result of chance individual encounters and by the witnessing and talk of miracles, which MacMullen adds to the martyrdom identified by Nock as significant.[70]

The most recent discussion has been a lively one, provoked by the writing of Rodney Stark in his work, *The Rise of Christianity.*[71] Stark is a renowned sociologist who has applied his considerable expertise in contemporary religion to the questions of why people converted to Christianity in the ancient world, an issue in which, on his own admission, he has no professional credentials as either a New Testament scholar or an ancient historian.[72] The result is a stimulating, insightful, speculative and provocative book.

Having estimated the numerical growth of Christianity[73] and stated that its appeal was to 'the solid citizens of the empire' and that it did not take the form of a proletarian movement,[74] he gives a series of explanations of its growth. The Hellenized Jews of the Dispersion were, he claims, marginalized as they were neither Greeks by birth nor Jews in the purist sense and, since they had accommodated culturally. Christianity offered them a way of resolving this tension that had the advantage of continuity with their former Jewish beliefs.[75]

As to Gentiles, Stark suggests the way Christians handled disasters and epidemics led to its successful growth for three reasons.[76]

1. Christianity offered a more satisfactory explanation of why such disasters befell people.
2. Christians coped with disasters better than others because of their commitment to caring for the helpless and needy, and also because of the strength of their community solidarity. This, in turn, he argued, led to a significantly higher survival

rate among Christians than among other religious groups. This may have been seen as a miracle and as a result led to even more conversions.

3. As victims succumbed to the disaster or epidemic so those who survived inevitably had their previous social links loosened and were open to join new networks.

The attitude to women was another significant factor in the growth of Christianity.[77] The status of women was considerably higher than in other religions and they were granted roles in leadership positions. Together with the outlawing of infanticide and abortion among Christians, this made Christianity considerably attractive to women and caused a rapid increase in its numbers.

Stark, like those who have worked previously in this field, also discusses the role of martyrdom.[78] His approach, however, is somewhat different from the discussion of Nock and MacMullen. For him, faith led people to face death bravely: a matter of considerable relevance to the precarious nature of life in the ancient world. Martyrdom was not the act of crazy fanatics or of masochists, but of people who made a rational choice to lay down their lives because the rewards of doing so as they entered God's presence, and the rewards received en route to doing so, in generating 'immense shared emotional satisfaction', outweighed the costs they paid.

Although it only becomes evident in his chapter on martyrdom, Stark's work is informed throughout by 'the rational choice theory' of religion of which he has been a leading exponent.[79] Rational choice theorists controversially argue that people make choices about religion rationally, by weighing up the rewards that they will gain from their decision and measuring them against the cost which is involved, in a manner which is akin to the economic or consumerist choices they make. Failure to appreciate this partly explains some of the reaction to Stark's proposals.

Opinions differ widely about Stark's work. William Garrett, commenting on some of Stark's earlier but related publications, called those essays 'perspicacious' and concluded they offered 'a substantive payoff' in our understanding of early Christianity, even though they have only largely confirmed earlier studies.[80]

The most sustained critique is found in Jack Sanders' study of
*Charisma, Converts, Competitors: Societal and Sociological Factors in
the Success of Early Christianity.*[81] He sees some parts of Stark's
work as 'a marvellous accomplishment'.[82] For the most part, however, his reaction is less than enthusiastic for two distinct reasons.
First, there is a methodological criticism. A good historical sociologist analyses the evidence carefully and then formulates models
to fit the evidence. But Sanders accuses Stark of operating the
other way around, that is, of making the evidence fit models
formulated on the basis of twentieth-century America and dis-
torting (or, to use Sanders' word, 'misunderstanding') the evidence to make it fit.[83] He does this not only in his application of
rational choice theory generally but when, for example, he
applies knowledge about the growth of contemporary new religious movements to New Testament times.

The second criticism is curiously back-handed. Stark's
methodology may be highly questionable but his conclusions
prove remarkably similar to those of others. Sanders writes,

> The fact that Stark has failed in his attempt to make certain points
> about early Christianity should not obscure the fact that his
> approach has underscored other points previously made. (Christ-
> ianity was not primarily a lower-class movement, Christianity
> offered benefits that made joining the movement a reasonable
> choice, Christianity filled a need in the society of the early Roman
> empire, most conversions came through networks, the place of
> women in Christianity abetted its growth) and has brought two
> others to the surface for the first time (Christianity could have
> grown to take over the empire without miraculous or dramatic
> activity, Christianity was more cohesive than its competitors).
> While all these social factors were important in the growth of
> Christianity, only the care of the ill, the (early) status and role of
> women and the greater cohesiveness can begin to explain
> Christianity's triumph.[84]

Sanders' own research suggests that the love command which
was at the heart of Christianity was key to their triumph since, in
seeking to put it into practice in their attitude to all and especially in caring for the sick and meeting material needs, Christians

'created a transnational civil society [and so] gave the religion a social role that no other religion of the day approached'.[85] It was this, together with the genius Christianity had for being both cohesive and adapting to its surroundings,[86] rather than martyrdom, that proved significant to it growth.

Conclusion

There is little of direct reference in Colossians that helps the discussion of the issues discussed by Nock, MacMullen and Stark one way or another. The concern of the letter is to ensure that the Christians at Colossae remain cohesive[87] with the rest of the Christian movement as expressed in the apostolic teaching of Paul, rather than assimilate too much to their surrounding culture. Those who were unsettling the church there may have been following the path of adapting to culture too far. Other evidence is minimal and incidental. The church is presented as a transnational (3:11) and caring society (3:13–17) where people of differing generations, genders and social classes respect each other and serve each other mutually 'in the Lord' (3:18 – 4:1). The single reference to a woman, Nympha (4:14), suggests she has a leadership position within the church at Laodicea, and it is probably therefore safe to deduce that women more generally would have had an elevated status and role within the church than elsewhere.

To the extent that we have any evidence at all in Colossians, and it is meagre, it confirms the picture drawn by Sanders and others as to why Christianity might have won converts in a world where it was costly to confess that 'Christ Jesus is Lord'. It also supports the fruitfulness of Chester's structuration approach to conversion.

4

Identity: The Construction of Personal and Social Identity

In a post-modern world our identities are particularly open. We are continuously constructing and reconstructing who we are without feeling any need for our latest identity to be coherent with previous ones. Although there may be certain 'givens', such as the fact we are somebody's daughter, someone's grandson, born in a particular place, or carry a national identity, these factors are far less significant than once they were in shaping us. After all, our 'family' may well have been 'reconstituted' before we leave home, and once we leave home we may be passionately committed to this cause in our twenties, converted to something altogether different in our thirties, de-converted from that and become someone else in our forties and so on.

The unique openness of the contemporary world clashes with the counter-forces of bureaucracy and managerialism that seek to reduce people's identities and impose some degree of homogeneity or uniformity on them, through the use of regulations, computerized identities and procedures to which we must conform. Even so, individualism wins hands down when it comes to determining who we perceive ourselves to be. But it would be a mistake to think this is the way it has always been.

This unprecedented openness, which has come about because of our devotion to freedom of choice, has also meant a loss of community. The picture is graphically symbolized by the title of Robert Putnam's study of American community, called, *Bowling Alone*.[1] Contemporary society shows itself to be schizophrenic in wanting individual choice and yet longing at the same time for the old experience of 'community' and 'belonging' to be redis-covered.[2] This enduring quest suggests that connecting with others is still quintessentially human and therefore of great sig-nificance when we ask who we are.

The Construction of Identity in Contemporary Sociological Thought

The peculiar openness of the present world has stimulated much reflection on how we construct our identities. At the most basic level, Berger and Luckmann pointed out that 'Identity is a phe-nomenon that emerges from the dialectic between the individual and society'.[3] The balance between the two partners in this dialec-tic varies between societies and between generations. While the balance may be largely established within a particular culture at any given time, different individuals also vary in the degree to which they permit one partner in this dialectic to exercise more influence than the other. Some people are less adventurous and more conformist by personality than others.

The construction of our personal identity is a different issue from discussion about an identity 'type' (such as a Scotsman or an army officer). Such types are wholly a social product and are 'rela-tively stable' and consistent, although not completely set in stone.[4] An extreme form of an identity type is found in the 'stereotype'.

Personal identities are never formed in a vacuum. As Berger and Luckmann point out, they are 'always embedded in a more general interpretation of reality' and draw from the way the world is perceived more widely, and how our understanding of it is maintained. Cultures that are framed by a scientific world-view shape identities very differently from those which frame them according to a supernatural world-view.[5] The impact of this wider interpretation explains why, for example, it is incredibly difficult for Western individualists to understand the mindset of those brought up in a culture of Chinese collectivism, where the individual's rights do not matter in comparison with the right of the social body as a whole.

Social psychologists have particularly looked at the part played by the group in the formation of personal identity. We are by nature people who long to connect and be a part of a wider and meaningful set of people. Our total identities, as we have noted from Berger and Luckmann, are formed by a combination of a personal component and a social component. The personal component has to do with our biological relationships and how we understand our personal characteristics, such as whether we are industrious, laid-back, intelligent or dim, loving or annoying, and so on. The social component consists of the groups to which we belong and roles we play in society such as whether we are a father, a teacher, a trades union official, a social activist, a Christian or whatever.

Hogg and Abrams stress the importance of this social component when they write 'Personal identifications are almost always grounded in relationships with specific individuals.'[6] Our identity, they argue, emerges as a result of our belonging to groups that help us define more sharply our understanding of the 'nebulous' world.[7] It is in the group that we find meaning and direction for our lives.

Our focus is sharpened because any group differentiates itself from other groups and causes its members to engage in social comparison. Groups accentuate the similarities and differences between themselves and other groups, highlighting their distinctiveness especially from those that are close to them. So, for example, both groups may be Baptist, but one group is Southern Baptist while another is American Baptist, or European Baptist. While Baptists as a whole are distinguished from Catholics or Episcopalians, they also are distinguished from each other and, to the outsider, seem to magnify the differences between them. But it is this that shapes their sense of identity and strengthens their belonging to each other.

As a result we feel much more comfortable with and we favour those in our group over those outside the group and view the group to which we belong as superior. We may even discriminate against those of other groups and build stereotypes in our minds: 'We are Protestant, so we are not Roman Catholics who all believe heresy'; 'We are Manchester United fans, not thugs like Millwall fans', etc. The reality may well be very different, but these are the social constructions groups place on the behaviour and identity of 'out-groups'. Increasingly we conform to the norms of the group we have joined and prefer the friendship of its members as opposed to that of the strangers who belong to other groups.[8] In its most naked form this can be seen played out in the rivalry between the supporters of different football or other sporting teams.

None of this should imply that a group's identity is fixed or its boundaries non-negotiable. They are not. The identity of the group requires ongoing social maintenance which occurs in a number of ways. Its rituals reinforce its values and beliefs, as does its particular use of language and the labelling of others. Arguments are advanced both to articulate its positions and to defend them. If members stray or offend the group, the group may exercise discipline, the most extreme form of which is exclusion.[9]

A group's boundaries are subject to constant renegotiation as circumstances change. Witness, for example, the way in which die-hard members of one particular Christian denomination, who in days when they were strong anathematized those of another denomination, end up 'marrying the enemy' when serious decline sets in. The boundaries are then redrawn, no longer on denominational lines but along the lines of Christian versus secular humanism.

The danger of the above is that it stresses the negative aspect of defining identity; that is, that we define our identity over against others. Henri Tajfel had earlier cast the discussion in a more positive light. He argues that 'groups need to establish a positively valued distinctiveness from other groups so as to provide their members with a positive social identity'.[10] Tajfel elaborated his understanding of the group further in saying it had three dimensions to it, which Philip Esler has summarized as:

1. 'The cognitive dimension', which is the simple recognition of belonging to the group;
2. 'The evaluative dimension', which covers the positive or negative connotations of belonging;
3. 'The emotional dimension', which refers to attitudes members hold towards insiders and outsiders.[11]

If we reduce our understanding to these dimensions we have only a partial picture of group dynamics. Groups, by their very nature, have shared beliefs and convictions, share collective memories, develop particular rituals, impose behaviour patterns, work towards a common goal, demonstrate varying degrees of passion and adopt specific ideological frameworks.

People also vary in how they perceive themselves within groups, an observation which led to the development of categorization theory by John Turner.[12] This closely related theory regarding identity sees people's self-concepts as more 'mobile' than social identity theory originally suggested. It focuses more on the psychology of the group and how members perceive (or categorize) their 'selves' in the balance between personally oriented and group-determined definitions of who they are.

Application to New Testament Studies

In addition to Christian Smith and his team, who have convincingly explained the strength and vitality of contemporary evangelicalism in the United States by using these theories,[13] they have been put to good use by Philip Esler who has applied them to the interpretation of John's Gospel,[14] and the letters of Paul to the Romans[15] and Galatians.[16]

Both Romans and Galatians are concerned with the identity of the early Christians but, in Esler's view, in two different respects. The major theme of Romans is that of ethnicity or, more specifically, the respective place of Jews and Gentiles in relation to God's purposes in Christ. 'Central to Paul's communicative purpose,' Esler writes, 'is to strengthen the social identity that his addressees in Rome gain from belonging to the Christ-movement, particularly by emphasising its supremacy over other identities, ethnic especially, on offer'.[17] Among the Christians in Rome are those who categorize themselves as Jewish Christians and others who categorize themselves as Gentile Christians. This leads them to interpret past events differently (Rom. 1 – 4); understand the workings of God differently (Rom. 5 – 6); evaluate the place of the law differently (Rom. 7); understand their identities in Christ differently (Rom. 8); and envisage the future, especially of the Jews, differently (Rom. 9 – 11); as well as place different values on a range of religious practices (Rom. 12 – 14).

The tensions, then, lie between two subgroups within the one Jesus group. Paul's strategy is to seek 'to bring them together by reminding them of the single category that they have in common – faith and righteousness in Christ'.[18] In each area, Paul sets out to provide a careful description of who they are as those who are loved by God and 'called to be saints' in Rome (Rom. 1:7).

Using the concept of categorization, there are, Esler explains, basically three ways in which he could have achieved his objective of instructing them in their true identity as those who were 'in Christ Jesus' (Rom. 8:1). He could either use the way of re-categorizing them; or de-categorizing them; or cross-categorizing them.[19]

Re-categorizing means that the subgroups involved in a conflict situation are called to perceive of themselves as belonging to a larger, more significant category. In United Kingdom terms, people may define themselves as Welsh, Scottish, White English or Asian English but, when facing a global conflict, most would redefine themselves as British. De-categorizing occurs when the particular boundaries in dispute are dissolved, by being rendered insignificant, and then people identify themselves more by personal and individual traits. Esler applied this approach to the parable of the Good Samaritan and demonstrated that the unease caused by him being a Samaritan was cancelled out in the light of the compassionate service he rendered the injured traveller on the road to Jericho.[20] Cross-categorization involves the cancelling out of the identity over which people differ by another which they share. The difference between this and re-categorization would appear to be that in re-categorization the secondary identities remain and are not obliterated.

Leaders such as Paul are 'entrepreneurs in social identity'[21] and have an obligation to seek to turn the language of 'you' and 'me' into the language of 'us'.[22] This is not to suggest that Paul was 'a good social identity theorist' but rather that he had learned a number of lessons about reconciling conflicting groups.[23] As a result he adopts the strategy of re-categorization whereby Jews remain conscious of their Jewish identity and Gentiles remain conscious of their Gentile identity, but they come to appreciate that both these identities are subsumed under a superior one, that of being in Christ. As a result, Jews may still treasure their heritage of circumcision and of having been 'entrusted with the laws of God', but must realize that they too are sinners. They sin with the law, while Gentiles sin without having had the benefit of the law, but they are both 'held accountable to God' (Rom. 3:19) and stand in need of justification. They may look back with a sense of pride to Abraham as their father, and rightly so, but must realize that Abraham was accepted as righteous not because of his works but by believing God (Rom. 4:3) – the same basis on which Gentiles are accepted. Or, to jump forward to Romans 14, they may differ over their diets or the observance of special days but they must realize that on whichever side of those debates they stand, both sides are welcomed by God, both are accountable to God, and him alone, both are called to live in peace and avoid putting stumbling blocks in each other's way, and both are called to act in faith and have clear consciences. Romans 14:19, 'Let us then pursue what makes for peace and for mutual edification', is the practical outworking, then, of what it means for both to identify themselves not primarily as Jews or Gentiles, but as those who belong to Christ.

The Galatian situation is different. The conflict here is not within the Christian group but is generated from outside by a group who wish to engage in vigorous boundary maintenance on behalf of the Jews. They see what they advocate as a gospel, albeit different from what Paul was preaching and one that he regards as a perversion of the true gospel of Christ (Gal. 1:7). The result of their preaching is that the Gentiles who are following Christ are made to 'have a threatened or even negative social identity in relation to the house of Israel'.[24]

Members of a group whose identity is threatened like this may respond in a number of different ways.[25]

1. Some may choose to leave the group or the group may even be abandoned.
2. A more likely strategy is that they may choose to change and re-evaluate their stance in relation to the dominant threatening out-group. This, in turn, might lead to a third or fourth response.
3. Some may seek to redefine their situation. For example, in Galatians, some may wish to point to the work of the Spirit

among them (Gal. 3:2–5). Or, not infrequently, groups redefine what was hitherto considered a weakness to be a strength. Esler cites the 'Black is beautiful' saying that redefined the issue of colour in the 1960s as an illustration. More recently still the highjacking of the term 'gay' for the homosexual community has placed a positive spin on what once was a despised lifestyle. In Galatians this may be happening through the positive explanation of freedom in Christ.

4. The final strategy may be that of competition, which is the strategy Esler essentially believes Paul adopts in Galatians.

Social competition refers to 'the efforts by the subordinate ingroup to improve its actual social location vis-à-vis the dominant group, especially in relation to their respective access to status and resources'.[26] In his letter Paul counters the claims of the threatening group by arguing that Galatian Christians, whether Jews or Gentiles, are the true offspring of Abraham and children of promise who can enjoy their status, no longer as slaves under the law, but as sons of God who have a close and accessible relation with the one they call 'Abba! Father!' (Gal. 4:7).

A competitive approach to social identity usually involves the use of stereotyping and Esler believes a good deal of it, both positive and negative in form, can be found in Galatians.[27] Positively, for example, his converts are called 'descendents of Abraham' (Gal. 3:7); 'children of God' (3:26); 'led by the Spirit' (5:18); and, most significantly of all, 'the Israel of God' (6:16). By contrast, those who disturb the peace are negatively stereotyped:[28] they are put under the curse (Gal. 1:9); said to be bewitchers (3:1);[29] children of the slave girl who deserve to be driven out (4:30–31); who live 'according to the flesh' (5:16–17) and those who delight in imposing a cosmetic spirituality (and surgery!) on others while they themselves live by a different spirituality (6:11–13). It is evident, as Neyrey puts it, that 'It would be an understatement to say that Paul is fiercely jealous of his turf'.[30]

While not agreeing with all the detailed exegesis that Esler offers, his overall approach demonstrates the value of reading the sections of the New Testament he has chosen through the lenses of social identity theory.

Social Identity in the Greco-Roman World

How ready should we be to apply contemporary theories about social identity to the Greco-Roman world? These theories assume, rightly, that a person today has a fair degree of freedom in constructing their identity. But was that so in the world of Paul's time?

The understanding of what it was to be an individual personality was altogether different then from our contemporary understanding, according to Bruce Malina and members of the Social Context Group.[31] Writing about the cultural anthropology of the first-century Mediterranean world, and consequently resorting to a high level of generality,[32] Malina has insisted that people perceived themselves not as autonomous individuals but as collectivist selves. Their identity arose from their relationship to others and their place in the networks of relationships they inhabited, rather than from individual choice or individual consciousness. The primary network in which they were embedded was that of the family but there were other networks as well, such as the political body, the ethnic group, or the craft or trade guild. In the early Mediterranean world 'a meaningful human existence depends on people's full awareness of what others think and feel about them, and their living up to that awareness'.[33] They were 'group-embedded and group-oriented' and showed no interest in individuality and autonomous self-consciousness.[34] In short, they formed 'their self-image in terms of what others perceive and fed back to them'.[35]

Expanding on the features of the collectivist personality, Malina lists, among other characteristics, that it led to a high degree of conformity; an acceptance of authority; reluctance to disagree with superiors; dependence on others for the vast majority; strong in-group ties but little faith in those outside the group; clear differentiation of gender roles; assessment of behaviour by what was outwardly observable; lack of introspection and refusal to expose the inner self; absence of self-determination and influence of social determination.[36]

The collectivist personality had implications for the practice of religion as much as any other area of life. Religion was enmeshed in the political and family systems of the ancient world and difficult to separate out from them. Conversions essentially took place col-lectively, through a household deciding to become Christian, rather than being an individual experience. The role of authority figures was accepted and, with that, the truth they taught was accepted too.[37]

One would expect this to lead to a highly static world where conversion to another religion and any redefinition of religious, social and personal identity would be very rare. Yet, manifestly it happened. How was it possible? The answer is implicit in the understanding of how we derive our social identity that was given earlier. The formation of identity is always a dialectical process between the individual and society. If in our society the dominant voice in the process is that of the individual, almost it seems, on occasions, to the exclusion of the voice of society, the reverse would have been true in the ancient world.[38] It cannot be true that there was no sense of individualism or of introspective consciousness. Creative individuals, like Paul, broke out of the confines imposed on them by their social networks. Personal emotions and individual passions are frequently mentioned in the New Testament and on occasions, albeit infrequent, the work-ing of individual psychological consciousness is evident. While the dominant component is undoubtedly the 'we' or the 'us', it is not so dominant that the 'I' and the 'me' are annihilated.

In the process of forming social identity the group certainly played a more significant role than it might today. It is possible today to identify oneself, for example, as a Roman Catholic while openly disagreeing with the church's teaching on abortion or contraception, and maintaining the right of individual conscious-ness, without feeling obliged to sacrifice the identification of being a Roman Catholic. We adopt a more consumerist approach even to groups to which we are committed than people of an ear-lier age did. Clearly people took independent lines and disputed what the apostles taught in New Testament times, otherwise there would have been no need for most of the New Testament letters. (When they did this they were, of course, reflecting the other or out-groups to which they belonged.) Yet, the sense of col-lective identity comes through the letters strongly and the appeal to 'this is what it means to be a Christian, now live it out' was much stronger than today when 'searching', 'journeying' and 'exploring' in a more open-ended way is encouraged. Colossians provides evidence of this in its use of the language of tradition and of '*the* gospel', as we have already seen.

So, while people were more collectivist personalities in the early Mediterranean world than today, they still engaged in the process of identity formation even if in a more restricted sense than would be common now. What, then, can we say about the identity of the early Christians on the basis of Colossians?

Colossian Christian Identity: Unimportant Factors

Four regular markers of social identity in the ancient world are evidently unimportant to the Colossian Christians. It is not that these identity markers have been obliterated. They still remain, but they are rendered insignificant in the light of the overwhelming identity that is formed by being 'in Christ'.

The first boundary marker which is insignificant is ethnicity. Colossians 3:11 says as much. Given the renewal which is taking place 'there is no longer Greek and Jew, circumcised and uncircumcised, barbarian, Scythian, slave and free; but Christ is all and in all'. People remained Jews and Greeks and they could not deny their barbarian or Scythian backgrounds. These identities, no doubt, continued to play themselves out in attitudes, education levels, cultural orientations and a host of other ways, but such identities had been eclipsed by being 'in Christ', and the usual ethnic boundary markers, which may have mattered much to others, were no longer of any importance to Christians. The church was an inter-ethnic body where people of different backgrounds found a common identity 'in Christ'. They had, in terms of our earlier discussion, been re-categorized.

A second identity marker which would have usually been significant in the ancient world, but which is surprisingly absent from Colossians, is that of being citizens of Rome, using that term in its widest sense rather than in its more restricted sense of being a Roman citizen. Philippi was a proud Roman colony and an awareness of citizenship is alluded to in Paul's letter to the church in that city. But even there, being a Roman citizen is set aside as unimportant in preference to the superior citizenship of heaven, most notably in Philippians 3:10. In Colossians, while there may be allusions to the lordship of Caesar and the powers and authorities of Rome,[39] they are not directly named and it is made clear that they are powerless when confronted by the Christ. Otherwise, being a member of Rome's empire was so insignificant as not even to rate an allusion, let alone a mention.

The third identity marker which would usually be significant, but which is relativized in the face of a true Christian identity, is that of social status. As with ethnicity, becoming a Christian did not abolish the reality that some were wives and some husbands, some children and some parents, some slaves and some masters. The roles continued and Christians were encouraged to work within the socially prescribed expectations which were inherent in them. There is no suggestion that the roles should be over-thrown in the interests of egalitarianism. But the instructions given in the household code (3:18 – 4:1) and in the related letter to Philemon draw the sting of the roles. Slaves have become 'brothers' in Christ (Phlm. 16) and are working for a divine Master, not just a human one, who will reward them justly one day even if they receive no justice on earth (Col. 3:23–5). Similarly, masters remain in charge, but must govern their slaves in a new way, always remembering that, just like their slaves, they are also answerable to a heavenly Master (4:1). Not only is their power significantly restrained, but their status is relativized. The same holds true for the other relationships mentioned in the household codes, each of which are invested with new meaning because of Christ. Again, in Esler's terms, this is re-categorization, whereby lesser identities are subsumed under a superior identity and consequently rendered insignificant.

The gender divide is included in the re-categorization just mentioned. This holds true even though there is no specific reference to male and female in 3:11, in contrast to the parallel statement in Galatians 3:28. The household code which speaks to the wife of what 'is fitting in the Lord' and imposes a restraint on the husband's behaviour (3:18–19)[40] alters, rather than merely reinforces, contemporary moral practices. The 're-categorization' of the gender divide is further supported by the reference to the place Nympha occupies in the leadership of the church in Laodicea.[41] Being a woman was apparently not an issue in her hosting the church in that near-by town. Thus, a fourth identity marker which was generally considered significant is eclipsed by the greater identity of being 'in Christ'.

Colossian Christian Identity: Important Factors

The problem and the strategy

The reason why Paul wrote Colossians is to combat the threat to Christian identity. The threat is described in 2:8–23. No label identifies those who threaten true Christian identity as Paul has taught it, and the threat may not emanate from an easily identified subculture, like the Judaizers, so much as from a more amorphous group who are infiltrating the church with their misguided and syncretistic teaching. We only have tantalizing glimpses of the nature of the 'aberration', which has been subject to a multitude of explanations.[42] The features of the misguided teaching involved 'philosophy and empty deceit, according to human tradition, according to the elemental spirits of the universe' (2:8). It involved the observance of food regulations and a sacred calendar (2:16), as well as the adoption of ascetic practices and visionary experiences which were somehow related to the worship of angels (2:16–23). The Jewish elements suggest that a channel through which these false demands were disseminated was the synagogue but other elements in the 'strange mixture'[43] point to some wider influences at work and the issue is clearly not identical to the false teaching Paul was combating in Galatians which arose from the Judaizers.

As Morna Hooker pointed out, the proponents of the false teaching 'are variously thought to be members of the Christian community spreading corruption from within, or outsiders attacking the Church's beliefs'.[44] The neat division, then, between the identity problems reflected in Romans, which arose from competing groups within the church, and the identity problems addressed in Galatians, which arose from a group outside the church, may not be as easy to maintain when it comes to Colossians. Andrew Lincoln believes that 2:18–19 suggests strongly that the person referred to is 'a believer who is in spiritual danger' and that attempts to suggest that the threat is external are incorrect. Given the description, he concludes 'It is quite possible that a Hellenistic Jew who had left the synagogue to join a Pauline congregation or a Gentile convert who had had some previous contact with the synagogue would advocate such a philosophy, and the writer evidently was concerned that it might appeal to others among the predominantly Gentile Christian readers'.[45] This certainly makes sense of Paul's reference to them 'not holding fast to the head' as if it were a connection they once had which they were now letting slip. But, even so, the situation is very different from both Romans and Galatians. On the one hand, the erroneous influence is less integral to the church than in Romans, while, on the other hand, it is less structured in form than in Galatians.

The combative nature of Paul's approach is certainly restrained by comparison with Galatians, so much so that Hooker refers to 'the extraordinary calm with which Paul confronts' them.[46] Paul does not stereotype or denounce his opponents in Colossians with anything like the same degree of anger as he uses in Galatians. No personal animosity or vindictiveness is expressed. Their arguments are said to be 'pseudo-philosophers', 'charlatans',[47] and 'deceptive' (see 2:4). They enslave those who follow them (2:8), and their beliefs are based on 'human tradition' and 'the elemental spirits of the universe' (2:8) rather than being based on any 'assured understanding' (2:2) of 'the word of the truth, the gospel' (1:5). The disturbers of 'truth' seek to 'condemn' and 'disqualify' (2:16,18) those who refuse to practise their rules and undertake their rituals. But, Paul suggests, the reality is that their apparent piety and wisdom amount to nothing and prove ineffective in transforming one's life (2:23).

The only category that matters: 'in Christ'

Rather than being competitive or polemical, Paul's strategy 'is predominantly positive and expositional'.[48] He advocates the superiority of Christian identity as found in the gospel he preached, and devotes most space to carefully explaining it to the Christians in Colossae. In contrast to the pick-and-mix approach of his opponents and the false teaching they are being offered, the gospel is reliable, attractive and effective. Their need was to remain true to it and apply it to every aspect of their lives, rather than to believe it needed supplementing in any way (2:6–7,9; 3:1–4). Central to that identity was their relationship to Christ. They are variously described as being 'in Christ' or 'in him',[49] 'with Christ/him'[50] or 'in the Lord'.[51] The complementary expression 'Christ in you' is also used (1:27).[52] Given the frequency of the terminology there can be no doubt about its defining importance as far as the identity of the Colossian believers are concerned.

The term 'in Christ' or the related 'in him/whom' is a distinctly Pauline phrase. 'It is important,' writes James Dunn, 'to grasp what a range of Paul's theology is contained within the motif.'[53] He helpfully distinguishes between an objective use, a subjective use, a use in describing Paul's own missionary activity and a use in exhortation. Only the third of these is absent in Colossians.

Much of the time it is used objectively to describe the act of creation or salvation, past, present and future which is accomplished through Christ. But it is also used in a more subjective way to speak of believers being in Christ. Both are evident in Colossians and have relevance for the question of identity. This objective element is particularly evident in the 'hymn' of 1:15–20 where the phrase 'in him' is used three times (1:16,17,19) and is supplemented by related phrases: 'through him' and 'for him' (1:16,20). The 'hymn' claims not only a unique status for Christ as 'the image of the invisible God, the firstborn of all creation' but also a unique role for him in creation and redemption. The identity of the Colossian Christians is governed by their having been united with this Christ: the strong Christ who is the originator, upholder and renovator of all creation; the one who is superior to all other powers; who is pre-eminent in all things and who is a completely sufficient saviour. This is the one in whose realm the Colossians now live and to whom they have become subject. To have given allegiance to a weaker Christ, whose creative power was inadequate, whose authority was inferior, and whose redemption was incomplete would have left them rightly cowering under the threats of alternative powers. They would then rightly have been living in fear of malevolent spirits, uncertain of their salvation and, therefore, have needed to adopt other ways of ensuring their wellbeing in this age and the age to come, such as observing rules or undertaking alternative religious rituals. What is important for their identity is not only that they have put their faith in Christ but also that the Christ in whom they have put their faith is the one described in the letter and defined as having 'first place in everything' (1:18).

The phrase 'in Christ' first appears in the opening greeting of Colossians (1:2) where it is used in the subjective sense to distinguish the readers of the letter from the rest of the population of Colossae. The word 'subjective' should not mislead us. Although the phrase has some personal, mystical or existential connotations, Paul uses it more to describe the position of the Christian community than individual Christian experience.[54] Because of our humanity, all people are 'in Adam' (cf. 1 Cor. 15:22) but because of their faith, the Colossian Christians may now be said to be 'in Christ'. To be 'in Christ' is to be 'within his sphere and power of influence' and to submit to his rule.[55] Schweizer put it well when he wrote 'Christ is the place in which the community lives, the atmosphere in which it thrives, and which does indeed permeate it.'[56]

So, the defining mark of the Colossian believers is that they are 'in Christ' and live therefore simultaneously in the natural realm of the city of Colossae and in an equally real but different realm of being 'in Christ'. Being 'in Colossae' means they are subject to ordinary life, need to earn their living, pay their taxes, obey the laws and enjoy the privileges the city offers. They are not exempt from this because they are simultaneously living 'in Christ'. But being 'in Christ' or 'in him' equally imposes privileges and obligations on them as much as being 'in Colossae' does. These have major implications for their 'ordinary' lives in Colossae.

The privileges may be summarized in terms of having an assured salvation because of the death of Christ (1:20; 2:14–15). This is variously and richly described as becoming inheritors (1:12); being 'rescued' (1:13), redeemed (1:14), forgiven (1:14), reconciled (1:21), and enlightened (1:27); given hope (1:27); being enriched in wisdom (2:3); made complete (2:10) and alive (2:13); being released from debt (2:14); and sharing in the triumph of the cross (2:15). They need no longer fear any power or authority that appears threatening to others and have no need of hedging their religious bets by worshipping others in addition to Christ.

The obligation, since they are living in his kingdom (1:13), is to live appropriately. That does not mean submission unaided to a new set of rules. If that were so, it would put them in the same category as the regulators whom Paul is opposing (2:20–23). On the contrary, it means living out the new life which they derived from their joining with the risen Christ through baptism (2:11–12,20; 3:1–4). Sharing in the resurrection of Christ[57] inevitably results in the living of a distinctive lifestyle. It is spelled out in detail in 3:5 – 4:6, where Paul shows the impact on one's personal character (3:5–10,12–14), social vision (3:11), church relationships (3:15–17), household responsibilities (3:18 – 4:1) as well as on their general conduct in a pagan environment and towards unbelieving neighbours (4:5–7). Their identity should be externally observable by the way in which they live.

The adoption of any social identity may usually be observed in the behaviour and lifestyle of those who adhere to it: a person speaks one language as opposed to another, eats one diet as distinct from another, wears certain clothes, a uniform, or badges not worn by others, spends time in certain company undertaking particular activities, and assumes a certain posture on issues and morality. In effect, Paul says it is not any different with Christians. The vocabulary of 'in Christ' is largely left behind, although in the household code he twice refers to being 'in the Lord' (3:18,20), an expression which is usually used in exhortatory sections. However, his concern is indisputably to reveal the outworking of being 'in Christ' in the ethical, moral and attitudinal aspects of life. This, he says, is what it means to truly identify with the risen Christ and it involves a radical change from one's previous way of life and a radical demarcation from those who live in Colossae but not in Christ. 'It is the sort of change,' Dunn writes, 'which follows from the complete identification with another person or cause, when the service of that person or cause becomes all consuming, the basic determiner of all priorities, the bubbling spring of motivation, resolution, and application which perseveres despite setbacks.'[58]

A different perspective: the proposal of Van Broekhoven

The basis for the rival understandings of the Christian gospel may well lie, as Van Broekhoven, has proposed, in the differing social bases on which Paul and his opponents build. Using Mary Douglas' grid-group framework,[59] Van Broekhoven[60] argues that Paul's understanding of the gospel is both high-grid and high-group while that of his opponents is high-grid but low-group. The grid axis refers to a group's conceptual understanding, or symbolic interpretation of reality. If placed high on this axis, the conceptual interpretation is widely shared. The lower people are placed on the grid axis the more room there is for individual and private interpretations. The group axis relates to the measure of social pressure which is applied and accepted. High-group tendencies mean individuals are highly controlled by the group, whereas low-group positions on this axis mean little or no pressure is placed on the individual to conform.

Paul and his opponents, it is argued, are both high-grid, and so do not particularly differ over the belief system. They share the basic Christology of the hymn (1:15–20) and the understanding of God's work in the world. Where they differ in their respective positions is on the group axis. Being high-group, Paul stresses the importance of group affiliation and the group's control over the outworking of the beliefs they share. He uses a great deal of the language of belonging; demonstrates great affection for his co-workers; provides detailed prescriptions for community and household life; and in his employing of baptismal language shows how Christians are already incorporated into the church, and therefore called to support its social structure and abide by its moral code.[61]

His opponents tend towards individualism and a loosening of the pressures exerted by the group. The difference lies in 'their respective social worlds and world views',[62] with Paul's opponents seeming to have a 'greater interaction with the outside world which accordingly frees them to be less loyal to the community'.[63]

So they differ from the lifestyle, behaviour and the application of beliefs, rather than the beliefs themselves. They agree about the importance of Christ but see his 'cosmic work as the *grounds* but not the fulfilment of their own spiritual ascent'.[64] They fit with Mary Douglas' observation that in facing cosmic evil, 'where grid is strong and group weak, magic is at hand to help the individual in a competitive society' and people typically resort to astral powers, observance of rules and feasts, to control their destiny and make their mystical ascent to God.[65]

This proposal raises a number of questions. While Van Broekhoven may have established in his detailed exposition that Paul and his opponents adopted different positions in relation to the group axis, he has not proved that they shared a common position on the grid axis. He admits that understanding 'the opponents' Christology (and its conceptual background) is trickier' than understanding Paul's, not least because we can only see them through Paul's eyes.[66] The plain reading of Colossians is that Paul and his opponents did not share a common belief in the cosmic supremacy of Christ. There is the danger that he takes some of the symptoms of the opponents' position which are evident in the letter concerning low-group commitments, sees that these fit with what might be expected of high-grid, low-group and therefore assumes they adopt a high-grid and so share in Paul's Christology. But that argument is somewhat circular.

Furthermore, it is not clear how Van Broekhoven's argument advances those of Hooker, who spoke of the need not 'to underestimate the pressures of the pagan environment, and to forget the background of these converts'.[67] Nor does it significantly advance the more grounded ideas of Arnold regarding the incursions of syncretistic folk religion into the church.

Having said this, it may be argued that Van Broekhoven supplements the approaches to social identity outlined above, by seeking to explain a detail of why the competing identities were different. It complements those interpretations in stressing that Paul is reasserting the boundaries of the Christian group and seeking to reinvigorate the cohesive nature of the church, in contrast to the onset of a disintegrating individualism.

Conclusion

While the early Mediterranean personality might have been essentially collectivist, it is still valid, necessary and, indeed, illuminating to speak of their construction of 'social identity'. While for much of the time people would have accepted the identities that were assigned to them by birth and social convention, some actively chose to dissent from those identities and were involved in constructing new ones. This is particularly so when Jews and Gentiles were converted to Christ.

In Colossians, as in many other New Testament letters, the identity of those who believe in Christ is contested. Paul is concerned that the distinctive social identity of the church in Colossae is being eroded and writes to revitalize their identity and reassert their boundaries essentially by setting out a positive statement of what it means for them to be 'in Christ'.[68] The Christ in whom they live is not one of their own creation but the Cosmic Christ whose person and work is celebrated in the 'hymn' of 1:15–20. He sounds a warning signal against giving space to the opinions of those who would compromise this identity and makes crystal clear, even if in a calm manner, the distinctions that mark them off from those similar but different religious practitioners who were troubling them. He re-categorizes the categories which would have generally been considered of significance in Colossae, such as race and social position, and stresses that being 'in Christ' is the only 'category' that matters. Once this is grasped, a stream of identity markers begins to flow, touching every area of their lives, and which plainly distinguishes the members of the Jesus group both from their would-be religious captors as well as from their pagan neighbours.

5

Theology: The Social Construction of Belief

The Sociological Perspective

Traditionally the Christian believer thinks that what they believe is a matter of revelation. God has made known to them not only the general shape of the faith but the particular details they are to accept. As a result what they believe is a matter of accepting 'truth' (1:5) rather than discussing opinion. It comes to them from the outside as both reliable and authoritative.

In reality, most believers would readily accept that the situation is not that simple for several reasons. First, Christians differ as to how they see the channel through which this revelation comes. For some it is the Bible, and the Bible alone; for others it comes through the teaching of the church; and for yet others through experience or reason, or through a varying combination of all of these. Second, differing positions are espoused even in a single channel of revelation which requires that the conflicts be harmonized and the tensions between them be reduced if not altogether removed. Third, it is recognized that all 'revelation' needs interpreting. What is said or taught is one thing. What it means and how it applies is another. Fourth, even the most literal of fundamentalists would see that within the Bible there are many passages which are in the form of testimony, reflection or uninterpreted narrative, rather than being a transparent declaration of 'thus saith the Lord'. The result of this is that even those who believe strongly in revelation accept that there is a human element in the way in which it is received and transmitted.

The concept of revelation is foreign to sociologists who come at beliefs purely from the human standpoint. To them, all 'truth' is a human attempt to make sense of the reality which humans experience and is therefore not a divine revelation but a social construction. For them it cannot be otherwise since they are committed to understanding culture and its social dynamics from within a human framework and have no way of handling anything beyond the social dimensions of human experience. This article of faith in the sociological canon is not especially directed towards religious belief. It applies to the complete range of human understanding and applies as much to mathematical concepts, scientific interpretations, psychological explanations, social analyses, historical reconstructions and philosophical speculations as to religious faith. Far from being intimidated by this approach, then, it puts religion on a par with other explanations of reality and means that religion need not be overawed by other disciplines that appear more authoritative. Such an approach is liberating and 'frees us from the tyranny' of the latest bullies[1] who wish to marginalize or eradicate religion. It 'relativizes the relativizers'[2] and humbles those who would claim impregnable superiority.

From this perspective, sociology cannot pronounce whether a belief is right or wrong, true or false. Such verdicts lie beyond its scope. The most it can do is to examine why beliefs are held and to what extent they make sense of the reality they seek to interpret.[3] Not all social constructions of reality are equally good. The test is how far our interpretations make sense of our human experience, and some interpretations make more sense than others. The sociologist does not deal with questions of validity but questions of plausibility, that is, of what people find it credible to believe. In particular, the sociologist is concerned with how a position is created and becomes plausible and how social support is essential for the maintenance of the belief.[4]

The Social Construction of Belief

The theoretical foundation to this is found in Peter Berger and Thomas Luckmann's seminal work, *The Social Construction of*

Reality, where they argue that all 'reality is socially constructed and that the sociology of knowledge must analyse the process in which this occurs'.[5] Peter Berger then applied this perspective specifically to religion and its place in the contemporary world in *The Social Reality of Religion*.[6]

Our initial experience of life suggests that reality is 'fixed' or 'objective'. We take it for granted. It is just 'there' and we can do little about it, or so we think. We are born into families and societies that have learned to interpret the world in particular ways, but these seem so strong and unchallengeable to us that we mistake these interpretations for objective reality itself. These interpretations encompass a number of levels of reality from the way we answer the ultimate questions of life (where did we come from, why are we here?), through the provision of a moral framework for life (the ten commandments), to providing an explanation for the things that threaten chaos on the margins of life (like dreams, suffering and death), on to the more mundane details of ordinary everyday living (don't eat with your elbows on the table!).

The truth is that we do not realize just how fragile this 'objective' world is and how precarious the interpretation of reality we are fed as children really is. This 'objective' world acts powerfully not only on but also in our consciousness because we 'internalize' it. It becomes so integral to us, certainly to begin with, that we do not question it. We see the world through the eyes we have been given. But it is as if we are seeing the world through a pair of spectacles – spectacles that are so much a part of us that we do not realize we are wearing them. Only later, as our world begins to expand, do we realize that the interpretation of the world we thought to be fixed has in fact been constructed by others and needs to be continuously maintained by them if it is to remain firm. Thus we are caught up in a continuous dialectical process 'composed of three moments of externalization, objectivation, and internalization';[7] that is, of our creating a world of meaning, its acting back on us as if it were 'really real', and its becoming a part of our subjective life. In other words *'Society is a human product. Society is an objective reality. Man is a social product.'*[8]

For our purposes, Berger and Luckmann's chapter on the origins and maintenance of 'symbolic universes', entitled

'Legitimation', is of most relevance. 'Legitimation' is the term for the way we give an integrated meaning to the social worlds we inhabit and involves both knowledge and values. The most comprehensive level of legitimation[9] involves giving meaning 'to realities other than those of everyday experience',[10] beyond the level of the mundane and ordinary, and which integrates the totality of things. The history of any society, or of a community, and even the biography of an individual, is made to make sense by being seen from this wider perspective and is understood 'as events taking place *within* this universe'.[11] A 'symbolic universe is the ultimate form by which communal life is rendered valid and real'.[12] It enables us to put what we encounter in everyday life (or even in every-night life, since it includes dreams) in the context of an 'overarching universe of meaning'.[13] In this way my little life is given significance and my ordinary and subjective experiences are given meaning by being placed on a much larger canvass than that of my individual story. It 'puts everything in its right place'.[14]

This comprehensive and overarching explanation embraces everything in life for which we seek a deeper explanation, whether it be suffering, the interruption of the world we take for granted by dreams, fantasies or paranormal experiences, the different stages of our lives which involve birth, maturing into adulthood, marriage and death. Our identities are 'ultimately legitimated by placing (them) within the context of a symbolic universe'.[15] We know who we are because we have a way of making sense of our changing, even confusing and contradictory experiences, and because those experiences are placed within an ultimate framework of interpretation.

To illustrate, sickness may be explained in a number of ways. Illness can be explained as a result of our foolish behaviour, or from a medical or chemical perspective, or perhaps using a psychosomatic framework. But these really deal with the 'how I got sick' question rather than the 'why I am sick' question. To say that we are ill because God has willed it, because it is an act of his discipline and he wishes to teach me through it or, to say, I am ill as a result of Satanic attack, or as a punishment for sin, explains sickness on an altogether higher plane. It seeks to give ultimate answers to the 'why' questions of life.

Symbolic universes not only account for our individual stories but, as mentioned, for entire societies and their history. 'It locates collective events in a cohesive unity that includes past, present and future.'[16] Symbolic universes give meaning to the events of the past, connect people with their predecessors, situate them in the present, giving them a sense of belonging, and also point forward to the future, explaining people's destiny. Since they are the ultimate explanations, symbolic universes legitimize other levels of interpretations rather than being legitimized by them. Yet, even 'symbolic universes' need maintaining or else they would collapse.

In Berger and Luckmann's view 'All social reality is precarious. All societies are constructions in the face of chaos.'[17] Therefore these socially constructed symbolic universes need people and institutions to service them, to keep them alive and to keep people believing in them, and there are a number of instruments they use to do so. People who inhabit them employ conversation, using the particular language and vocabulary appropriate to them so that people see the world through their eyes. They engage in rites and rituals that revitalize belief and revive people who may be beginning to drift in their commitments.[18] And they also engage in defending their interpretation of the universe in the face of threats and problems that might undermine it. So, when necessary, they bolster their constructions by explaining them in new (more or less consistent) ways and come up with new answers against their critics. This last instrument is particularly apparent within Christian theology, which is a key mechanism for maintaining a religious symbolic universe in the face of heresy or disbelief, and has often provided the impetus for a fresh conceptualization or articulation of the received faith.[19]

Ironically, the very institutions which work to maintain symbolic universes are themselves social constructions and, therefore, vulnerable to being replaced. They are caught in an unending dialectical process of legitimating the symbolic universe but, in turn, being legitimated by the symbolic universe they seek to uphold.

Initial Application to the Apostolic Gospel

The early Christians believed that Jesus and the events of his life were exceptional and demanded an explanation. Demonstrably human though he was, they reached for a number of frameworks that could help them interpret what they had witnessed. Given that the events took place in Judea among the Jews, it is not surprising that they initially reached back into the Jewish symbolic universe and particularly to their sacred Scriptures, a major element in the maintenance of that universe, for those interpretations. This resulted in various formulations like that of Peter explaining on the day of Pentecost that what people saw was the fulfilment of what Joel had predicted, that Jesus was 'the Messiah' who had inaugurated the coming age ('the last days') for which they had longed, and who through his death and resurrection was vindicated by God and installed on David's throne 'at the right hand of God' until all his enemies were finally defeated (Acts 2:1–37). Time and again they believed that they had seen Jesus do what their sacred Scriptures claimed to be God's unique work, so they drew the obvious implication about his unique relationship with God. They ransacked those Scriptures to explain Jesus in terms of 'the prophet', 'the servant', 'the high priest', 'the Son of God', 'the Son of Man', the 'word of God', the 'new Moses' and so on. The story of Jesus was not to them the story of a private individual but the key to understanding the whole of creation and of God's working within it and his future for it. Jesus, then, became the central figure in making sense of life and of constructing a new symbolic universe in which the experiences and puzzles of individual lives were given meaning and in which the course of history came to make sense as well.

Once the mission activity of the early apostles moved beyond Jewish circles and they began preaching to Gentiles, explaining the person and work of Jesus had to be reconstructed. The previous categories of interpretation made little sense to Gentile audiences, unless they were already associated in some voluntary way with the Jewish community by being a 'god-fearer' or sympathetic observer. So, consistent with what they believed to be the truth about Jesus, they came up with new social constructions of their gospel. This is clearly seen in the preaching of Paul, as recorded in the Acts of the Apostles. His explanation of the gospel takes on a very different starting point in Lystra (Acts 14:8–18) and Athens (Acts 17:16–34) than it did in a Jewish synagogue. Central to his gospel was the death and resurrection of Jesus, but what did those events mean?[20]

'The central emphasis of Paul's missionary preaching,' writes Ekhard Schnabel, 'was the proclamation of Jesus as the Messiah of the Jewish people and the Kyrios [Lord] of the world'.[21] The change in terminology was not a mere accommodation to the audience so as to make it more appealing, for the claims, whether cast in a Jewish or Gentile light, would have been offensive to the hearers. The message did not become less demanding or more attractive by being recast. It was a matter of making sense of the same message in a culture that had been differently socially constructed. So, Paul's preaching to the Gentiles was a new or at least revised 'social construction' of the life of Jesus of Nazareth.

Central to the proclamation was Jesus' death by crucifixion.[22] In Jewish eyes such a death meant the victim was cursed by God.[23] How then could a crucified man be 'the Messiah'? In Roman eyes such a death meant that he was a convicted criminal and identified him with slaves and the scum of the earth to be disposed of at will by the power of the day. How could such a person be 'Lord'? The contemporary understanding of crucifixion, in Greek culture as well as Jewish and Roman culture, was a very real problem for the claims made about Jesus. So it was necessary for the apostles to reinterpret the meaning of the cross, as Paul does most explicitly, but not exclusively, in 1 Corinthians 1:18–30. The cross is presented as God's ironic instrument of salvation. In Christ, God was embracing the weakness experienced by a victim of crucifixion and in doing so he displays his strength. In embracing folly, displayed in permitting his Son to be executed in such a humiliating fashion, God was paradoxically revealing his wisdom. In other ways too, the meaning of the cross is socially reconstructed so that it becomes good news, not bad. Thus, Galatians 3:13 claims that in becoming cursed Jesus is able to release those who justifiably are cursed by their failure to keep the law.

These ways of reinterpreting the cross are social constructs because they 'are part of a web of meanings embodied in social patterns and social relations'.[24] These ideas about the cross are not free-floating and have no existence apart from the group who believe them and live by them. The apostles are the 'significant' people whose authority to interpret the meaning of the cross is accepted by others. They have achieved this significance because they had been close to Jesus, witnessed his resurrection, and now demonstrated the same acts of power that he did. Their teaching answers the questions posed by the historical, social and personal experience of their hearers. It makes sense to them of the conundrums they daily face by portraying what Christ has done, as it were, on the widest screen of all. It is the overarching umbrella beneath which total shelter can be found. It is also a construct that determines the way people live in the daily routine of their lives. The motif of death and resurrection gives the clue to how they may personally relate to God and becomes the key factor in determining their behaviour, shaping their characters and controlling their relationships.

Scholars have been fascinated by the dating of Colossians because they think it may illuminate the way in which early Christian teaching developed, especially with regard to Christology, in the late Pauline or post-Pauline period. But Colossians is perfectly consistent with the earliest claims about Jesus. Peter spoke of him as '*both* Lord and Messiah' (Acts 2:36) in the first Christian sermon ever preached. What is happening in Colossians is that the initial claim is examined in greater depth and applied rigorously to the situation of the Colossian church. So, it reflects both the church's location in the vulnerable city of Colossae and the threatening influence of those who suggested that Jesus, however eminent, was not the supreme and solitary Lord. The theology of Colossians, then, is particularly constructed to maintain the Christian symbolic universe in a way that makes sense of their experience.

Application to Colossians

Colossians yields rich information when viewed from the perspective of social construction. While our primary interest lies in how Christian doctrine is constructed to supply ultimate meaning to the experience of its readers' everyday lives, there are other relevant factors which we should note first.

The maintenance mechanisms of Colossian theology

The significant other

As we have mentioned, any interpretation of the objective world that is to be considered plausible on an ongoing basis depends on various elements that compose its 'plausibility structure' being operative. First among them is the significant person or persons who adopt the interpretation for themselves and pass it on and explain it to others. 'Significant others,' write Berger and Luckmann, 'occupy a central position in the economy of reality maintenance.'[25] Some people matter more to us than others, perhaps because of their power, authority, experience, or because we are in love with them. As a result, we take more note of what they say than we do of those who mean less or even little to us. They become one of our primary, if not exclusively our primary, reference points.

While Epaphras (1:7) was the means by which the Colossians were initiated into the gospel's interpretation of the world there is a hint, in 4:12–14, that his authority was being questioned or his influence was not as significant as necessary if the meaning system embedded in the gospel he had preached was to be maintained. Consequently, one who is more significant is introduced, namely Paul, who greets them as 'an apostle of Christ Jesus by the will of God' (1:1). His credentials were greater than those of Epaphras, and his track record as the founding father of many churches put him in a different league from Epaphras, whose authority he seeks to bolster in 1:7. Epaphras was almost certainly a convert of Paul's and Paul would have been well-known among them even though they had not met him. People might suspect, however, that Epaphras had not fully understood Paul's gospel or had distorted it in some way in retelling it. But when Paul himself is brought into the picture they are connected directly with the apostolic gospel and so encouraged not to deviate from it. The letter not only intrudes Paul directly into the Colossian scene but also endorses the authenticity of Epaphras' teaching and therefore his significance among them,[26] while Paul's explicit objective is to use all his energy and skill to maintain and improve a true understanding of reality which is currently in danger of being undermined among the Colossians (1:28–9).

The significance of Paul is underlined by the way in which he presents himself in the letter.[27] Having introduced himself as one who was fulfilling a divine commission (1:1,25) in teaching 'the word of the truth' (1:5), he goes on to speak of himself as sharing in the sufferings of the Messiah (1:24), as a revealer of the mystery which has long-been hidden (1:26–7, 2:2–5), who operates according to the canons of wisdom (1:28) and without regard for ease or personal comfort (1:29 – 2:1). He is courageous and not afraid to confront those whose teaching lacks 'wisdom' (2:8–23). While the claim to be a model is more explicit elsewhere, there are several hints in Colossians that Paul embodies the message he preaches (4:3–4). Finally, Paul portrays his mission as anything but small and insignificant. His use of 'every', 'everyone' and 'all' (1:23,28–9), his reference to his struggle for those who have not met him personally (2:1), and awareness that the gospel 'is bearing fruit and growing in the whole world' (1:6), mean his 'mission takes on global proportions'.[28]

Conversation

Berger and Luckmann state that 'The most important vehicle of reality-maintenance is conversation'.[29] Conversation permits a particular view or reality to be continuously reinforced and strengthened as a result.[30] Conversations make the 'objective world' more real. If the conversation is only occasional then the firmness with which the subjective interpretation of the world is held is likely to be correspondingly lessened.[31] Even in crisis situations where the view of reality is under threat, conversation is often sufficient to re-establish it, although rituals too may well have a place. 'Talking through' the various questions of the doubters is usually sufficient to bring them back into the fold.[32] Conversations make firm what might otherwise be vague and brings 'reality' into a sharp focus. They enable us to share our subjective worlds with others and to refine them in doing so.

Conversation usually takes place face-to-face but the conversation between Paul and the Colossians takes place in the form of a letter. The moral teachers of Paul's day would frequently use letters as a means of instructing their disciples more fully in their teaching. It was considered a more personal and friendly means of communication than, say, the publication of a speech or discourse which was meant for a general audience and not about a specific situation. It was a means of instruction that the apostle Paul adopted and may even have pioneered among other apostles.[33] But it was, of course, a one-sided form of communication and is not amenable to ongoing adjustment in the way in which a live conversation would be.[34]

Most face-to-face conversations take place in a context where much is taken for granted and this is especially true of a personal letter. To usurp what Malina says about the gospels, Paul's letters may be described as 'high density' texts because, unlike 'low density' texts which are detailed and leave little to the imagination, they are 'sketchy and impressionistic texts' and leave much to the reader's imagination, just as in a normal conversation.[35] So we must look for what is assumed but unstated in the correspondence. What, for example, had Epaphras told Paul about the state of the Colossian church? And where, for example, did the false teaching that threatened to undermine the gospel according to Paul and Epaphras come from?

The particular language used in conversation shapes the way its members see the world. There is, by way of illustration, all the difference in the world between saying something was a 'mere coincidence' and saying that 'God providentially arranged it'. The one assumes an impersonal and random universe while the other assumes the intervention, either directly or indirectly, of a personal God in a person's life. But conversation, through its use of particular language, not only expresses the world as we see it and maintains a view of reality we have already accepted but has the potential to modify it too. In Colossians, Paul is not contradicting the gospel preached since the day of Pentecost, but his conversation brings it into sharper focus and refines it so that they might see it from a fresh angle and see new, hitherto unobserved, things in it. The conversation is, then, maintaining the gospel's view of reality, which is in sharp contrast to the general view of reality in Colossae, by coming at the gospel from a new perspective which is of particular relevance to the social experience of the Colossians.

Rites and rituals

Rites and rituals also play an important role in maintaining a group's interpretation of reality. Two 'rituals'[36] are mentioned in Colossians: that of baptism (2:12) and worship (3:16). There is no mention of the Lord's Supper, which Meeks describes as a 'ritual of solidarity'.[37] Baptism is only explicitly mentioned once but that belies its significance in Paul's argument. Baptism was 'the ritual of initiation',[38] a clear boundary marker which enshrined within it a whole world of subjective meaning. It was a spiritual 'circumcision' (3:11–12) and thus it gave those who underwent it membership within God's community together with all the markers of that community's corresponding identity. It symbolized their being made alive with Christ (3:13) and so of sharing in the exalted life he now enjoyed (3:1–3). It spoke of death to 'the elemental spirits of the universe' who therefore no longer had any sway over them or significance for them (2:20). It epitomized the life they were not to live, as well as the one they were to live. Just as in baptism they were literally unclothed and reclothed, so morally they were to 'put to death . . . whatever in you is earthly' and to 'clothe yourselves with compassion, kindness, humility, meekness, and patience' (3:5,12).

Colossians 3:16 gives a rare insight into the ongoing worship of the early Christians. Five elements are involved: (i) the word of God, (ii) mutual teaching and admonition, (iii) wisdom, (iv) thanksgiving, and (v) singing, which is addressed to God and is varied in form. It would be possible to read too much into these unexplained elements. The word of God certainly later involved the public reading of the Scripture together with its exposition (1 Tim. 4:13), and that is probably implicit here. The stress on mutual edification and the absence of any reference to instruction by teachers implied the church was still not formalized and institutionalized as yet.[39] It remained a community which, while not egalitarian,[40] was not especially hierarchical either. Wisdom refers to the manner in which the mutual edification is to be undertaken but it picks up the more major theme about wisdom that occurs throughout the letter.[41] Their manner has to be consistent with their message. Thanksgiving came to be particularly associated with the eucharistic meal but there is no evidence that it is used in this restricted form here. The need for gratitude is another running theme in the letter.[42] Lincoln speculates that the emphasis is 'because thankfulness and joy were in short supply in the philosophy, with its severe ascetic regulations'[43] but there may be other explanations too.[44] While the exact differences between 'psalms, hymns, and spiritual songs' may be debated, these ingredients of worship must have been a crucial means of conveying the theology of the early church. All of these play a key part in maintaining the 'symbolic universe' and function in the same manner as conversation does.

The construction of Colossian theology

John Barclay has commented on 'the dearth of theological analysis' of the letter which is evident among New Testament scholars.[45] Yet, as he admirably sets out, the letter displays a 'heightened Christological self-consciousness that is . . . sufficiently confident to claim the church's "secret" is the secret of the universe'.[46] Every aspect of its interlocking themes, he rightly suggests, 'may be viewed in terms of its relationship to Christology'.[47] He enumerates the themes as Christ in relation to creation, God, Christ, salvation, the powers, the church, the life of the community, the hope of glory and service in everyday life.[48] We shall explore the way in which three themes are socially constructed to provide a symbolic universe which addresses the actual situation of the Christians in Colossae.

Christ and his cosmos

The 'hymn' (1:15–20), as we now have it, celebrates the pre-eminent role of Christ in relation to the cosmos.[49] Consistent with John 1:1–5 and Hebrews 1:1–4, the 'hymn' ascribes the act of initial creation to Christ and asserts his ongoing role in upholding it. It was not only brought into being 'by him' or 'through him' but also 'for him'. He is both its agent and its goal. He has the place of supreme honour within creation as 'the firstborn' and as such 'thrones or dominions or rulers or powers' are subordinate to him. It is assumed and unspoken in the 'hymn' itself that although created by 'the image of the invisible God' and by the one in whom 'all the fullness of God was pleased to dwell', a flaw has crept into creation which has marred it so that a new start is required. This new start is occurring through Christ's 'body, the church', where, as with the rest of creation, he is supreme. The church, like Christ himself, will be the first in some future time to experience resurrection to a new life, a re-creation. Furthermore, this process of re-creation will climax in the reconciliation of 'all things', that is, of the totality of the disfigured cosmos itself, to God.

From what is said elsewhere, the flaw relates to the existence of sin and to powers that are hostile to creation. The theme of sin brackets the 'hymn'. The need for redemption from or forgiveness of sin is mentioned in 1:14 and as soon as the 'hymn' is completed Paul describes his Gentile readers as having once been 'estranged and hostile in mind, doing evil deeds' (1:21).[50] The 'powers' are variously described in the 'hymn' itself as 'thrones or dominations or rulers or powers',[51] while 'every ruler and authority' is mentioned in 2:10. These twin factors of sin and of 'powers' are said to be dealt with by the cross of Jesus Christ in 2:14–15.

F.F. Bruce suggests 'They [the powers] probably represent the highest orders of the angelic realm.'[52] But even if ancient metaphysical systems distinguished between these terms – Dunn refers to them as 'a hierarchy of heavenly powers[53] – Paul is not interested in doing so. His only interest lies in the superiority of Christ to them.[54] These 'supernatural beings'[55] are invisible and occupy the heavenly realm. They are not specifically said to be hostile and may have included good spirits and beneficent angels. But the weight of evidence suggests that their hostility to human beings is of primary concern. An earlier reference, in 1:13, to 'the power of darkness', and a subsequent reference in 2:15, where Christ is said to have disarmed them, combine with the climax of the 'hymn' in 1:20, which speaks of 'making peace', to suggest they were hostile.[56] Other parts of Paul's argument support this. His reference, for example, to their potentially being taken captive 'according to the elemental spirits of the universe' may well refer to 'the physical components of the cosmos – earth, fire, water and air' – which 'in Hellenistic thought . . . were believed to be under spirit powers'.[57]

Given that at least some may have been hostile, the picture fits with what we know, *contra* Carr,[58] of the world to which Colossians belong. W.T. Wilson summarizes it well when he writes that there were

> feelings of dislocation and loneliness among Hellenistic people. It seemed that the universe, in all its vastness and intricacy, was beyond human comprehension or control, being governed instead by a host of wrathful gods and indifferent supernatural powers. Human beings could do little more than struggle against the relentless tide of 'Fate'. For them, personal and material insecurity, not to mention moral and spiritual indeterminacy, characterized the human condition, which often amounts to little more than a fruitless search for meaning that ends in death and oblivion.[59]

Pagan religion was directed towards appeasing these forces by honouring the gods. At the core of these practices was 'the belief that the very fabric of the universe suffered from some sort of irreparable rift. The two fundamental realms of reality that make up the universe, the celestial and the terrestrial, are set in opposition to one another on account of some cosmic crisis variously described.'[60]

W.T. Wilson was writing before Clinton Arnold published his monograph on *The Colossian Syncretism* and, among a wide range of scholarly resources, bases his work on the research of Robin Lane Fox in *Pagans and Christians*.[61] Arnold's research has only served to confirm the picture.

Scholarly interest has focused on the 'origin' of the hymn and, most recently, on its relationship to the figure of Wisdom, known to us through Proverbs 8 and the writings of Philo, which was a common discussion theme among Hellenistic Jews of the time.[62] If so, Paul is taking the symbolic universe found there, which had Wisdom at its heart, and is reconstructing it to apply to Christ. But our interest is more in how already extant teaching about Christ, as revealed in Paul's letters and what we know of his preaching from Acts, is 'socially constructed' to address the particular situation in everyday Colossae.[63]

There is certainly nothing in the hymn that is in any way in conflict with Paul's other writings. But it puts a particular spin on the understanding of Christ that heightens what Paul has said about Christ before. He takes the previous elements of his teaching about Christ – that he was Lord,[64] that God was in Christ,[65] that he came to reconcile people to God,[66] that he was the firstborn from the dead,[67] that he is our peace,[68] etc. – and combines them in a new way while at the same time adding novel elements to do with Christ's role in creation and re-creation.

1. Christ 'is the image of the invisible God, the firstborn of all creation' (1:15). He has been previously presented as the second Adam (Rom. 5:12–21) but this is the most explicit statement by far of Christ as the image of God. The terminology embraces his perfect humanity (Gen. 1:27) but suggests more than that. He is the one who makes the invisible God visible and 'he does not belong to what was created'[69] but exists with God before it to bring it into existence. So, 'he is absolutely superior to the cosmos, i.e., the whole creation on earth and in heaven'.[70]
2. He is the creator of all things including the 'powers' which the Colossians find so intimidating (1:16). As their creator they are inevitably inferior to and subordinate to him. Creation not only came about by his past activity but continues its existence because of his present activity (1:17). This must include the 'powers' whose continuing existence depends on him.
3. He is the goal of creation (1:16). It exists for his pleasure and glory but he will also serve as determinative of its future destiny. In this capacity he will overcome the rupture in creation and renew it, restoring it to its original design and intention.[71]
4. He occupies the pre-eminent place in the cosmos (1:18). He is unmatched in his supremacy and unique in the position he occupies and the power he exercises. His position of 'first without equal' (and not 'first *among* equals') extends to his being the first to be resurrected from the dead as the 'firstborn' of the renewed creation (1:18).[72]
5. The new humanity is coming into being through the church, which he relates to as a head to a body (1:18). This extends the

previous metaphor about the church as a body, found in 1 Corinthians 12, which majored on the body functioning as an integrated organism, and focuses on the head that gives life and direction to the body. In Colossians 2:10, the term 'head' is applied to Christ's position not only over the church but vis-à-vis the powers as well. The claim is made use of in 2:19 where the opponents are accused of being disconnected from the head.

6. Previous statements about the deity of Christ are surpassed by the claim that 'in him all the fullness of God was pleased to dwell' (1:19). The claim is repeated in 2:9, which suggests the key point at issue is not whether 'the whole fullness of deity dwells bodily' in him so much as what the Colossians make of that claim and how they themselves can access its implication for their own lives.[73]

7. It is through the death of this 'supreme one', the 'power' which is above every 'power', that the reconciliation of 'all things, whether on earth or in heaven' is achieved (1:20). The location 'on earth *or* in heaven' of the things to be reconciled suggests that 'the powers' are specifically in mind, whereas the 'all things' suggests they are not the total picture. His death is mentioned more fully in 2:14–15. 'Reconciliation' does not necessarily imply that they will change their minds and become friends of God but that they will be pacified[74] so that the flaw in the cosmos is overcome and its intended state of being in harmony with God is recovered.

So, Christ is presented in a weighty and wide-ranging way as the clue to the two-fold mystery of the cosmos, that is, the mystery of its creation and the mystery of its re-creation subsequent to the fracturing it has undergone through sin and the activity of hostile powers. Reality – ultimate substance and meaning – is to be found in him (2:17).

While some scholars are cautious about seeing this 'hymn' too narrowly as a response to the problem faced by the Colossian Christians, partly on the basis that the letter does not itself make the explicit link, the connection seems obvious and the caution unwarranted. It is hard to imagine a better way for Paul to expose the folly of the Colossians' need to appease the 'powers' than this; namely, to take the raw materials of Christology which are found elsewhere, even in the Wisdom tradition of the Old Testament, reflect further on them, and push them in a new direction in terms of creation and eschatology.[75] In it he encompasses the problem of personal sin and of creation's fall and reconstructs traditional material. Since Christ is Lord over all, the Colossians can rest assured that their salvation and that of the world is already accomplished by the crucified Christ. He, in himself, and through his death and resurrection, gives them an assured hope of glory (1:27). And they have access to him not through laws and rituals but by standing firm in their faith in Christ (1:4) and the tradition of the gospel they have received (2:6).

Christ and his cross

The message of the cross is presented in a new way in Colossians in 2:14–15. Again, it is perfectly consistent with what Paul had claimed previously but, instead of the categories of justification, righteousness or atoning sacrifice coming into play, a new theology of the cross is constructed. The categories in which the cross of Christ is presented in this letter relate to those of power versus weakness and wisdom versus folly which are found in 1 Corinthians 1. Even so, Colossians is not content merely to repeat what is written there but reframes it in ways which meet the exact situation of the Colossians.

It is said that the cross, on the one hand, erases 'the record that stood against us with its legal demands' and, on the other hand, that it 'disarmed the rulers and authorities and made a public example of them, triumphing over them in it' (2:14–15). While the detailed exegesis of both phrases is problematic, as the commentators mention at length, the overall thrust is clear. The former relates to the forgiveness of sins and the latter to the defeat of the evil powers, both of which have been identified as the problems that lay at the heart of the spoiling of the cosmos (1:13–14). And both are decisively dealt with by the death of Christ on the cross.

The Colossians were in debt and needed to wipe out 'the record that stood against [them] with its legal demands'. The metaphor had a long-standing Jewish background[76] and assumes the legal practice of keeping a written record of debts which, when paid, would be cancelled, once and for all.[77] What this 'record of debt' refers to is uncertain. Many believe it to be the record of good and evil kept in heaven for the final judgement, as mentioned in various apocalyptic writings.[78] In one apocalyptic writing it is said that this book is in the hands of an accusing angel, which seems more than pertinent.[79] The reference to legal demands, though, introduces the suggestion of the law.[80]

The problem referred to here seems in one way or another to resonate with the way in which the Colossian Christians were being invited to supplement their faith in Christ. False teachers were encouraging them to pay off their debt by keeping the regulations concerning diet and holy days, and in some way being involved in the 'worship of angels',[81] and having visionary experiences (2:16–23). But while this may appear a wise course to take, Paul explains that adopting it has 'no value' and is, in any case, completely unnecessary because the 'certificate of debt' was destroyed by Christ through his death by crucifixion. As his body was nailed to the cross so, metaphorically, their debts were nailed to it as well and thereby entirely cancelled.

The second interpretation of the cross is equally expressed in a way that relates specifically to the Colossians' experience of life. As we have seen, they encountered the flaw in the cosmos in the form of the presence of powers who, with malevolent intent, threatened to destroy their lives. They lived in fear of these powers. But the death of Christ, Paul asserts, means they had no need to cower before these powers because they have been vanquished through the cross. Again, despite exegetical complexities, the metaphor of 2:15 is clear. The victim of crucifixion was stripped naked[82] and held up to public ridicule. Paul explains that in submitting to this humiliating ritual, God in Christ[83] was ironically stripping the unseen forces – the very powers that had combined together to humiliate and defeat him – of their power. He casts them aside as one might cast dirty clothes aside at the end of the day. And, having done so, he then parades them as a victorious Roman general would parade the opposing army and its commanders whom he has defeated.[84]

Since the cross has vanquished the rulers and authorities in this way, there is again no reason for the Colossian Christians to be in fear of them, and no need to seek additional assurance by placating them through undertaking the religious and ascetic practices that have been recommended to them. Jesus Christ is a decisive and sufficient saviour and his death on the cross a totally adequate means of overcoming the rift at the heart of the cosmos.

The sufficiency of his death is what one might expect from one who was supreme in the universe (1:15–20). By enduring violence and submitting to the full force of the hostile powers, Jesus Christ confronted them and defeated them. The Colossians, then, needed to have more confidence in the gospel and take their stand on the claim that 'through him God was pleased to reconcile to himself all things . . . by making peace through the blood of his cross' (1:20). They had no need to supplement the work of Christ in any way because it was not in any way deficient.

Christ and his resurrection

The way in which Christians are described as already having been 'raised with Christ', in Colossians 2:12 and 3:1, is seen by many as a further theological innovation. So much so that several use it as evidence that Paul cannot be the author of Colossians.[85] In Paul's earlier writings, 'rising with Christ', the third element of the believer's union with Christ, was still spoken of as future. Romans 6:1–4 speaks of the believer's union with his death and of being 'buried with him by baptism into death' but joining in Christ's resurrection is essentially seen as something to anticipate in the future: 'For if we have been united with him in a death like his, we will certainly be united with him in a resurrection like his' (Rom. 6:5). Similarly in Romans 6:8 Paul uses the future tense: 'we will also live with him'. The resurrection has 'not yet' been experienced, at least fully, in the life of the believer.

In speaking of the believer's resurrection as future, however, Paul has something of a quandary. He has no desire to espouse a negative theology and spirituality which stresses the believer's death and burial but stops short there. His point is that believers are dead to sin and have buried their old lives and so are free from them. But he also positively wants to stress that they are walking now 'in newness of life' (Rom. 6:4) and that they are now 'alive to God' (Rom. 6:11). How can the resurrection, then, be future?

Paul's answer in Romans is to say that believers have to consider themselves 'dead to sin and alive to God in Christ Jesus'
(Rom 6:11). Using a mathematical or accounting word, he
instructs believers to study the balance sheet and calculate how
to live accordingly. Joining in the death and burial of Christ and
the resurrection, which has already happened to Christ but which
is yet to happen to them, has placed an immense amount of grace
in their account so they owe nothing to the claims of sin or the
law. Instead, they can already live in the new life *in anticipation* of
their fully uniting with Christ and experiencing the third element
of their union with him sometime in the future. They may 'not
yet' have fully experienced what it means to be raised with
Christ, but his past resurrection and their future resurrection has
'already' unmistakable implications for the way in which they
currently live. It is not wishful thinking to believe that those who
have faith in Christ may one day rise, since Christ's own physical
resurrection from the dead makes it certain.

In Colossians Paul balances the tension between the 'already'
but the 'not yet' of the believer's resurrection differently and
advocates a realized resurrection. The resurrection is no longer an
event that lies in the future that they will eventually experience,
but a past event in which believers have 'already' been united
with Christ. Significantly, this Christ is described as 'seated at the
right hand of God' (Col. 3:1). He is already in the seat of power
and they live in his presence and share in his powerful life.

The need of the Colossians is different from the need of the
Romans. Their problem is not the threat of antinomianism (that
is, living having rejected laws) but the threat of hostile unseen
powers believed to live in the heavenly realm. Their problem is
not that they are casual about sin, far from it – keeping the law
worries them – but that they lack confidence in their Lord's
supreme position in the universe: a position which is his both
because of his role in creation and because of his victory over the
powers on the cross and his subsequent resurrection and exalta-
tion. So greater stress is laid on their already participating in
Christ's resurrection.

Those who were circulating false teaching were concerned
about how believers were to access heaven and they advocated
various legalistic, religious and cultic practices which would

open the door. They were 'obsessed' with the heavenly realm. Paul does not tell them to 'forget it' but rather exposes their false assumptions and directs the Colossians to reframe their understanding of the upper realm and how to access it. 'Here,' writes Henry Chadwick, 'is one more instance of the typically Pauline method of outclassing his opponents on their own ground.'[86] Unlike his opponents, Paul does not start on earth and see how he can ascend to heaven but travels in the reverse direction, starting with heaven and seeing how what happens there affects how people live on earth.[87] In heaven, Christ is 'seated at the right hand of God', which underlines his superiority over any other authority, whether in the lower or upper realms. Furthermore, 'nothing can prevent [the Colossians'] access to this realm and to God's presence and there can be no basic insecurity about the salvation they have in him and its final outcome'.[88]

Once the Colossians can be persuaded to look to the true situation in the upper realm they will see not only that they have no need to placate the powers that threaten them but also that it is fundamentally erroneous to do so.

Having moved the resurrection in the life of the believer forward, as it were, Paul is still left with the double conundrum that he faced in Romans. The first is the conundrum of the 'so what'? The ethical implication of the future resurrection in Romans is resolved by Paul instructing his readers to 'consider yourselves . . . alive to God' (Rom. 6:11) and so live ethically in accordance with their status and no longer as slaves to sin. The 'so what' question still remains in Colossians. It is not removed by their 'hav[ing] been raised with Christ' (Col 3:1). Paul resolves the issue in Colossians by instructing them to 'seek the things that are above' and to 'set your minds on things that are above, not on things that are on earth' (3:1–2) and work these out in the earthly realm. While he rejects the asceticism of his opponents, he has no embarrassment in introducing his own ascetic teaching,[89] but it has an entirely different place in his understanding from the place it occupies in theirs. It is not the means by which the upper realm may be accessed but the coming down of heaven, which is already the true home of the believer, to earth.

Whether it is the resurrection as a future event or as a past experience that comes to the fore, the ethical implications are the same: Christians are to live as if it will happen or has happened. It makes no difference to the ethical lifestyle to be adopted which tense is used. The latter simply bolsters the encouragement given in Romans 6:1–4 to live out their baptismal confession (Col. 2:11–12) more fully.

The second conundrum is the sense Christians had that the present experience of life does not live up to what might be expected if Christ truly has risen from the dead and Christians are already raised with him. If this is true, why do the Colossians still feel intimidated by hostile powers and sense the need to experience God more fully through the practices suggested by the false teachers? And why are they not recognized now for who they are? In Romans the same dissonance between the claim of the gospel and the experience of the believers' present life exists, even though the emphasis is on the 'not yet' element of the resurrection. Their frustrations are caused by the enduring power of sin and the threat of the law, as well as by suffering.

Paul's answer to this dissonance is very similar in Colossians and Romans. In Colossians he explains that the life of believers 'is hidden with Christ in God' (3:3). In other words, the true reality of their situation and position within the order of creation is not yet evident to others but 'when Christ who is your life is revealed, then you also will be revealed with him in glory' (3:4). In Romans 8 as Paul reviews the 'sufferings of the present time' and the frustrations of the present creation he gives a not dissimilar answer. These frustrations, he says, 'are not worth comparing with the glory about to be revealed to us. For the creation waits with eager longing for the revealing of the children of God' (Rom. 8:18–19). In all the frustrations and weakness of the present life, he explains, God is at work for good (Rom. 8:28) and Christians can be certain that nothing can 'separate (them) from the love of God in Christ Jesus' (Rom. 8:39) that will one day lead to glory. Significantly, among the instruments which might try to force a separation between the believers and God's love Paul mentions 'neither death, nor life, nor angels, nor rulers, nor things present, nor things to come, nor powers' (Rom. 8:38). It is as if he were writing a commentary on and explaining the background to the briefer comments which were to be penned in Colossians 3:4.

In Colossians, then, Paul constructs the concept of the resurrection and its place in the Christian life differently from in his earlier writings. But the differences can be overstressed, and have been. The contrast is not as great as it might at first appear.[90] Both the earlier and later letters accept the twin poles of the 'already' and the 'not yet' of resurrection hope. In the earlier writings the need of the readers was to stress the 'not yet' pole so that they did not fall into the trap of 'cheap grace', whereas for the Colossians the need was to stress the 'already' pole and build up their confidence in the supremacy of Christ. What Paul writes to them was already implicit in his earlier letters. There is no conflict in the writings, but simply a different focus according to need. In many respects Colossians is an elaboration of Romans.[91] What Paul is doing, then, is to take the same building blocks of eschatology as he has always had to hand, but to reconfigure them to address a particular situation.

Conclusion

The theology conveyed in Colossians demonstrates all the hallmarks of having been socially constructed. It legitimates a particular symbolic universe and works to maintain it through a 'significant other' (the apostle Paul) having a conversation (admittedly a one-sided conversation in the form of a letter) with those who have come to inhabit its plausibility structure. He refers to the meaning inherent in their rites and rituals (especially baptism) by way of explanation. But mostly, he takes the already-established Christian gospel and reconstructs its theology in such a way as to deal directly with their social situation and the problems that it poses. In doing so he seeks to remove the threat posed by those who wish to call the gospel's counter–cultural symbolic universe into question and regain their united loyalty to the gospel Epaphras passed on to them.

6

Institutionalization: From Charisma to Institution

When something is entirely new, there are no patterns to follow, but as soon as any group of people begin to meet on a regular basis routine settles in. The spontaneity and novelty of a situation gives way to familiarity. The situation is no longer entirely open and as time passes patterns emerge which exercise a hold over those who meet. To begin with, questions are encountered for the first time and there are no ready-made answers and no precedents to guide the answers. The moment the same question is confronted a second time, there is a precedent that someone is bound to mention and, even if a different answer is given, before long, it becomes obvious that there are only a limited number of options in answering the same question. Before too long, traditions grow and options are closed down.

This easily recognized picture of confronting questions a second time and the impact of meeting together on a regular basis gives a little inkling into the complex process that sociologists refer to as institutionalization. It is a process to which religious organizations, by their very nature, are particularly prone.

From Max Weber to Bengt Holmberg

Max Weber

Max Weber (1864–1920), the most creative genius of the classical sociologists, laid the foundations for our understanding of the process of institutionalization in his discussion of charismatic authority.[1] Weber distinguished between three types of legitimate authority, although he specifically denied that they ever existed in pure form.[2] Authority was based on rational or legal grounds, traditional or hereditary grounds, or on the basis of a person's charisma Weber defined 'charisma' as applying 'to a certain quality of an individual personality by virtue of which he is set apart from ordinary men and treated as endowed with supernatural, superhuman, or at least specifically exceptional powers and qualities'.[3] The definition, however, may be slightly misleading for Weber's chief concern was not the 'individual personality' and its magnetism in isolation, but on the way in which this exceptional person drew a following and provoked a response which resulted in a movement being formed. For Weber the exercise of charismatic authority was a *'social* phenomenon; without acknowledgment from a group of believers charisma does not exist'.[4]

The 'charismatic leader', of which the Old Testament prophet was a prototype,[5] usually arose in times of crisis[6] and 'preaches, creates or demands *new* obligations'.[7] This revolutionary force 'is thus specifically outside the realm of every-day routine' and is anti-establishment in tone and practice.[8] Consistent with the shunning of the ordinary, pure charisma may be seen as a response to an overpowering call that cannot be resisted and which sets its recipient off on a mission or vocation, from which none of the usual financial and other rewards are expected.[9] The charismatic leader has a narrow focus, is 'sold out' to it and calls for others to show extraordinary allegiance to the cause. Those who join him need no rules to protect them. They live communally. The movement is marked by great fervour.

At first sight, Weber's concept of charisma seems strongly opposed to institutions but that is partly because Weber's method is to work with 'ideal types' which he was aware never exist in reality. Eisenstadt has also rightly argued that 'the analytical distinction between charismatic and routine is not complete or extreme' and that Weber was concerned with the bridges that connect them. The result is that charisma can become enshrined in an office or a family or in more traditional structures.[10]

By its nature, charismatic leadership is inherently unstable and 'the desire to transform charisma and charismatic blessing from a unique, transitory gift of grace of extraordinary times and persons into a permanent possession of everyday life'[11] leads to its institutionalization, that is, to its taking on a structure or organizational form. Several factors are involved. If charismatic leaders are to maintain their authority, they must continue to demonstrate the characteristics which gave them authority to begin with. So, if they were the recipients of divine revelation, or a worker of great miracles, the revelations and miracles must continue to flow, otherwise their authority evaporates. But when they do so, the revelations and miracles lose something of their novelty and these unusual events themselves become routine.

The greatest pressure comes, however, from the need to leave a legacy in the form of an ongoing body of followers and this pushes the charismatic leader towards forming institutional structures. A stable community is essential if their authority is to be anything other than transient. Without leaving this behind, their work would simply not survive. But in achieving the legacy, 'it is necessary for charismatic authority to become radically changed'.[12]

Weber says another main pressure for transformation comes from 'the ideal' interest of the movement, the desire to use every resource to continue to broadcast its message, and from 'the material interests of the followers' and of 'the administrative staff' who emerge as the movement grows. These people become more concerned about the need for economic support than the original band of disciples, and begin to require rules to define their roles, and to look for status and a pecking order.[13]

Weber also identifies the demise of the original charismatic leader and the problem of succession as providing a major impetus along the road to becoming an institution.[14] The second-generation leader may be chosen in a number of ways: by a search for one who bears the qualities of the original leader, by revelation, by designation by the original leader, charismatically by existing staff, or even be 'transmitted by heredity' or 'by ritual'.[15] Whichever route is followed, the charisma becomes 'routinized' and the new leader commands less awe and gifts than the founder of the movement. Staff interests also develop[16] and they become protective of their position and exercise increasing control over the recruitment of new leaders. One direction this takes is in the separation of the 'laity' from the 'clergy'.[17] Developments are usually not without conflict. Charisma, thus, changes and, to the extent it survives, is found within the office of the leaders of an increasingly structured organization. In all these ways, 'the hot flowing lava of the charismatic eruption soon cools and hardens into structures of normal solidity'.[18]

Weber's ideas were political as well as religious and several scholars have applied them to contemporary religious movements,[19] as well as to the emergence of the early church. It is easy to picture Jesus as a charismatic leader whose band of disciples maintain something of his charismatic power for some time but to a decreasing degree, and to see how that charisma gets increasingly channelled more and more into offices and structures. The free community of brothers and sisters thus becomes an institution that is defined more and more tightly.[20]

Peter Berger and Thomas Luckmann

Berger and Luckmann's *The Social Construction of Reality* is again of great significance. Their particular focus is on how 'any action that is repeated frequently becomes a pattern, which can then be reproduced with an economy of effort and which, *ipso facto*, is apprehended by its performer as the pattern'.[21] On the one hand, this process makes for efficiency and stability; people are not constantly having to re-invent the wheel. On the other hand, it means that 'choices are narrowed' and that it leads to institutionalization.[22]

Institutions are about people who are qualified to do so undertaking repeated actions in an authorized manner which then become typical of that group.[23] These 'typifications' are shared by members of the group and begin to define it and give it its own identity. Before long, the group looks to a shared history and develops systems of control which establish 'predefined patterns of conduct' to protect their identity.[24] If these controls are unsuccessful, more controls are put in place and controls are spelled out more and more as the changing circumstances of the group require.

In what looks like a fascinating bypath to their discussion, but which proves germane, Berger and Luckmann spend time showing how this applies not just to groups but even to two individuals as they interact with each other.[25] They build the picture step by step until they 'imagine' these two individuals who came from different social worlds having children. The arrival of a child inevitably changes the patterns they have developed and makes them less flexible and more fixed. Parents are eventually called upon to explain and justify the world they have created and legitimate their interpretation of it. '"There we go again" now becomes "This is how these things are done".'[26] The child experiences this family world 'as an objective reality'.[27] So it is with institutions. They are simply there and have an external existence that shows resistance to change.[28] Institutions are formed by actions being repeated and becoming habitual, by a looking back to (often selective) history, by developing traditions, by adapting legitimations, by hardening expectations and defining boundaries.

Thomas O'Dea

Thomas O'Dea has made a broader contribution, setting out the benefits and disadvantages of institutionalization, which has proved extremely stimulating.[29] He identifies five dilemmas which religions face when they become established and routine sets in, all of which were implicit in Weber and the first of which was explicit.

1. The dilemma of mixed motivation

When a new movement commences, a charismatic leader is able to rely on the total dedication of his disciples and their willingness to make sacrifices for the leader and the cause. They do not look for reward. But with the need for stability disciples are granted status, which soon becomes graded and complex, and roles become increasingly defined in their function. These have implications for the obligations of the disciples and also for their rights. So, 'there arises a structure of offices which involve a stratified set of rewards in terms of prestige, life opportunities and material compensation'.[30] The early single-mindedness is replaced by the more mixed motives of wanting to serve but be rewarded for it, until material rewards become the overwhelming motivation.

While the primary location of this dilemma is among the leaders, it is also found among followers when those who are born into the movement come to replace those who were converts to it.

2. The symbolic dilemma: objectification versus alienation

Religious experiences have to be translated into symbolic forms if they are to be shared by those outside the original recipients, and also if they are to be repeated, which is usually necessary if they are to be shared with others. Hence there develop rituals of various kinds: ceremonies, words, spaces, times, actions and songs become sacred. So the experiences are objectivized and these objective symbols make an impact on the worshippers. Over time 'a loss of resonance between the symbol and the attitudes and feeling from which it originally derived' creeps in.[31] The symbols begin to lose their power to elicit a response from the worshippers. 'Objectification,' writes O'Dea, 'necessary for continuity leads finally to alienation.'[32] This is Berger and Luckmann's habituation and typification.

3. The dilemma of administrative order: elaboration and alienation

A further cause of alienation is the development of an elaborate bureaucratic structure. Bureaucracy develops as a way of handling problems and in response to opportunities of growth. Again it is initially a necessary and beneficial response to the changing need of the movement and can make for great efficiency. But once established, bureaucracy is notoriously difficult to change and adapt. When new problems or situations arise, new layers of bureaucracy are laid on top of old ones, which are often irrelevant and dysfunctional. One of the reasons for this is that people who manage bureaucracy come to have vested interests in their territory and ways of doing things. So, the machine becomes over-elaborate and less efficient. Furthermore, it distances office-holders from the rank-and-file members.

4. The dilemma of delimitation: concrete definition versus substitution of the letter for the spirit

The inner ethos (or 'spirit') of a movement needs to be translated into specific guidelines for everyday life, to be expressed in a way new converts can grasp, and to be protected from those who would abuse it. Without this translation it remains an abstract ideal, probably beyond the reach of most would-be adherents. Consequently the pressure mounts to define a movement's belief system and ethical teaching in ever-increasing detail. The moment people ask, 'Is this belief compatible with the spirit of the moment?', the process of transforming the spirit into the letter of the law has begun. So orthodoxy and heresy become defined. The same question is asked in terms of behaviour and so an original ethical insight, such as Augustine's 'Love and do what thou wilt', becomes a set of rules applied with ever-increasing rigidity. Freedom is lost and a moralistic judgementalism becomes a temptation. The boundaries with the world outside become drawn ever more tightly.

5. The dilemma of power: conversion versus coercion

Those who gathered around the original charismatic leader were attracted to him or her by personality, actions and insights. There was no need to work at maintaining allegiance and obedience since they had voluntarily surrendered to the leader's authority. Later generations consist of those who have grown up in the movement and different methods of ensuring compliance become necessary, especially when authority is challenged. Various coercive measures are then adopted, including everything from social pressure to violence as, for example, in the Inquisition. Another factor in this dilemma is the increasing alliance which religious movements experience with power, especially when their first flush of radicalism has passed and when they become numerous. The alliance between church and state means that orthodoxy in religion becomes equated with loyalty to the state, and doubt and heresy are equated with treason. The state then brings its own instruments of coercion into play.

To these five dilemmas, Keith Roberts[33] has added a sixth: the dilemma of expansion when rationalized structure supplants the sense of community that is evident in the first phase of the movement's life. The group needs to grow 'or the members' morale may waiver, and the sense of mission and destiny fade'.[34] But in doing so it inevitably surrenders the value of being a small, face-to-face community where members know all the other members, and it loses the sense of ownership of the group which members once had. They have become participants in a more impersonal society and the relationship to the group, and to each other personally, differs from what it used to be.

These dilemmas are of course a statement of general principles and no particular movement will demonstrate all of them, or all to the same degree.[35] Yet, most movements become organizations over time and most communities become societies, to a greater or lesser degree. If the process proceeds on its full course, it may eventually prove fatal but, before that happens, it may bring as much benefit as harm, as much strength as weakness, to a movement. That is precisely why O'Dea has termed the institutional dimensions he has highlighted as *dilemmas*. Movements would not usually survive without making the transition and certainly not enjoy a sense of stability. Yet, at the same time, much is lost, and the second generation of a movement cannot usually hope to retain the vitality, single-mindedness and purity of its original phase. As Keith Roberts wisely says, institutionalization is 'a mixed blessing'.[36]

Bengt Holmberg

Bengt Holmberg was the first to give an extended treatment of the relevance of institutionalization to the ministry of the apostle Paul. His analysis begins with Weber and provides an excellent critique of his views, especially charging him with a sense of vagueness. Seeking to establish some priority among Weber's numerous reasons for institutionalization, Holmberg states, 'The real driving force of the routinization process is the staff and its strong ideal and material interest in the continuation of the community'.[37] He asserts more strongly than Weber that charisma carries within it an inner impulse towards institutionalization:

charisma is not a passive victim of institutionalization but actively seeks it.[38] He seeks to distinguish the driving force of institutionalization from the dilemmas that O'Dea has set out.

Holmberg finds a more secure foundation for institutionalization in the work of Berger and Luckmann and builds helpfully on it by introducing the idea of complex institutions resulting from 'cumulative institutionalization'.[39] Illustrating it from the institutions of marriage, he suggests that what starts as a simple relationship develops over time into something complex in which one part of the institution might even be legitimated by another. Hence, in marriage, custom institutionalizes behaviour and is enshrined in law which then, in turn, justifies the custom, so reinforcing its institutionalization.

The primary institutionalization that occurs during the lifetime of the charismatic founder and his interaction with the times,[40] is distinguished from secondary institutionalization that occurs after the founding leader departs from the scene.[41] Contrary to Blasi,[42] who speaks of Paul's charisma as socially constructed and enhanced after his death, Holmberg regards it as a natural part of the process that 'the leader's words, his message and example, the rituals and institutions he created' enjoy more authority after his death than before, because 'he is not there to complete, interpret or change them'.[43] A key moment in secondary institutionalization is when the original leader's teachings are collected together, transforming 'unconsolidated verbal tradition into a body of normative texts'.[44] In doing so they become more fixed and the status of the staff who 'conserve, expound, develop and systematize what has already been given' is consolidated.[45] With it, the movement becomes more rationalized and traditionalized.[46]

To Holmberg, the early church is an example of secondary institutionalization.[47] Primary institutionalization occurred in the lifetime of Jesus, but his disciples continue the process into its second phase after his death and resurrection. The church in Jerusalem[48] was already institutionalized by the time Paul visited it and the 'council of Jerusalem' and the collection among the Gentile churches for the Christians there are symptoms of that. The new churches founded by Paul did not claim independent authority but recognized the precedence of Jerusalem. 'Thus,' he concludes, 'even if all apostles of Christ are equals theologically they are not equals sociologically.'[49]

What of Paul's authority? How charismatic and how institutionalized was it? Paul is fundamentally in line with the traditions of Jerusalem and to that extent is not a primary charismatic leader. Although he derives his charisma from Christ he shows some dependence on Christ's original followers in Jerusalem. In spite of this, when Paul begins his ministry 'the tradition was relatively "open" and variable, especially in regard to new conditions and problems',[50] and he becomes a significant charismatic authority in the churches he founds. Holmberg draws attention to the way Paul limits his own authority:[51]

- He makes clear his authority 'is delegated from a higher source to which, in principle, they themselves have direct access (cf. 1 Cor. 3:59; 21b–23)'.[52]
- He presents himself as 'father' of the churches he founded, not as prophet or head. The father image is the warmest and most personal of the images he might have chosen.
- He refuses to exercise his right to financial support.
- His aim in instructing his churches is to get them to make their own decisions about their ethical and corporate lives, within the overall tradition they had already received. He 'motivates and explains his admonitions and instructions' and so 'implicitly rationalizes his authority', rather than seeking to keep them dependent. 'The apostle's letters are thus both an exercise of apostolic authority and at the same time a diffusion of this authority into the local churches.'[53]

What we have in the New Testament, Holmberg acknowledges, is a statement about the theology of Paul's authority, not a sociological description of it.[54] The same is true when we look at the leadership Paul appointed or recognized in local churches where he may have played some role in institutionalizing 'intra-church authority'. But the evidence is very limited as Paul shows little interest in the questions and therefore the assumption that he aided institutionalization in this way 'represents only an educated guess'.[55] But we can say his attitude to institutionalization 'is positive'.[56] He supports local leaders and portrays practical gifts as gifts of the Holy Spirit as much as the more supernatural or extraordinary gifts. In doing so he contributes to the rationalizing and institutionalizing of the church.

Paul's role in institutionalizing the early church is complex and too many judgements about it have been superficial. Holmberg's judicious conclusion is that 'we cannot say that the institutionalization of intra-church authority or the inception of offices occur independently of Paul, even if he did not "institute" them in any simple sense of the word'. His legitimizing of the developments consolidates the institutionalizing process.[57]

Holmberg's specific focus was on the power dimension of Paul's leadership. He was right to reach the conclusion that Paul's role in it was complex. Had he added other dimensions and investigated the process of institutionalization beyond the Pauline letters which are generally considered to be authentic, it would have been more complex still.

Institutionalization in the Pauline Churches: the work of Margaret MacDonald

The widest study of institutionalization in the early church so far is that undertaken by Margaret MacDonald. She derives much from the studies we have reviewed but extends the discussion much further. She shows acute awareness of the difficulties involved in historical reconstruction in general and of the relationship between ideas, social context and sociological institutions in particular, and proposes 'a cautious union' between history and social sciences.[58] The advantage of employing sociological tools is that they will provide us with a more complete understanding of the process of transformation that the early church underwent.

MacDonald adopts the consensus position among New Testament scholars that only some letters which bear Paul's name are authentic. She divides the Pauline corpus into three categories each reflecting a different period of development. The genuine letters (Romans, 1 and 2 Corinthians, Galatians, Philippians, 1 Thessalonians and Philemon) belong to the initial phase of community formation and show only initial signs of institutionalization. The deutero-Pauline letters, essentially Colossians and Ephesians,[59] belong to a second phase of community-stabilizing and show more advanced signs of institutionalization. But the most advanced stage belongs to the third phase of the Pastoral Letters that she terms a 'community-protecting' stage. MacDonald then traces what each of these groups has to say about ethics and their attitude to the world, ministry and the structure of leadership and congregations, ritual, and belief and doctrine.

The first stage provides evidence of the early church being 'a sect in the early stages of institutionalization'.[60] The sect is a voluntary religious community with clearly defined boundaries that, at least in its New Testament form,[61] requires its converts to undergo a conversion experience and to separate themselves from the corruption of the world. The shared conversion experience and shared beliefs build Jews and Gentiles into a coherent community. Many of Paul's writings seek to justify (give legitimation to) this new community. But the conversionist sect does not withdraw its members from the corrupted world and tensions arise as to how its members are to continue to live in the midst of evil. Issues of eating food offered to idols, of marriage and sexual relationships and of the religious calendar are all matters of extended comment in Paul, as are issues of leadership. The patriarchalism of the wider society is transformed by the adoption of love-patriarchalism within the community.[62]

MacDonald rightly rejects the idea that the early Pauline churches were charismatic communities, formless in structure.[63] Once the dialectical 'relationship between beliefs, social structures and social setting' has been taken into account it is evident they were not structureless. While those with the charismatic gifts of prophecy, tongues and wisdom may have been granted authority and looked to for ministry in the early communities, there were signs of other authority structures, including Paul's own role as a father to those communities. Offices had not been formalized and ministry had not be solidified, but his ranking of 'apostles, prophets and teachers', and recognition of some as household leaders, suggests some structure is present and will emerge further.

Using Clifford Geertz's definition of ritual as 'consecrated behaviour',[64] MacDonald sees it as performative action that brings members of the community into contact with the sacred. Sociologically rituals define boundaries, 'stimulate group solidarity' and 'both induce an ethos and define a world view'.[65] The two rituals of importance in these early letters are those of baptism and the Lord's Supper. They encapsulate early Christian belief in the one being baptized proclaiming that 'Jesus is Lord' and the Lord's Supper as a means of remembering the central acts of their faith and of being united by Christ. MacDonald perceptively concludes that at this early stage ritual 'is a blend of the spontaneous and the customary'.[66] Only later is the spontaneity reduced and the traditional liturgical element hardened.

Beliefs, as seen previously, have to do with the building of a symbolic universe. In Paul's early letters they have to do with the events of Christ's life and their relevance for living in Christ in the context of the wider Greco-Roman society.[67] They are also about explaining the current experience of the believing community and providing a legitimation as to how they are to relate to the Jewish law and why, for example, they continue to suffer. Hence, the eschatological thrust of Paul's teaching assumes importance. Central to their belief was that salvation was to be found only in Christ. Ironically, MacDonald observes, the grand vision of evangelizing the world involves it happening through the small sect to which they belong. Hence, 'The Pauline communities may be described as a conversionist sect which is characterized by a tension between remaining separate from the world and saving the world'.[68]

During this initial phase, matters remain quite fluid, although they already show some signs of solidifying. Those signs become more apparent and the process of solidifying – of options being shut down – advance as time progresses. The second phase, that of Colossians and Ephesians, concerns the existence of the church after the apostle Paul has departed from the scene. We summarize it only briefly at this point because we will examine it, at least in regard to Colossians, further in the final section of this chapter.

Briefly stated, on the ethical front[69] there is clear continuity between what is said in these community-stabilizing letters and what was said in the earlier letters. If they are expressed more woodenly, as Käseman thought, it is because the need of the church is different. The clear identity of the Pauline churches has already been established and the need is not to be creative but to match the tradition to the new circumstances the churches faced. So, the image of the body of Christ is used in a new way. Innovative teaching is rejected in favour of continuing in the tradition concerning Christ. The language of belonging and incorporation into Christ is frequent, even if the personal family language of 'brothers and sisters' is absent. The same universal vision is evident, only the claims about it are even more expansive. The same tensions between separating from the world and saving it are evident. The hierarchical nature of society is taken for granted and Christians are encouraged to work within it. The expression of the tradition is 'more conservative' and leaves less room for 'exceptional behaviour' than the earlier letters, but it is clearly the same tradition which is being propounded.[70]

As to ministry,[71] Paul's apostolic and charismatic authority is reinforced, even in his absence. He continues to play a crucial role as a teacher and the one who prevents believers from going astray. In his absence 'his associates could speak in his name'[72] and their work and authority is commended. The church is built on 'the foundation of the apostles and prophets' (Eph. 2:20) and the gifts of grace are now spoken of as being given to apostles, prophets, evangelists, pastors and teachers (Eph. 4:11). No mention is made of other charismatic gifts although worship appears to be highly participatory and ministry mutual (Col. 3:16). Respect is shown to household leaders.

With regard to ritual,[73] the new dimension concerns the place of hymns in worship and the use of hymns, especially the 'Christ-hymn' of Colossians 1:15–20, in doctrinal teaching and the education of the believers. No mention is made of the Lord's Supper but baptism assumes an important role, and one that is different from previously. It is tied now to the resurrection of Christ and his cosmic reign rather than to either an initiation into the body of Christ on earth or merely to union with Christ in death and burial. It now symbolizes the fullness of salvation that believers experience in the present through the risen and exalted Christ. It continues to have implications for a believer's lifestyle and lies behind the plea for them to 'put off their old natures'. On the basis of the institutionalization theory, it might be expected that the ritual dimension would receive fuller treatment in these letters than it does. The fact that it is spoken of so little does not seem, however, to dent the theory in MacDonald's eyes.

As to belief,[74] the way in which traditional doctrine is reformulated has been outlined in the previous chapter and MacDonald justifiably accounts for it 'in terms of the social situation underlying these writings'.[75] Belief and the social situation are held to be in a dialectical relationship and therefore bound to be constantly re-expressed. Consequently, some aspects of teaching, such as about the place of the law and justification, are no longer of major concern whereas the cosmic rule of Christ and the completeness of his victory and salvation are.

The third phase that concerns MacDonald, which she labels that of community-protecting institutionalization, relates to the Pastoral Letters. She dates these around 100–40 AD and argues they reflect 'the continuation of the Pauline movement into the second century, after Paul's death'. It is, she claims, 'indisputable that we find a more established or institutionalized church in the pastorals than can be found in other Pauline or deutero-Pauline writings'.[76]

Ethically,[77] the body of believers are taking on the nature of a church rather than a sect.[78] They appear in general to live in a more comfortable relationship than previously with the corrupt world.[79] There is concern about the church's reputation among 'outsiders' and church leaders are said to need the respect of those outside, whereas previously the views of those outside would have, at best, been considered irrelevant. The perspective of the householder is adopted throughout. While the position of the wealthy is eased, 'the position of slaves and women in particular seems to have worsened'.[80] The Pastoral Letters seem to present a picture, it is said, of 'bourgeois piety'.[81] Teaching about love-patriarchy, however, connects these letters to the earliest letters of Paul.

Paul's own authority is even more vigorously defended than before even though he is no longer alive. He is presented as an authoritative teacher whose teaching is no longer as open-ended as once it was. Faith has become 'the faith' and clear instruction is given so the readers 'know how one ought to behave in the household of God' (1 Tim. 3:15). Coupled with that is the development of local leadership or 'offices' as they are often termed, which are aimed at protecting the institution, although MacDonald wisely states that 'no simple solutions can be given with respect to the origin of offices in the Pastoral Epistles'.[82]

Instructions regarding prayer, the place of women in worship and the need for public reading and teaching of the Scripture relate to ritual. These show that 'the predominant concern evident . . . is the need for control'.[83] Some claim an indication about ordination is to be found in 2 Timothy 1:5 (and implied in the discussion of the qualities of bishops and deacons) but it is by no means clear that this is a reference to anything like an ordination ceremony and the context seems to relate it to the exercise of charismatic gifts.

False teachers are seen as a real threat to the church and energetically denounced. The letters suggest a development in the understanding of orthodoxy as distinct from heresy, but MacDonald is concerned to argue that this is not purely a doctrinal issue but a social one. 'The notion of universal salvation, the purifying significance of the Christ event, and the promise of future salvation' are key elements in these letters, but are very much in line with traditional teaching. What is new is the way they are used ethically, which reflects the social context in which the church now operates. Great concern is shown throughout about protecting community life and defining belief more clearly, as well as upholding the authority of the leaders, which is seen as a way of doing it.

MacDonald's overall approach has been widely welcomed. It convincingly demonstrates the need to understand doctrine not just as a history of ideas but of it developing in relation to its social context. She is commended for her understanding of the complexity of the relationship between theology and social sciences and the restraint of the claims she makes and the nuancing of the judgements she reaches.

Even so, her thesis is not above criticism. It builds on a number of questionable assumptions regarding the dating of the letters, which are significant for her theory. She argues, for example, for a very late date for the Pastoral Letters and asserts that they were pseudonymous. Their pseudepigraphic character is then taken as evidence of institutionalization. But the real symptoms of institutionalization, if they exist, would still be evident if these

letters were late Pauline. The very late date and pseudonymous
authorship is unnecessary to her thesis. And, as Luke Johnson has
pointed out, she does not relate these letters to the much more
developed picture of ministry we find in Ignatius, even though
Ignatius' letters date from the same period, according to her dating. By contrast with Ignatius, the structure of church order in the
Pastoral Letters is 'remarkably simple and functional' and show
no signs of the hierarchy Ignatius advocates.[84]

The chief criticisms, however, relate to the selectiveness of her
evidence and that there are more similarities between the earlier
and later letters than she admits. For example, is the teaching in
the Pastoral Letters about the wider world really any different
from Romans 13; and why is the reference to deacons necessarily
a sign of development when they are mentioned in Philippians
1:1? I have argued elsewhere that it is possible to overstress the
difference between the charismatic ministries of the early letters
and the 'offices' referred to in the Pastoral Letters.[85] The chief criticism against MacDonald, then, is that 'she may overextend the
evidence'.[86] E. Elizabeth Johnson concludes that 'the thesis seems
to run away with the evidence' and that the problems with it
'suggest that it is not the weight of the evidence found within
these letters that demands a developmental explanation, so much
as the use of a developmental model that selects and shapes the
evidence'.[87]

Application to Colossians

Subsequently, MacDonald has applied her skills to writing a full-
length commentary on Colossians and Ephesians in which the
stated aim is to use sociological tools to 'comprehend the challenges faced by the Pauline circle in the face of the imprisonment
and death of its central leader'.[88] Several themes are relevant to
the question of institutionalization.

Charisma

MacDonald is uncertain as to whether Paul is still alive when
Colossians is written but she is certain the letter was not written

by him. Whatever Paul's personal situation, the letter makes his continuing charisma central in a number of ways.

First, the letter seems concerned to establish Paul's charismatic credentials not only in his assertion of apostleship in 1:1, but particularly as he writes about that apostleship more fully in 1:24 – 2:5. There, his call and commission (1:25), his suffering (1:24, 4:3), his receipt of revelation (1:25–6, 2:3), his preparedness to toil and live without the normal comforts for them (1:29 – 2:1) and his authority (2:4–5) are all signs of that charisma. It would seem that the 'symbolic universe . . . created under Paul's leadership is being threatened and requires efforts to ensure its maintenance'.[89] Part of that effort concerns reminding people of his apostleship.

Charisma, however, as Weber taught, is not simply possessing extraordinary personal qualities but having those qualities recognized by followers. From the very first verse of Colossians Timothy is mentioned and a network of relationships becomes evident. Timothy is the central figure among a group who work with Paul and seek to propagate his teaching. His name is quickly followed by that of Epaphras (1:7), the missionary founder of the church at Colossae but who does not act independently of Paul (4:12). Whatever measure of charisma he possessed in himself, 'in Weberian terminology, Epaphras is part of the staff of the charismatic leader'.[90] Others, too, are part of the network and in his greetings (4:7–17) the writer seems keen to establish their authority by letting it be known how close they are to Paul. The message they heard from Epaphras and the ministry they received from others is not their own but Paul's. They provide access to him and his teaching. They are neither self-appointed, nor self-sufficient, but part of an emerging charismatic train which traces its origin back to Paul and beyond him to Christ.

Two other observations MacDonald makes about their position are relevant. First, Epaphras is referred to as *diaconos* ('minister'; 1:7). It would be a mistake, however, to take this as a sign that he 'occupies an institutionalized office' because that development had not yet taken place, even though it was 'a title reserved for leaders'.[91] Second, sociologically she comments that Paul's praise of the various network members is significant in a society where honour and shame were key values and where 'the public demonstration of reputation is vital to the establishment of identity'.[92]

At some stage, the original charismatic leader is bound to pass from the scene and a second generation to assume control. MacDonald believes Colossians gives evidence of this happening and that Paul's charisma is beginning to be transformed into a tradition.[93] This is especially true if the letter is pseudonymous, as she believes it probably is.[94] If so, Paul's name is being used not only to establish the authority of the letter's contents but also so that his followers can augment his reputation and continue to ensure attention is given to his teaching. Even if it is not pseudonymous, the differences between it and Paul's earlier letters are sufficient to justify the thought that Timothy, 'our brother', may have actually written it. This would mean more than that he acted as Paul's amanuensis and that he had considerable input into the content of the letter.[95] If so, Paul is already passing on the baton and charisma is passing from its original carrier to a younger colleague. At that stage the charisma was bound to change and to some extent evaporate and a tradition which looks back to his original charisma comes into being.

Sect

The sect-church dichotomy was introduced by Ernst Troeltsch in his *The Social Teaching of the Christian Church*. 'The Church,' he wrote

> is that type of organization which is overwhelmingly conservative, which to a certain extent accepts the secular order, and dominates the masses; in principle, therefore, it is universal, i.e. it desires to cover the whole life of humanity. The sects, on the other hand, are comparatively small groups; they aspire to personal inward perfection, they aim at a direct personal fellowship between the members of each group. From the beginning, therefore, they are forced to organize themselves in small groups and to renounce the idea of dominating the world. Their attitude towards the world, the State, and Society may be indifferent, tolerant or hostile, since they have no desire to control and incorporate these forms of social life; on the contrary, they tend to avoid them.[96]

Since then, although the dichotomy has been debated and elaborated, it has become a commonplace in the sociology of religion.

Troeltsch gives little theoretical attention to how a sect transformed itself into a church, which he saw as the 'mainstream' of
the 'two channels', but he does comment on the way in which
'the tendency towards conservatism was prepared by
Paulinism'.[97] The theory of institutionalization parallels this in
that, from a different angle, it argues that new religious movements often start as sects and then eventually develop into
churches.

The Jesus movement had all the hallmarks of a sect to start
with[98] but, certainly after the Emperor Constantine's 'conversion'
in 312 AD, it assumed all the characteristics of a church and it had
exhibited many of them long before that. By the time Colossians
was written the Christian communities still displayed the characteristics of a conversionist sect.

The evidence for this is seen in the strong sense of belonging
and separation that comes through in the letters. It may lack the
more personal warmth of family language – only Paul's col-
leagues are called 'brother', never members of the church except
in 1:2 – but that is easily explained in their not having face-to-face
relationships (2:1). But the letter speaks of their belonging when,
for example, it speaks about their sharing 'in the inheritance of
the saints in the light' (1:12). Their incorporation into Christ is a
major theme. The letter clearly aims to bring divided voices into
harmony and produce coherence and unity in the fellowship, as
3:12–17 demonstrates. If the ethical stance it advocates is becoming more conservative, as some suggest, this does not outweigh
other factors. There is still a strong sense of their mission to convert the world (1:6; 4:5–6).

The language of separation also abounds. They are 'the saints',
the 'set part ones' who, unlike many others, 'are *faithful* brothers
and sisters in Christ' (1:2, also 1:4,26). It is explicitly said that they
have been 'rescued . . . from the power of darkness and transferred
. . . into the kingdom of his beloved Son' (1:13), while implicitly the
ethical commands concern their being 'God's chosen ones' (3:12)
and so they are required to live differently from those who are not
elect. The language of 2:8 and 2:20 draws boundaries of a different
kind, those between genuine followers of Paul's gospel and the
false teachers, behind which perhaps lurks the Jewish synagogue.
There is also the mention of 'outsiders' in 4:5.[99]

So, given the continuing sharp sense of belonging and separation, if the process of institutionalization has advanced, it has not
advanced much.

Ritual

As mentioned previously, two rituals are apparent in Colossians.
The first is baptism and, second, that of 'routine' worship.

Interpretations of baptism usually focus on it as a rite of initiation and of transformation of one's status. Through it people
come to belong to the community and by it a community draws
its boundaries.[100] Baptism in Colossians achieves these things[101]
but, in MacDonald's view, also serves a different, more special-
ized, function. The church at Colossae was a church in conflict
and she argues throughout her commentary that the conflict was
'centered in the significance of what is experienced in the midst
of ritual', especially that of baptism.[102]

MacDonald has a tendency to see a reference to baptism even
where such a reference is not obvious.[103] The indisputable reference in 2:11–13 'recalls the dramatic re-enactment of salvation
attained through Christ's body', stresses the 'finality and com-
pletion' of their dying and rising with Christ and 'rebukes the
repetitive rituals and practices of the opponents'[104] and their
desire for ritual purity as outlined in 2:16–19. This leads her to
assert that 'baptism was at the heart of the conflict at Colossae. It
may be that competing visions of baptism were under dispute.'[105]
But this is by no means a necessary or even obvious inference to
draw. It was surely the meaning of the work of Christ, not the rite
of baptism, that was in dispute.

Having established to her satisfaction the importance of
baptism in the Colossian conflict, MacDonald then employs sociological insights to explain what was happening. Sociologists,
following the work of the anthropologist, Victor Turner,[106] see a
rite of passage as involving a three-act sequence: separation from
existing status, a liminal transition (that is an unstructured
threshold stage), and reintegration. Thus, in marriage, bride and
groom leave their parents as single people, enter into a process
which varies from culture to culture but usually involves an in-
between stage where they are either engaged or married but

away on honeymoon, before being reincorporated into society as a married couple.

Baptism conforms to this pattern as one leaves one's old life, is buried in water and then re-enters as a new person into a believing community. The issue, that is 'at stake in Colossians', says MacDonald, is precisely the working out of that third stage. What does it mean in terms of everyday living to belong to the alternate community? How does that affect food laws and sexuality? And 'how should one rekindle the powerful experience that led to building an alternate community . . . ?'[107] How does baptism, which would have offered a deep religious experience, connect with everyday living?[108] Paul begins to answer these questions in 3:1–4 and in doing so contradicts the false teachers who want to insist on repeated religious rituals, humiliations[109] and experiences (2:16–19).

The forty-six references MacDonald lists in her index to baptism, in the Colossians section of her commentary, stands in sharp contrast to Paul's single explicit reference (2:12) and suggests the significance of ritual has been inflated, even if baptism is sometimes implicit rather than explicit. No case can be built that Colossians increases the importance of the rite of baptism in comparison with earlier letters, as one might expect if institutionalization was advancing apace. In spite of these qualifications, it should be stressed that the ability of a ritual symbolically to capture the meaning of a spiritual experience and clarify the implications that follow from it is beyond question.

It is unfortunate that more attention is not paid to the more regular rituals of worship, mentioned in 3:16, but MacDonald's emphasis on baptism blinds her to the importance of this.[110] Although she offers some insightful exegetical notes,[111] MacDonald says little about the sociological significance of this verse except for scattered, brief comments which confirm that rituals, including singing, play an important part in educating members of a community in their beliefs.[112]

It is highly significant that Colossians makes no mention of the Lord's Supper. The later institutionalized church certainly emphasized this ritual, but although Colossians mentions the need for thanksgiving – a word associated with the celebration of the Eucharist – on several occasions, it is never connected with the Lord's Supper, and nor does MacDonald do so. Furthermore, much of Colossians is about reinvigorating the memory of the events of their faith, one of the purposes of the supper according to 1 Corinthians 11:24–6, but Colossians never mentions this. This suggests that Colossians has not advanced far down the road of institutionalization.

Doctrine

MacDonald's approach, as we have seen, conforms to the exposition of belief in the previous chapter. Doctrine is about the creation of a symbolic universe which legitimates the distinct identity of Christian believers in their given social context vis-à-vis others. The new challenges faced by the Colossian believers result in the person and work of Christ being defined more sharply and an increasing gap opening up between what is orthodoxy and what is heresy. The definition of doctrine relies increasingly on tradition and remembering, which, in themselves, are symptoms of institutionalization.

While supporting what others have said about the social construction of their beliefs, MacDonald draws particular attention to the 'body symbolism' that is introduced in the 'hymn' and then becomes an important theme throughout the letter.[113] The author initially develops the body image beyond its previous use by presenting Christ as the head of the body, whether it is the body of the universe or the body of the church. The problem is that the Colossian believers currently experience the universe as fractured and the church as divided. Both find their unity and coherence in Christ. His body is 'central to the vision of cosmic and social integration in Colossians'.[114]

A great deal is made of Christ's physical body (e.g. 1:22, 2:9–15) because the false teachers stress the need to subdue the body by diet and other ascetic practices (2:20–23). But the way of peace, that is, the way to cosmic and social harmony as well as personal integration, does not lie in what happens to their bodies, but what happened to Christ's body. The foundation is to say that 'you who were once estranged and hostile in mind, doing evil deeds, he has now reconciled in his fleshly body through death' (1:21–2). The way he achieved this is a little more complicated and involves the image of circumcision (2:11–15). Circumcision involves the removal of a small piece of flesh and is the symbolic rite by which a Jewish male becomes a member of the Jewish community.[115] Here circumcision is said to apply not to the stripping off of a little flesh but the whole body of flesh (2:11). It is unclear what 'the circumcision of Christ' refers to but the most likely interpretation is that it refers to the death of Christ.[116] It is a metaphor, writes Douglas Moo, 'for violent death' and the body of flesh, mentioned in 1:22, being stripped off him when he died on the cross.[117] Believers have not undergone physical circumcision and have no need to treat the flesh harshly. By uniting with Christ's burial through baptism, they have undergone a 'spiritual circumcision' and have done with 'the body of flesh' (2:10–12) as a step to sharing in Christ's resurrection life. It is through his body, not theirs, that peace comes. But once it comes, they then have the duty of manifesting that new life in the physical world, not to escape from it to some form of ethereal existence.

Whatever exegetical conclusions are reached, not only is the main thrust of these verses clear but the sociological purpose is transparent. Throughout, the image of the body serves a 'central unity-generating function'.[118]

A second particular aspect of the institutionalizing of belief that MacDonald highlights is the reformulating of eschatological hope. There is still an emphasis on future hope in Colossians, not least in 3:2–6, and this is sometimes neglected in a desire to prove that a development had taken place in Paul's theology. Nonetheless it is true that 'the emphasis in Colossians [is] on the present nature of salvation' and on the eschatological hope already having been fulfilled.[119] Playing down the future dimension of Christian experience and the imminent expectation of the return of Christ, which was evident in the earlier letters, is usually seen as a sign of the church becoming more comfortable in its environment and thus of institutionalization.

In further defining and re-expressing Christian belief, as Colossians does, the process of institutionalization is beginning to be apparent.

Ethics

Attention will be given in the next chapter to the question of ethics and, in particular, the household code (3:18 – 4:1). Suffice it to say

here that in MacDonald's view the code shows a more conservative stance than previous ethical statements, and this would be a
sign of the sect settling down in the secular environment and
becoming less sectarian. There is, she readily agrees, continuity
with earlier teaching on women and slaves, 'but the rule-like statements are much more categorical, leaving less room for exceptional behaviour on the part of some members'.[120] She supports the
view that the code fosters a 'double consciousness' among the
women and slaves. In the religious realm they are made conscious
of their 'equal' status, while at the same time in the social realm
they are made conscious of their lower status. Overall, her verdict
is 'the Colossian household code functions to sustain the patriarchal order of society and may contribute to a double consciousness
[but] it may be that this double consciousness was part of a strategy for survival for Pauline Christians in a hostile environment'.[121]

The issue is not, however, a straight line push towards the ethical right. Not only is the stance of the ethical code possibly the
only viable strategy for survival, but it might also be an effective
mission strategy. The false teachers are concerned about spiritual
experiences that encourage withdrawal from the world, but this
teaching is firmly rooted in the reality of everyday life in the
world in which they lived. Obedience to this code will lead them
to love in a way that commends their faith and makes Christians
attractive and accepted in many households, even the households of nonbelievers.[122]

A further complexity MacDonald helpfully mentions is that
'texts that appear only to reinforce conventional attitudes may in
fact include elements that challenge the status quo'.[123] The role of
Nympha as patroness of the church at Laodicea (4:15) and the influence which believing wives can exert on unbelieving husbands (1
Pet. 3:1–6) are tiny glimpses of the way in which women may not
have been passive victims as a result of this teaching.[124] No simple
linear projection of institutionalization seems to fit the evidence.

Conclusion

The process of institutionalization is an important concept that is
amply supported by wide historical evidence and contains many

practical insights for religious groups. The passing of the original apostles from the scene meant the early Christians to some degree unavoidably experienced it. The charisma of the original disciples inevitably became more routine and the spread of the gospel to new environments as well as to another generation raised questions of definition and organization. The later church provides ample examples of institutionalization which, even if it is not always detrimental, suggest a lively, radical community was transformed eventually into an institutionally hidebound and ethically compromised society.

To what extent there is evidence of this process in Colossians, however, is more debateable. It needs to be remembered that Colossians was not written as an essay in institutionalization and therefore to prove its presence requires the use of scant and incidental allusions rather than direct evidence. Colossians provides an interesting case study because it comes from late in Paul's ministry. It makes an even more interesting case study if it is dated later and comes from a period immediately after his ministry. On the whole, Margaret MacDonald is modest in the claims she makes for institutionalization in this community-stabilizing phase, as she terms it. Clearly the Christian church is facing a new phase and, with it, new challenges. Even so, sometimes the facts seem to be stretched to fit the theory. In using this theory, great care needs to be exercised so that the institutional tail doesn't wag the Colossian dog.

7

Household: Its Significance for Ethics, Mission and Organization

With very rare exceptions, relationships do not occur in a random or haphazard way. They are channelled and managed in ways determined by the culture in which they take place. The recurring patterning of relationships gives rise to institutions, such as the family or the body politic, which are invested with rules that stipulate how people are to interact with each other within and outside the institution. These institutions are laden with expectations about people's behaviour and roles. While many of these expectations are assumed and unexpressed, rather than articulated, some aspects of these expectations are enshrined in law. These institutions are not inflexibly set in stone and they adapt over time, as the history of the family and marriage demonstrates, but they do exert enormous influence over the way people live in society at any given time.

The Significance of the Household in the Greco-Roman World

In the world of the early church, the household served as the basic social institution in society and had done so for many centuries. Although there were variations between Greek, Roman and Jewish households,[1] they demonstrated a common pattern which was patriarchal and hierarchical in character. A household included not only intergenerational family members, their stewards and their servants (slaves), but also possibly clients, day labourers, freedmen, other dependents, and sometimes even business partners, fellow tradesmen or voluntary friends.[2] Many would have been relatively small, with perhaps only one slave, but their constitution made them larger and more inclusive units than the contemporary family. Ruled over by the *paterfamilias*, the senior father figure, who had legal powers (*patria potestes*), each member knew their place which was prescribed by custom, justified by reference to morality, and was, in some particulars, upheld by law. Typically, the key relations were those between husband and wife, parents and children and masters and slaves.

This does not imply the household was a cold and formal institution, as there is plenty of evidence of affection between its members, and also that it provided emotional satisfaction for those who belonged to it. Nonetheless, the household had as much to do with business and economic wellbeing as with emotions,[3] and questions of self-esteem and individual psychological wellbeing, as we have seen, were not high on the agenda. 'The household, like the republic, expressed its solidarity in a common religion' and its bonds were strengthened by its religious practice.[4] Which deities the household worshipped was, of course, determined by the *paterfamilias* and religious tradition was passed down from generation to generation.[5]

The Roman world saw itself as one vast household, composed of myriads of lesser households which were the key components of its citizenship. The Roman emperor exercised authority as the *paterfamilias* and it was to him that gratitude was to be expressed for the benefits of his protection and provision. It made no pretence of being a democratic structure. As with the smaller households, it was the rituals of religion, in the form of the imperial cult, which bound the whole imperial family together.[6]

Households in the New Testament and at Colossae

The world of the household is taken for granted in the parables of Jesus and comes to the fore in the Acts of the Apostles as a main channel through which the early Christian mission was established. It was the natural structure to adopt as the basis for their worshipping communities, once the gospel moved beyond the confines of Judaism. The significance of the household becomes most explicit, however, in the New Testament letters where it is evident that the early Christian groups were based on the households of some of the wealthier converts. It is more than probable that a large city like Corinth or Rome would have had several such household-based Christian groups that occasionally met together as a visible expression of the more comprehensive church.[7] Floyd Filson, in an early, seminal article on the significance of the house churches,[8] argued that the existence of these several 'house churches' accounts for the divisions which appear in Corinth.[9] There were certainly some disadvantages but the advantages of the institution for the Christian church seem grossly to outweigh any of the disadvantages.

It is not clear how many household-based Christian groups there were in Colossae. We definitely know of one such group that met in Philemon's house (Phlm. 2). Paul sends greetings to Nympha's house church, but that was located in nearby Laodicea (4:15), and no other householder is mentioned in connection with Colossae. Wayne Meeks may be right in saying 'the household assembly in Philemon's house was apparently not the whole of the Colossians church'[10] but he bases this on the assumption that the pattern in Rome and Corinth would have been the same in Colossae and he provides no evidence for it. Perhaps, on the contrary, the church in Colossae (and Laodicea) was based on a single household at the time. After all these cities were much smaller than Rome and Corinth. If so, the Christian community would have been quite a small gathering of people since, according to archaeological evidence, the villas of averagely wealthy Roman merchants would have been able to accommodate between thirty and fifty, certainly no more that fifty people, in the public parts of the house, which would have been used for their worship gatherings.[11]

With Meeks, Gehring rather assumes the Colossian church was composed of more than one household. He advances the argument that the household code of Colossians was written because the number of Christians could no longer be accommodated in one household and so a set of 'general rules' had become necessary to ensure uniformity of behaviour across the various house churches.[12] This, again, is a supposition, but that does not make it inevitably wrong. The fact that Paul only mentions Philemon does not necessarily undermine the argument either, since it would be natural for Paul to mention the household he knows in Colossae rather than others with whom he was not acquainted.

Paul's use of the word 'church' does not help us to resolve how many households composed the church at Colossae since he switches freely between using 'church' to apply to a single household (4:15), to apply to all the Christians who lived in Laodicea (4:16), that is what Gehring terms 'a local church',[13] and to apply to the worldwide church or church universal (1:18).

Whether the Colossian church consisted of one or more household churches is uncertain, but the existence of even one household church is highly significant for several different reasons.

The Colossian Household Ethical Code

The fundamental importance of the household meant that the writing of a household code (*haustafeln*) became a common device for presenting instructions about managing close relationships within it. They were seen by many as a vital way of ensuring social stability and discouraging any unrest which might jeopardize the peaceful living thought to be one of the benefits of the Roman Empire.[14]

The household code in Colossians 3:18 – 4:1 has been the subject of much interest partly because it is probably 'the first and most precise form of the domestic code in the NT'.[15] The wide agreement about the importance of the Colossian code soon crumbles under the weight of disagreement about virtually every other aspect of it.[16] The two main disagreements concern the origin of Paul's code and, second, the related matter of its interpretation. This chapter will introduce both of these debates but, sociologically speaking, our interest is wider and is as much concerned about the implications of the household itself for the organization and mission of the church as for the church's ethics.

Its originality

Although Paul gives no editorial heading referring to 3:18 – 4:1 as a 'household code', the structure of his guidance is readily identified as akin to other known household codes and can, beyond question, be classed as belonging to that genre. Like other codes, the Colossian code covers three sets of relationships: those between husband and wife (gender); child and father (generation); and slave and master (social status) and is thought to stress the subordination of the weaker partner in each pair to the *pater-familias*.

Earlier suggestions that Paul derived the contents from Stoic philosophers[17] have now been abandoned in favour of thinking that Paul was dependent on Aristotle because a very similar pattern of code is found in his *Politica I*.[18] Aristotle is credited with originating this form of structured approach to domestic relationships, and doing so in a way which was both widely applicable and conveniently resonated with the social philosophy of the Emperor Augustus, who perceived the whole empire through the lenses of structure and subordination. The Colossian code may also be said to be consistent with the tradition of moral exhortation found in Hellenistic Judaism, as seen, for example, in Tobit and Philo.[19]

While there can be no doubt that Paul's framework is traditional,[20] the fact that a number of others devised their own formulations of how to manage households suggests that several streams contribute to shaping Paul's approach, rather than it having a single source. Given this, it is better to see all the writers in this field as addressing a common concern rather than slavishly following one recognized model.[21]

Several have sought to establish the particular cause which may have led to the inclusion of this household code in Colossians. The suggestions have been numerous. Cannon believed it was an attempt to bring order to 'an unruly church'.[22] Gehring, as mentioned, believed it was an attempt to standardize behaviour across a growing number of house churches in Colossae but there is no way of proving or disproving this suggestion.[23]

Another suggestion that has attracted much attention is that of J.E. Crouch.[24] He observed that the address to slaves is out of proportion to the way others are addressed and so argued that Paul is seeking to quell social unrest and dampen the ambitions of those who think the gospel's liberation extends to their social situation as well as their spiritual standing. Paul's teaching here, Crouch claims, appears conservative and unadventurous, when compared with the manifesto of freedom found in Galatians 3:28.

It is true that the by-product of the Colossian *haustafeln* is to demonstrate that Christianity is not immediately disruptive of normal social arrangements and that Christians can be good citizens and fit comfortably with the expectations of the wider society. To that extent the code does perform an apologetic function and may seek to rebut the criticism of those who see it as politically destabilizing.[25] The instruction which almost immediately follows to 'Be wise in the way you act towards outsiders . . . Let your conversation be always full of grace, seasoned with salt, so that you may know how to answer everyone' (4:5–6, TNIV), lends support to there being some apologetic motive at work.

Yet, there are several reasons for questioning Crouch's particular thesis.[26] First, Galatians 3:28 has a parallel in Colossians 3:11, and so it is hard to conclude that Colossians is less revolutionary than one of Paul's earlier letters, notwithstanding Schüssler Fiorenza and others arguing that Colossians changes the claims of Galatians 3:28 'considerably'.[27] Second, there is no evidence of restlessness among slaves. The case of Onesimus would appear to be the case of an individual runaway slave rather than symptomatic of wider unrest. Wider unrest might have been at least alluded to in the letter to Philemon had it existed but there is no whiff of it. Third, the question of the degree to which Paul's household ethic is conservative or revolutionary is a moot point to which further attention needs to be given.

It is safer to conclude that the Colossian *haustafeln* addresses a topic which was of common concern during the period, that it does so in a manner which is readily understood, and with a framework which was readily available. Since such a code was a matter of common currency, it seems unnecessarily speculative to seek to posit a more particular cause for its inclusion.

Regressive or progressive?

The discussion that the household code was written in response to a particular situation leads to the second and related area of debate, which has been about its interpretation. Does it go back on the earlier and more revolutionary claims of Christianity, does it merely justify the status quo, or is it more progressive?

Several scholars, 'some in harsh tones, others in resignation, point to the household code in the Letter to the Colossians as a prime example'[28] of stifling the original emphasis on freedom with all its revolutionary potential for the wider society. Chief among such critics are feminist theologians who see the emphasis on wives *submitting* to their husbands (and equally children and slaves *obeying* their father or master respectively) as a major step back from Galatians 3:28.[29] That text, it is argued, has more than soteriological significance; it has sociological significance as well. It promises that in the church the less powerful will find freedom from patriarchal dominance and social liberation. The effect, it is claimed, of Galatians 3:28 was to bring about the end of dominance by one gender, one ethnic group or one class, and the abolition of any order based on such distinctions, at least among the followers of Jesus. Those who take this position often assume that the text predates Paul and argue, on the basis of 1 Corinthians 7:20–24, that Paul himself never truly bought into it. If this is so, then the Colossian *haustafeln* genuinely does appear to be a backward step and an attempt, for whatever reason, to re-impose conservative positions and renege on the freedom many thought the gospel offered.

It has to be questioned, however, whether this was the intent of Galatians 3:28, or of the parallel Colossians 3:11.[30] It is indisputable that in terms of status before God the divisions are abolished and that all people, irrespective of gender, social status, ethnic background (and by extension age) are of equal worth and have access to the same salvation. This, in itself, must have implications for the way people from either side of those divides relate to each other in the church. Initially, this was bound to lead to a great deal of uncertainty and to the re-establishing of new relationships. This much is evident in the letter to Philemon where Paul encourages the slave owner, Philemon, to welcome his runaway slave back 'no longer as a slave, but better than a slave, as a dear brother' (Phlm. 16). Some masters, no doubt, were reluctant to behave towards their slaves in this way, whereas others might have been more egalitarian in their approach. But though Paul has a clear objective in mind, in writing to Philemon he couches his words carefully, suggesting rather than demanding, never condemning the institution of slavery as such, and never setting out a social programme that leads to the instant abolition of slavery.

As Gehring acknowledges, there is certainly a tension here, but 'The author to Colossians obviously does not see a contradiction between asserting, on the one hand, that in God's eyes (soterio-logically) religious and social differences are nullified, and maintaining, on the other, the continued existence of creational differences among Christians in the family and in the church'.[31]

Having exercised caution about the arguments that view the Colossians *haustafeln* as a regression, equal caution needs to be exercised about arguments that see it as a reassertion of patriar-chal conservatism. In a debate which is highly charged with emo-tions, Dunn wisely cautions that we should neither soften the guidance nor exaggerate it. Paul's plea for submission is a plea for 'subordination' not 'subjugation'.[32] It is an appeal for volun-tary submission and does not justify imposing obedience or exer-cising tyranny over an unwilling partner.[33]

Some argue that Paul is reinforcing the contemporary social status quo with its emphasis on patriarchal privilege and merely rephrasing it for use in a Christian context. The 'interest of the owner and the patron class is obvious'[34] and this code, they argue, softens Aristotle and others at the most by teaching 'love-patriarchy' in place of full-blown patriarchy.[35] It is true that Paul is reflecting conventional social patterns, but closer examination suggests that he is not merely reinforcing them. Several features distinguish the Colossian guidance from other contemporary household codes.

Balch's research concludes that it is highly unusual for ancient codes to address all these social classes, even if it is not without precedent. The direct address to slaves is particularly significant. 'What is most notable,' he writes, 'is not the subordination of the slaves, but that they are addressed in the codes.'[36] In doing so it becomes evident that slaves, along with wives and children, are seen as full members and participants in the church, regardless of whatever other restrictions their social status may impose on them elsewhere.

The element of mutuality in the code is immediately striking and calls into question those who see the code as a one-way street, or as merely conventional advice. Wives are to submit, but husbands are to love. The command for Christians to love their wives is fairly infrequent in such codes, to say the least, and the use of *agapaō* to define the quality of love to be expressed is unique.[37] Children are to obey, but fathers are not to cause resentment. While the advice to fathers to exercise moderation is found elsewhere, it is unusual that there is no stress on the father's authority and even more unusual that children are treated as persons in their own right who have a place in the church and their own relationship with God.[38] Moreover, there is truth in the claim that 'the psychological sensitivity that is expressed here is surprisingly modern'.[39] Slaves are to obey, but masters are reminded that they are also accountable to a greater master. This is quite unconventional and overturns the idea that slaves are mere property to be disposed of at the master's whim. Balch points out that 'this integrating power is something entirely new in social history: masters and slaves have the same Lord and judge (Col. 3:25b)'.[40]

The key factor is the inclusion of the repeated reference to Christ. Seven of the fourteen references to *kurios* (Lord) in Colossians occur in this code. Wives are to submit to their husbands, 'as is fitting in the Lord'; children to obey, 'for this pleases the Lord'; slaves to serve with 'reverence for the Lord . . . as working for the Lord', knowing that they 'will receive an inheritance from the Lord', and as serving him; masters are reminded they 'also have a Master in heaven' (3:18 – 4:1, TNIV). The impact of these simple words should not be underestimated. They transform conventional patterns and give an entirely new colour to any ethics of relationship derived from the ancient world.

For people to relate to each other 'in the Lord' defines the motivation which underlies all relationships. All living is to be lived under the watchful eye of Christ and all relationships are to be conducted as an act of worship which pleases him. It also defines the kind of relationship Christians are to have. Obedience to Christ prevents any person in the relationship from mistreating another and ensures that weaker partners in a relationship are never going to be abused. They can no longer be treated as mere property, they are people, made in the image of God and born anew by the Spirit of Christ. As Gehring points out, too often the Colossian *haustafeln* is interpreted without any consideration being given to the context in which it is set in Colossians. That, perhaps, is the danger of seeing it as something of a distinct literary unit that owes its existence to an external source. In the immediate context, 3:5–17 defines what it means to live 'in the Lord'. Christians are exhorted 'to practise heart-felt compassion, kindness, humility, gentleness, and patience in interpersonal relationships',[41] in the household as well as in society generally.

The cumulative weight of these arguments leads to the conclusion that the Colossian *haustafeln* is anything but merely conventional and certainly not regressive. It is true that neither here, nor elsewhere, does Paul set out a programme for social or political reform. Paul does not advocate social egalitarianism, nor does he command masters to set their slaves free. He works within the legal framework of his time. But the expectation that he should set out a manifesto for social, legal and political reform is an anachronism. Ideas of reform which belong to a post-Enlightenment world and the context of modern democratic societies would have simply made no sense to those living in the Roman world.[42] 'Paul is not interested in mere social reform or in replacing one order with another' but only in bringing people to surrender to Christ as Lord.[43] That has major practical implications for the way people lived and related, as is seen in the christianizing of the household code, which is no mere adaptation of conventional wisdom but a radical transformation of it from within and which lays the seeds which were eventually to blossom into radical social change.

The Social and Missionary Implications of the Household in Early Christianity

The structuring of society around the household has many practical implications for the development of the early church, in addition to its implications for ethics.

Implications for mission

It may legitimately be argued that Paul's missionary objective was not so much the conversion of individuals as the conversion of households and the formation of new Christian communities.[44] The household was the raw material out of which such communities were constructed. The Acts of the Apostles identifies the households of Mary (12:12), Lydia (Acts 16:14–15), the Philippian jailer (Acts 16:31–4), Jason (Acts 17:5–9), Priscilla and Aquila (Acts 18:1–4), Titius Justus and Crispus (Acts 18:7–8) as all crucial to the expansion of the Christian mission. Paul's letters equally testify to the importance of converted households serving as the base for newly formed Christian communities, as seen, for example, in Romans 16:5,14,15,23; 1 Corinthians 16:15–18,19. This wider picture illuminates the role Philemon played in the Colossian church and gives some colour to the reference to 'Nympha and the church in her house' (4:15).

As an itinerant missionary Paul would have needed a base for his operations in the cities he visited. Jewish travellers would have avoided staying in inns, which were the customary place to seek hospitality, because of their association with magic and the provision of sexual favours for their clients, and looked instead for members of their own community to accommodate them in private homes.[45] Initially the synagogue provided a platform for Paul's message but, given their hostility to his message (e.g. Acts 18:4–11), it was necessary for Paul to find other platforms. He occasionally hired a public meeting place (Acts 19:9) and made, of course, good use of the marketplace and public square (Acts 16:16–21). Other itinerant philosophers and teachers attached themselves to households and used the house as a platform to propagate their views and Paul seems to have done this in a number of places but, as Hock comments, this could prove expensive for the householders.[46] Paul seems to have been conscious of the expense involved and sought to pay his way by continuing his trade as a leather-worker or tent-maker (1 Thess. 2:9). Indeed, it was the fact that they had a common trade that made him seek out Aquila and Priscilla in the first place (Acts 18:2–3).

The relationship with Aquila and Priscilla may also point in the direction of Paul using the workshop as a place from which the gospel could be broadcast. Workshops, which also served as shops, came in all shapes and sizes. Sometimes they formed the lower storey of a house and sometimes they were separate from a house. It would appear from the writings of Socrates that they often served as the location for intellectual discussion, assuming Socrates does not place some of his discussions there merely as a literary device. While there is not a great deal of evidence of philosophers engaging in manual labour, there is some and, after careful investigation, Hock concludes that Paul was likely to have used it as a setting for his missionary activities.[47]

Planting missionary cells in some of the major cities of the ancient world enabled the gospel to spread rapidly and flexibly. It is safe to assume that similar dynamics operated in the founding of the church at Colossae and that Epaphras (1:7; 4:12) would have made Philemon's house the setting for his missionary preaching and found in it a home for the small group who came to follow Jesus, although it must be conceded that there is no direct evidence of his being so. Schüssler Fiorenza rightly concludes 'House churches were a decisive factor in the missionary movement in so far as they provided space, support, and actual leadership for the community'.[48]

Implications for conversion

A second implication of the use of the household relates to conversion. Mention has already been made of the way in which members of a household were bound together by practising a common religion and, as with any major decision a household would make, the responsibility for choosing which religion would lie with the *paterfamilias*. If the householder decided to become a devotee of a local deity, the house would follow suit. Equally if the householder was converted to Christ, the household would become a Christian house.[49] In Meeks' words, a household would become 'Christian more or less en bloc'.[50]

This explains the phenomenon of household baptism which we encounter in Acts 16 where, after coming to faith, first Lydia's household and then the Philippian jailer's household were baptized (Acts 16:15,33). The practice of household baptism is also mentioned in 1 Corinthians 1:16 where Paul states he baptized the household of Stephanus. Modern questions, generated by contemporary individualism, are not usually relevant to these accounts. Household baptism expressed the new allegiance the household had to Jesus Christ and was not intended to indicate that every individual member of the household, including young children, shared the same degree of understanding or commitment. It was an expression of where the primary social unit stood rather than of each individual's commitment.

It is, therefore, unlikely to mean that all individuals believed to the same degree, or that they all participated in the Christian activities equally.[51] Some Christian householders would surely have been more tolerant than others in enforcing compliance, and enforcement seems to have varied with the size of the household and over time.[52]

From the reverse angle, we see from the New Testament that some who were Christians belonged to households that were not Christian (Rom. 16:11; 1 Cor. 7:12–14; 1 Pet. 3:1) and that a Christian gathering was one that unbelievers might attend (1 Cor. 14:23). The household was neither an isolated nor a totalitarian institution, but one with a permeable interface with other households and would have interacted with other groups, such as the trade guilds and voluntary associations, in a locality. Slaves from different houses would congregate together in the course of doing their work in the marketplace and some from non-Christian households would have been converted through the witness of fellow slaves. Masters would meet others of all ranks in the course of their business and in various other social contexts. When conversions took place the new convert would attach themselves to a Christian household for worship, in so far as their obligations permitted.[53] The household structure does not explain everything.[54] But, in spite of this qualification, it is still one of the most important channels of conversion.

Implications for social integration

Roles within the household were clearly delineated and status was vertically differentiated. Everyone knew their place which was defined by social custom and culture, reinforced by law. Yet, paradoxically, this highly stratified structure provided a place where the different strata of society not only interacted but also integrated. Larger households would have mirrored the pyramid form of society generally with the *paterfamilias* alone at the top and with increasing numbers the lower down the social scale one went, with a larger number of slaves at the bottom. Having a base in the household meant that the early church was socially mixed, as is apparent in the household code. The presence of some house owners who were wealthy enough to travel and accommodate Christian worshippers supports the recent consensus that the early church was not exclusively a movement of the poor and of slaves, while at the same time making it obvious that the majority of members would not be drawn from among the wealthy. The use of the household as the major framework for mission and association meant that the Christian church was naturally a socially integrated body from the start to a considerable degree.

The house was considered to be private space and the women's domain while men did business in the public world.[55] By using the household as the meeting place for the church, the old stereotypical gender divisions were challenged and men and women found a place of integration in their worship of Christ.

The household functioned as a 'fictive family' as the frequency of family language and warmth of cross-gender and cross-status relationships testifies. Families, even 'fictive' ones, are very different from voluntary groups which people opt into as a matter of making a conscious choice. Voluntary associations, then as now, generated a very different kind of relational ethos from that found in a family. They usually had more limited goals and foci, and, consequently, a more limited appeal. This resulted in voluntary associations being less socially homogeneous and if the church's configuration had been influenced by them, instead of the institution of the household, it would have been almost certainly less socially inclusive and more socially fragmentary.[56]

Implications for leadership

Voluntary groups, especially newly formed groups of a novel religion such as Christianity, needed patrons who would provide resources to enable them to function, with accommodation where they could meet, and apologists who would represent them in the wider society. This function was performed in the early church by significant householders, such as Stephanus (1 Cor. 16:15–16), Philemon (Phlm. 2) and Nympha (Col. 4:15).

In the household, leadership indisputably lay in the hands of the *paterfamilias* and it would appear that this too naturally carried over, in some respects, into the early Christian communities.[57] Colossians does not refer to Philemon, but the more personal letter Paul wrote to him explicitly refers to his role as host and benefactor of the church there (Phlm. 2). And if Archippus was Philemon's son,[58] it would have been natural for him to assume a leading role in the church as heir apparent in the household.

However, the conventional form of leadership in the household was not adopted neatly by the church, nor without it undergoing significant changes. While the early church may have worked largely within the normal social patterns, it saw the need for the gospel to transform them in significant ways. First, household leaders were used to being served by others, but in the church they became the servants of others (1 Cor. 16:15).[59] The usual concerns with position, privilege, titles and status are entirely absent when the New Testament refers to these household patrons. In Christ a role reversal has taken place and they have become servants too. The conventional understanding of status has been radicalized and assumes a very different model which has been termed one of 'eschatological equality'.[60]

Such a change obviously posed a number of problems and it is evident that it took some time to work out the implications of it and get the balance between living with present social realities and eschatological hopes right. So, on the one hand, Paul had to encourage people in Corinth to continue to show respect for Stephanus and not abuse his newly adopted status as their servant in Christ. The same issue may lie behind the lengthy clauses addressed to slaves in the Colossians *haustafeln*.[61] On the other hand, Paul had to encourage Philemon to work out what it meant to have his fugitive slave back home no longer as a slave but as a brother.

In addition, our understanding of the transfer of leadership from the household to the church needs to be carefully nuanced because leadership or patronage is not to be wholly equated with ministry. While households exercised great influence in the fledgling churches, it does not mean to say they served as its ministers. The qualifications for ministry (used in a general and inclusive sense) depended on spiritual gifting rather than social position. Alongside household leaders, others exercised spiritual leadership who were gifted as prophets, evangelists, pastors and teachers.[62]

In the Colossian correspondence (4:7–16) we have reference to Paul's team, which MacDonald describes as 'a mixed group . . . and most likely people from a variety of social strata'.[63] In the Colossian church, spiritual leadership was initially, and on an ongoing basis, supplied by Epaphras (1:7) who, as a colleague of the apostle Paul, serves as church planter and 'minister'. While he was absent from Colossae at the time the letter was written, Epaphras continued to work on behalf of the church there and those at Laodicea and Hierapolis (4:13). Presumably, on his return, he would function alongside Archippus in leading the church. There is no evidence that Epaphras was a significant member of Philemon's blood family, even though Archippus may have been, but they shared in ministry together.

An even more interesting, or perhaps intriguing, example from Colossae relates to Onesimus. While at the time of writing, Onesimus' status as a fugitive slave, though 'faithful and dear brother' of Paul's, was still to be resolved, it is possible that it was solved in such a way that he was not only released from slavery but encouraged to exercise ministry. Around the year 107 AD, Ignatius of Antioch wrote a number of letters on his way to martyrdom, one of which is addressed to the church at Ephesus. In its opening paragraph he mentions that the bishop's name is Onesimus. We cannot be sure that it was Onesimus, the runaway but converted slave, and maybe the timescale weighs against it being so, but what is not improbable is that a former slave should 'rise' to become a spiritual leader, even bishop, in the church.

A particular issue which this discussion of the relationship between leadership in the church and household leadership raises is that of the role of women. In the Roman world there were a number of women in charge of their own houses and running their own businesses, some of whom were presumably widowed but others may never have been married. In Pompeii, for example, the largest house so far excavated belonged to Julia Felix and was associated with baths, shops and gardens which were maintained by many slaves. The largest building in the Forum in

Pompeii was built and owned by Eumachia, daughter of Lucius, who had business connections with fullers, wool dyers and international trade in pottery.[64] Here were situations when a woman acted as if she were the *paterfamilias* at the time. Furthermore, some wealthy women used their houses to accommodate various religious cults, especially of an ecstatic nature.[65]

Given this wider context women, like the businesswoman Lydia (Acts 16:14–15), the hostess and teacher Priscilla (Acts 18:18–26; Rom. 16:3), the benefactor Phoebe (Rom. 16:1–2) and the house owner Nympha[66] (Col. 4:15) do not seem all that unusual.

Within this overview of women householders in the New Testament, the reference to Nympha 'is striking' because it is 'the only unambiguous reference to a woman house church leader [which] is indisputable'.[67] We do not know whether she was widowed or never married but, in the light of 3:18 we must conclude that she was not currently married. We only know that the church in Laodicea was 'in her house', which indicates she was a woman of some wealth. Given this, and interpreting it through the lens of the wider context, Robert Banks is right to say, 'it seems unlikely that she . . . would take an insignificant part in the proceedings in favour of socially inferior male members who were present'.[68] Rather, it seems much more likely that she would have acted in a similar way to men like Stephanus and Philemon who hosted churches in their houses. She would have done more than opened the door and served the drinks if, given the presence of her slaves, she did that at all. She would have exercised influence as a leader.

Conclusion

The significance of the household for the advance, formation and ethical stance of the early Christian church is hard to underestimate. It did not stand on its own but it stands in the most significant place in configuring the corporate life and growth of the early followers of Jesus.

8

Culture: Values and Arrangements

Cultures are composed of a number of elements including values, customs and day-to-day arrangements, as well as major institutions. Previous chapters have surveyed a number of cultural components which are of importance to our understanding of the letter to the Colossians but there are a number of other elements which also deserve attention.

Since 1989, an international group of scholars known as the 'Social Context Group' have produced a series of publications which use social-scientific tools, mainly from anthropology, to interpreting the New Testament.[1] They have, as previously mentioned, particularly concentrated on the pivotal values of Mediterranean cultures and constructed a series of models which both demonstrate the social arrangements of the ancient world and contrast them with the social mechanisms of contemporary Western society. Social scientists always need to be alert to the danger of imposing their models on unique systems of social relationships and of transferring models from one culture to another that they do not really fit. Yet the work of the group has been very illuminating, even if it has been criticized for being somewhat repetitive and inflexible.[2] The criticism that they operate at a fairly general level of abstraction and that they impose a coherence on Mediterranean culture which may not have existed in reality in the more particular subcultures of people to be found in the Mediterranean basin is less cogent. Cultures can be analysed at different levels and to different degrees. So, for example, while there are distinct Welsh, Scottish and English cultures, together they can be legitimately understood as having so much in common that the concept of British culture is valid. So it was with the Mediterranean world and the individual peoples who had been shaped by first the Greek and then the Roman civilizations.

Chief among the cultural values and arrangements that the Social Context Group have researched, in addition to that of the understanding of personality, are those of family and kinship, honour and shame, purity, the body, limited good, patronage and literacy.

Earlier chapters in this book have given explicit attention to the perceptions of collectivist versus individualist personality, and to questions of household and family, while some of the other cultural values have been dealt with tangentially or implicitly. This chapter reviews those issues which have not been addressed directly in order to discover their helpfulness, or otherwise, in our understanding of Colossians.[3] There is no particular significance in the way in which the topics are reviewed.

Honour and Shame

'Honour,' writes Richard Rohrbaugh, 'understood as one's reputation in the eyes of the public, was the core value of the ancient Mediterranean world. It was the goal, the passion, the hope of all who aspired to excel. To many, but especially the elite of ancient society, it was dear as life itself.'[4]

Honour was about one's status in the community and the esteem one was accorded. It affected every area of life including how one behaved, who one married, who one entertained, how one did business and even how one dressed. Honour was the crucial factor in determining one's social interaction. Care was taken to guard one's honour, so a person would not marry beneath them or entertain guests who could not reciprocate in kind. It mattered whether one received public recognition of one's honourable status or not. Honour was stoutly defended and any challenge to it met with a vigorous riposte. Retaliation was the order of the day, including violent retaliation, especially if the honour of the family had been impugned. Honour was felt in one's city and people and these too would be robustly championed. It was usually ascribed on the basis of one's birth and family lineage although it could also be acquired where a consensus thought a person worthy of it because of their achievement, virtue or contribution to the community.[5]

The cultural value of honour is implicit and assumed in Colossians rather than being directly addressed. It relates first to the honour of God and second to the honour of the apostle Paul.

The honour axis between God and the Colossians was a two-way street. Paul publicly recognized that God had bestowed honour on them as the gospel came to them and was accepted by them (1:3–8). Their status in relation to God has changed from that of alienation to reconciliation (1:21) and so, as 'God's chosen ones, holy and beloved' (3:12), they bask in God's reflected honour. This new status means they have come under God's protection with a view to their being eventually presented 'holy and blameless and irreproachable' (1:22). Margaret MacDonald explains that 'An understanding of the core values of honor and shame in the ancient Mediterranean world is essential to a full appreciation of how [their] new identity is envisioned in Col 1:21–23'.[6] The idea of 'presenting' the Colossian Christians may seem strange to modern ears, as if they are debutants to be presented to the king at a royal ball at their 'coming out'; a practice which belongs to a past age. It would have been a more familiar concept in the ancient world. 'God is here understood as acting like an honourable Mediterranean male who protects the reputation of his bride (the community) and presents her worth to the world outside'.[7] In an honour-shame culture, shame was to be avoided at all costs.

Becoming a Christian did not appear to bring honour to believers in New Testament times but rather the reverse and often involved opprobrium and persecution. Although this is not explicit in Colossians the believers there were subject to the ignorance, if not downright misunderstanding, of their neighbours. They cannot be said to receive the public respect which they deserve as those who have been 'raised with Christ', who 'is [already] seated at the right hand of God' (3:1). Colossians explains that this is because their true status is now 'hidden' (3:3) from view. In not being accorded honour, their experience is identical to Christ's experience, just as they might expect since they are 'in him'. The majority of people in Colossae did not attribute honour to him, so they did not attribute it to his follow-ers either. In the future, though, they will receive the public recognition that is rightly theirs, when Christ himself is revealed in his full glory (3:4).[8] In the meantime, they are not to respond to this disrespect in the culturally conditioned way by defending or promoting themselves. Rather they are to exercise compassion and humility and to forgive those against whom they might have grievances (3:12–14).

Since God has honoured them, it is now for them to honour him in return. They do this by living a life that is consistent with the wishes of their master and by not bringing shame on his name. This is the context in which the emphasis on being 'wor-thy' in Colossians 1:10 ('so that you may lead lives worthy of the Lord, fully pleasing to him') would have been understood.

Margaret MacDonald also draws out the way in which the rela-tionship between Paul and the Colossians involves honour. On the one hand, MacDonald argues Colossians is written to defend Paul's authority as a teacher,[9] and that of Epaphras as his 'faithful inter-preter',[10] against false teachers who would undermine his honour. This battle is certainly more evident elsewhere, say, in 2 Corinthians and Galatians, but it is present here as well, even if it should not be overstated. It is more of the subtext than the main text. On the other hand, Paul publicly bestows praise on the Colossians for their 'faith, love and hope' (1:3–8) and 'read social-scientifically, Paul's praise takes on new significance as an assertion of legitimacy of the church mission. In an honour–shame society like the first-century Medit-erranean world the public demonstration of reputation is vital to the establishment of identity.'[11] They are granted credibility by being acknowledged in this way.

The values of honour and shame are taken for granted in Colossians because they are part of the wallpaper of Medit-erranean culture. The honour-shame axis is still a core value in some cultures, as we see positively in the pride many take in their family's solidarity and as, negatively, the sad episodes of honour killings remind the Western world from time to time. But since they are no longer central to 'modern' cultures their significance for a reading of Colossians easily escapes our attention, whereas an understanding of them can illuminate the text and aid us to a more accurate reading of it.

Patrons, Brokers and Clients

Social roles in the early Mediterranean world

In our discussion of the significance of the household, mention was made of the role of the householder in serving as patron of voluntary religious groups.[12] In fact, the role of the patron is much broader than that and pervasive throughout the Mediterranean world of the early church. Patrons were also part of a complex network of relationships that does not permit any straightforward explanation.

Patrons were those who were in a position to act as benefactors, those who could confer favour or donate gifts to others. The chief patron was, of course, the emperor himself, but many others acted as patrons at different levels. Communities depended on patrons, often called 'benefactors' in this role, to finance public buildings, the games or public festivals, much as many today depend on businesses to sponsor their community activities. The difference is that in the ancient world such sponsorship was personal. In stark contrast to the contemporary impersonal world, where 'fairness' and 'objectivity' reign, the wheels of the ancient community and business were unashamedly oiled by whom you knew, rather than what you knew.[13] Patrons functioned in both the public and the private world. They might donate the money for a building, as several ancient inscriptions testify, or they might aid a client in doing business, or they might give to the support of the poor. The gifts they conferred might be material, or they might involve rendering a service of some kind, such as offering protection, influence, prestige or access to someone who mattered.

Richard Saller identified three features as central to an understanding of patronage in the ancient world.[14] First, it involved an exchange of goods and services. It was, therefore, a reciprocal, not a one-way relationship. The patron gave, but also received something in return. Second, the relationship between the patron and recipient, who is usually called a client, was personal and more than a brief and temporary relationship, leading to a sense of solidarity. Third, it was a relationship between parties of different status rather than a relationship between equals. Where the reciprocity was between equals, patrons and clients referred to each other as friends.[15]

The relationship was reciprocal because clients were expected to repay their patrons 'in kind'. They were usually not in a position to repay financially, but there were other ways in which gratitude could be expressed.[16] First, the client was expected to honour the patron and speak well of them to others. Testimonies to their generosity and virtues were expected. Second, they were expected to be loyal to their patron and not seek to play one patron off against another. There was a sense, perhaps more innocent than it sounds, in which a client was 'bought' by a patron. Third, the client could reciprocate by performing some service for the patron.

Sometimes a client would need a third party to facilitate an introduction to a patron and those who did this were (and are) known as brokers.[17] Brokers had to look in both directions at once: from one viewpoint they knew and represented the patron and his interests, from another, they stood and interceded on behalf of the client.

Application to Colossians

To date, New Testament scholars have applied the concept of patronage principally to the gospels,[18] 1 Corinthians,[19] and James,[20] but it affects most of the New Testament and is often the unspoken assumption behind various parts of the letter to the Colossians. A study of Colossians shows how complex the network of relationships between patrons, brokers and clients can be.

The chief benefactor throughout Colossians is God. In the opening prayer Paul thanks God for the believers (1:3) and for the grace or favour they have received and grasped from God (1:6).[21] The conferring of God's grace on the Colossians was not exhausted at their conversion, which is why Paul prays that God will fill them further with his gifts to enable them to live worthy lives (1:9–11). The favour they have already received is one through which they have been rescued from 'the power of darkness' and brought under God's protection (1:13–14). God bestows life (2:13) on sinful human beings and also continues to supply life to the church, enabling it to grow (2:19). He chooses people to be his own (1:2; 3:12) and spares them from the judgement that is coming on others (3:5–6). He not only adopts people into his family but also gives them a significant part to play as servants in his kingdom (4:7–17). The grace he has already conferred on the Colossians is only the beginning of his generosity. Therefore Paul concludes his letter by praying for them to continue to experience God's favour (4:18).

What is true of God the Father is also true of Jesus Christ the Son, since the fullness of deity is in him (2:9). As a member of the divine trinity,[22] therefore, he is inevitably a benefactor of the believers in Colossae. In his own person, however, he is said to be the benefactor as the one who provides people with the fullness of God (2:9); who is the source of reality (2:17); who is glorious in his own nature (3:4); and giver of peace (3:15) through his message (3:16).

Under God, the most obvious human patrons are the householders who host the church in their properties. While only Nympha is expressly mentioned in Colossians (4:15) – and she is the patroness of the church at Laodicea – Philemon obviously served as patron to the church in Colossae (Phlm. 2), perhaps alongside other converted householders in Colossae. Their conversion to Christ as Lord also entailed, as Bruce Winter has put it, 'the conversion of [their] patronage'.[23] 'Under Paul,' he writes in reference to 1 Corinthians, but it is no less true of Colossians, 'patronage values had been inverted, with a patron and patroness now serving people without respect for their *persona* and their usefulness for any personal political aspirations typical of patronage.'[24] They may remain among the wealthy and influential in conventional terms but in the church, alongside all the other members, they were servants of Christ and brothers and sisters of one another.

Paul often presents himself in his letters as a client, in receipt of the gifts of others, as when he writes of Phoebe one who 'has been a benefactor of many and of myself as well' (Rom. 16:2). Philemon, as Paul's letter to him testifies, clearly gained from having Philemon as his personal patron on occasions (Phlm. 6–7,22), even if the relationship was one of 'friendship', a relationship of partners (Phlm. 17) rather than a superior-subordinate relationship. Yet this should not blind us to the way in which

many would have seen Paul as a patron.[25] Even if some in the
church struggle to see Paul in this light, Epaphras, who brought
the gospel to Colossae and now seems to be in need of support
(4:12–13), and Onesimus (4:9, Phlm. 12–16), are both spoken of as
if they were clients of Paul's sponsorship. He invests a great deal
in both of them.

If God is seen as the divine benefactor, perhaps it is reasonable
to say that Jesus is chiefly presented as the divine, and also
human, broker. Jesus is the person through whom God brought
the creation into being (1:15) and mediates life to it still (1:17). He
is also the broker of God's grace and becomes the agent of reconciliation, between God and his alienated subjects (1:21–2). His
unique qualification to serve in the role of the broker of grace is
summarized in the claim that in Christ 'the whole fullness of
deity dwells bodily, and you have come to fullness in him' (2:9).
Union with Christ is the means by which sinful human beings
receive God's grace (2:13–14); are protected from their accusers
and enemies (2:15–23); and may already participate in God's ultimate triumph (3:1–4).

Paul fulfils not only the role of patron but that of a broker as
well. In writing of his commission as an apostle he speaks in the
language of brokerage (1:24 – 2:5). His calling is to disclose 'the
mystery that has been hidden throughout the ages and generations', that is, to reveal to the Gentiles 'the riches of the glory of
this mystery', the gospel which is 'Christ in you, the hope of
glory' (1:27). The task may be demanding, involving suffering as
well as toil, but his objective is clear: in the social terms of the day,
it is to be the broker who introduces sinful clients to the riches of
the divine and gracious patron. The great privilege of his role is
not principally that of making the connection between God and
those clients who might be considered to be in a privileged position, namely, the Jews, but between God and the most unexpec-
ted clients of all, namely, the Gentiles and even the barbarians
and the Scythians (3:11).

A second broker in the letter to the Colossians is Epaphras who
introduced his own people to Paul's gospel, serving, as Paul
states (1:7) either 'on our behalf' (NRSV margin) or 'on your
behalf' (NRSV). Either way, he continues to serve as a bridge
between them and as a mediator and guardian of the truth Paul

taught. Archippus (4:17) might prove to be a broker of the gospel, if he fulfils his potential. Equally, Onesimus (4:9), in view of his own experience, might come to be seen in that light too, if Paul's plans and wishes for him as he returns to Philemon come to fruition.

The chief clients in Colossians are the brothers and sisters who are called to be 'God's chosen ones' (3:12). All the hallmarks of the conventional obligations of clients towards their patrons find parallels in how the Colossians are instructed to relate to God. First they are to be faithful, not deserting the God who has conferred his grace on them, nor compromising their allegiance by showing devotion to other faiths. This is the thrust of the central argument of the letter, starting at 2:6 where they are told 'As you therefore have received Christ Jesus the Lord, continue your lives in him', through the explanation of why it is foolish to give any credence to the religious teaching of others (2:16–23), and on to the call to them to set their hearts and minds on 'things that are above, where Christ is, seated at the right hand of God' (3:1–2). Second, they are to honour their patron by living in a way that would enhance his reputation and serve his honour rather than shame him (1:10; 3:5 – 4:6). Third, there is the repeated call for them to be thankful (1:12; 2:7; 3:15,16,17; 4:2). This is not Paul's attempt to employ the power of positive thinking so that a grumpy and depressed group of Christians in Colossae would buck their spirits up. It is rather the language of reciprocity: clients would have been expected to express gratitude to their patrons.[26]

The customary relationships of patron, broker and client are all evident in Colossians, although not in any simple way. Some members play more than one role in the network of relationships in the newly formed community of Christ. Moreover, their common dependence on his grace transforms the way in which those who continue to act as human patrons and benefactors perform their duties, regardless of their social rank.

The Body: Physical and Symbolic

Anthropologists have identified attitudes to the physical body and bodily behaviour as an important key to unlocking how a society perceives itself.[27] Beyond the basic biological functions, there is no such thing as natural bodily behaviour. Bodily behaviour is learned, deeply shaped by the cultures in which people are educated, and consequently reflects, albeit unwittingly, the values, customs and self-understanding that culture has. From an anthropological perspective, the way people handle their physical bodies is symbolic of the way in which they handle the social body. The one is a microcosm of the other.

In her various writings, Mary Douglas[28] has highlighted the symbolic importance of the body and given particular attention to people's attitudes towards its boundaries, internal structure, control, pollution and wholeness. The topic has a close connection with questions of purity, which will be addressed in the next section.

Modern Western Christians are heirs to an earlier age which emphasized the need to control the body and suppress its expression, as can be seen in attitudes to sex and discipline. With hindsight they often appeared to live in denial about its importance relative, at least, to 'the spirit'. By contrast the New Testament has a surprising amount to say about the body from a variety of perspectives. The many references to physical healing, sexual practices and the dangers of polluting the body are obvious in this connection. But there are also many references to members and organs of the physical body – heads, minds, eyes, ears, hands, hearts, feet, tongues, stomachs and even 'less honourable' and 'less respectable' parts[29] – some of which are mentioned repeatedly.[30] References to the body, whether it is referred to literally or symbolically, are deeply revealing of the early Christian's understanding of the church.

Body language plays a major role in 1 Corinthians where it is something of a recurring theme,[31] and where the body is chiefly seen as a microcosm of the church.[32] But it is also evident in other letters of Paul. Colossians mentions the physical body three times. Once it stresses that reconciliation has occurred through the death of 'Christ's physical body' (1:22, TNIV).[33] The second refers to Paul's physical absence (2:5) and the third to the harsh ascetic treatment with which some treated their bodies, which Paul regards as misguided (2:23).[34] The body is the assumed reality behind 3:5–14. The letter also refers to the mind (1:21; 3:2), heart (2:2; 3:22,23), head (2:19), hands (2:11), and eye (3:22). These terms are used in a natural, which ironically usually means metaphorical as opposed to physical, sense and they are not of major significance.

Some texts, however, are of great significance. Colossians 1:18 refers to Christ the Son as 'the head of the body, the church'. Consistent with this, although somewhat of an extension, is the claim of Christ's headship over 'every ruler and authority' (2:10). Consistent, again, is the condemnation of people who indulge in the esoteric and false religious practices who are described as 'not holding fast to the head, from whom the whole body, nourished and held together by its ligaments and sinews, grows with a growth that is from God' (2:19).

The body image in Colossians is a significant development on the use of the image in the earlier letters of Paul. In 1 Corinthians 12, the emphasis is on the internal structures of their relationships in the church and the need for its varied members to function in a coherent and unified way in the here and now.[35] In Colossians[36] the emphasis is on the relation of the body to its head, now identified as the pre-eminent Christ, and pushes the earlier image much further with the result that it is used to teach a different lesson. The cosmic Christ, who rules over all, is the one in whom the various believers, cowering under the malign influence of various 'rulers', find their destiny and integration, as will the whole of the creation in the future. They are all too well aware in the present of the breakdown of creation and its fragmentation. One day, however, 'all things, whether on earth or in heaven' (1:20) will find renewal and reintegration in him.

The body and headship motif in Colossians is employed to envisage an eschatological future in which the entire cosmos is brought into harmony under the rule of the Father in an eternal kingdom of light. The vision's purpose is not to suggest that utopia lies in the future and in the meantime believers have no option but to put up with the fallenness of the world and get on with it. The vision is precisely designed to affect their present behaviour, by giving them confidence in Christ and hope to persevere, and encouraging them to live as those who are vitally connected with the one who is the firstborn of this new, coming creation (1:18). As his body on earth they serve as vital witnesses and examples of the future reconciliation of all things. In their current lives they have already begun to experience their anticipated futures (3:1–4). In MacDonald's words, 'When Colossians is understood as a result of the dialectical relationship between social actors and the symbolic universe, its cosmological perspective emerges as fundamentally tied to the realities of community life.'[37]

The symbolic world produced by the body metaphor in Colossians, then, is not only of integration between members of the church in Colossae, but is a much grander vision, a vision of integration or reconciliation which is of truly cosmic proportions.

Purity: Clean and Unclean

A major element of any culture is its concern for purity and order.[38] All societies perceive the world as composed of people, animals, places, food, body parts and acts which are labelled and categorized by vocabulary like clean or unclean, pure or impure, holy or polluted. Those that are pure, clean or holy create a symbolic world which is ordered and whole, whereas those which are labelled unclean, impure or polluted threaten to destroy life and reduce the wider world to chaos. Between these two categories there exist a number of things which are labelled 'common', things which are necessary to life but seen as somewhat neutral on the spectrum between a creation that is whole and one that has been heading for chaos. Regulations and customs about purity mirror in miniature how people see the world in which they live: a world composed of a number of overlapping circles which include that of creation in general, the society or nation of which they are a part and a particular subculture within it. Approaches to purity symbolize people's wider world-view and help to create and maintain their symbolic world of meaning. They also distinguish one community from another as they create coherence within a community and create distance and mark boundaries from those outside it.[39]

Much religion concerns the maintenance of the boundaries between the pure and impure. Religious rituals serve a number of functions. They remind people of their community's particular symbolic world and reinforce commitment to its laws. They also provide a way of correcting what has gone awry through rituals of cleansing or sacrificial offerings. In the extreme, they provide a way of expelling anything which threatens chaos if it is not amenable to correction and restoration.

The people of God in the Old Testament and the New Testament show a persistent concern with issues of purity. An early and comprehensive exposition of the topic is found in Leviticus, but the issue is one that continues down the centuries and dogs the early church as we see, for example, in Peter's vision at Joppa (Acts 10:9–23), the discussion of the so-called Council of Jerusalem (Acts 15:1–29), the argument between Peter and Paul at Antioch (Gal. 2:11–21), the advice given in Romans 14, the many questions addressed in 1 Corinthians, and finally in the vision of judgement and re-creation in Revelation (e.g. 18:1–3; 21:8,27). But what of Colossians?

Questions of purity surface in Colossians in three respects. Paul first uses the language of purity when reminding his readers that their reconciliation is the start of a journey and that when they reach their destination they will be presented to God, 'holy and blameless and irreproachable' (1:22). The words for 'holy' (*hagios*), 'blameless' (*amōmos*) and 'irreproachable' (*anegklētos*) all belong to the same semantic field about purity.[40] The vision is of the Colossian believers being separated from the world and continuing to be loyal to the same gospel they received at the start of their Christian lives since that is the way in which they will be transformed into the 'perfect' sacrifice, prefigured by the Levitical sacrifices, which can be offered to God.[41]

Second, and perhaps more obviously, 'the conflict at Colossae has to do with the question of purity'.[42] Paul's condemnation of those seeking to take the Colossians Christians 'captive through philosophy and empty deceit, according to human tradition' (2:8) is a condemnation of those who still have a symbolic world-view which is constructed on the basis of the obsolete purity regulations of Hellenistic Judaism. Their concern, as catalogued in 2:16–23, with food laws, sacred days, ascetic practices and other ritual regulations belonged to the old era, not to the new and eschatological age which had already dawned in Christ and in which Christians now lived (3:1–4). These old regulations mapped a symbolic universe in which Gentiles were seen as impure and unclean outsiders. But in Christ the map of the symbolic universe has been redrawn and the Gentiles have had the mystery of the glorious riches of Christ made known to them (1:26–7).

This leads, third, to the question as to whether the boundary between the pure and impure is not situated in a different place or abolished altogether. Colossians makes it clear that the boundary is not abolished. Colossians 4:5 speaks as a matter of course about 'outsiders',[43] showing they still believe there is a boundary. Insiders are defined as those of any nationality, age, social position or gender who have been reconciled to Christ.[44] Their purity is asserted in labelling them as 'saints' (*hagoi*) and 'faithful (*pistoi*) (1:2) and is now demonstrated not by the keeping of ritual laws but by the transformation of their character and the reformation of their moral behaviour (3:5–14). So the question of purity is still germane but has been reformulated in Christ.

Limited Good

The economy of the contemporary world is built on the premise that we should always be producing more in the future than in the past. If resources in one area are limited (like the unrenewable resources of energy we are said to be rapidly depleting), we have the confidence that scientific and technological advances will soon identify new sources and that there will always be a way of satisfying our ever-expanding desires. Those in the peasant economies of the ancient Mediterranean world perceived the world in very different terms. It seemed to them that they spent their lives in the rural areas producing food and other goods to supply those who lived in the cities, at cost to themselves and without gain. For them, 'good' was available only in finite quantities and, what is more, it had already been distributed.[45]

What they meant by 'good' was material possessions, physical resources and wealth but they extended it beyond the material to include immaterial assets like honour, praise, love, friendship, prestige, fame and safety. Since the quantity of 'good' could be neither increased nor decreased, any more than the amount of land could be increased or decreased, it meant that if someone

increased in any 'good' unavoidably others would suffer a reduction. The bottom line of the balance sheet was always the same. It
could not be increased. All that could happen was that the assets
could be transferred from one account to another but the overall
capital remained unchanged. It was a 'zero-sum game'.[46]

This perception had a major impact on life and meant people
worked hard to maintain what they had, saw those who became
more successful as robbing others since they would be depriving
others of what they owned. Although honourable people would
not seek to acquire more, the perception of limited good inevitably
became fertile ground for the vice of envy. The perception of limited good especially affected the way people sought to defend their
family's property and inheritance and, above all, their honour.

Of all the concepts spoken of by the Social Context Group, this
one is constructed on the least substantial foundation. There is no
direct evidence of this perception though it must be said it makes
reasonable sense and appears to be a credible way of joining up
the dots.[47]

How does it help us interpret Colossians, if at all? It helps to
interpret the question of honour, especially in relation to God and
his Son, Jesus Christ. Paul places Jesus Christ in the pre-eminent
place of honour in the universe (1:15–20; 2:9–10). His status in creation, past, present and future, is not only unsurpassed but other
powers or authorities simply do not compare. He has no competition. Given that all honour belongs to him it would be an act of
extreme folly for Christians to accord honour to these lesser
'thrones or dominions or rulers or powers' (1:15). Since honour is
limited, if they were granted recognition and status, by praying
to them or observing the religious rituals associated with them, it
would be robbing the Lord Jesus Christ of the distinction which
belonged to him alone. To credit others with the need for religious respect was not a sign of tolerance and wisdom but was
rather totally incompatible with the supremacy of Christ.[48]

Reading

The postscript in Colossians gives a fascinating glimpse into the
life of the early church when Paul writes 'And when this letter

has been read among you, have it read also in the church of the Laodiceans; and see that you read also the letter from Laodicea' (4:16). The instruction, which gives to the letters a significance beyond their immediate recipients, has caused curiosity and controversy in equal measure, not least because of questions about the identity of the letter to the Laodiceans.[49] Our interest lies in a different area, which is in what it says about the cultural context of reading and the social function which reading achieved.

The use of a letter to communicate or extend a philosopher's teaching was a well-tried technique in the ancient world. The style, form and objectives of Paul's letters were consistent with 'hortatory letters in the traditions of Greco-Roman philosophy'.[50] Such a letter was seen as overcoming the distance of separation and an extension of, in this case, the apostle's ministry to a community with as little change as possible.[51] Of course, the distance between writer and recipient was greater if, as again in this case, Paul had not founded or yet visited the church. In our minds, the distance might be greater still if the letter was pseudonymous, but Esler argues that even then 'If the recipients of such a letter believed the sender was still alive, the dynamics of his or her presence would have been similar to the dynamics of a community who had received a letter by Paul'.[52] However, letter-writing was inevitably different to some degree from the apostle personally being present since it could not avoid being a one-way communication.[53]

In the ancient world, reading was overwhelmingly a social act. We must divest ourselves of misleading contemporary connotations when we read the word 'reading' in the biblical literature. Since the printing press, reading has become an individual act in which a person reads silently, decoding the symbols on the page with their eyes. In the world of the early church only a minority of people would have been able to read in this way; few would have been literate, as we understand the term.[54] At that time, reading usually meant listening to a document being read in a group context by one who was an able reader, maybe the householder or an educated slave, or even a trained lector.[55] It was reading with the ears, rather than the eyes.[56] Letters were written to be heard, rather than seen and, as Paul Achtemeier has insisted, they were 'oral to the core, both in the creation and in their performance'.[57]

The fact that they were oral documents, transcribed by one of Paul's literate friends and read orally to the gathered church by a competent reader, has an impact on the way they would have been understood. In discussing how these documents would have been heard by their original recipients, Bruce Malina[58] rejects the idea that they would have been interpreted in the propositional way in which contemporary readers, trained to exegete languages, would do. He does not dismiss the value of contemporary tools of linguistics and exegesis. They have their value in helping us to understand the text to some extent but they also have the danger that they may leave it fragmented, abstracted and atomized on our desks. Rather, he argues, they would have read (heard) the text as part of a larger story and focused on its meaning as it evoked connections with other scenes, frames and schemes. He puts it perhaps most helpfully when he says that it would be much more like the way we read 'situations' rather than read a dictionary. The reader plays a significant role in how a situation is interpreted because:

> As a rule, people carry in their heads one or more models of 'society' and 'human being' which greatly influence what they look for in their experiences, what they actually see, and what they eventually do with their observations by way of fitting them along with other facts into a larger scheme of explanation. In this respect, every human being, tutored or not, is no different from any trained observer in our society.[59]

When we read 'situations', as readers, we read them through the lenses of our previous experience, wider knowledge and cultural expectations. So it was with the readers of Paul's letters. Living in the same world as Paul and being part of the same developing story, they would have interpreted the text not in a vacuum but in a shared context and tradition. They were participants in a social system that provided them with the clues they needed to read between the lines and fill out the implicit meanings that the writer had no need to spell out. If the letters had been to those who did not share the common context of apostolic faith, much more would need to have been supplied to interpret the meaning for the reader. Being part of the apostolic community presented the readers of Paul's letters with a privileged position in inter-preting what they heard. Since we do not share the same social and immediate religious context easy interpretation is not so readily available to us.

The writings of the New Testament perform a number of par-ticular social functions depending on their genre. Gospel writ-ings may be designed to perpetuate the teaching of Jesus or to be apologetic, letters to be pedagogical, and apocalyptic writings to encourage people to persevere, and so on.[60] But since the letters were read to the community as a whole, they also perform the function of increasing social solidarity and reinforcing their understanding of collectivist personality. The fact that the letter was read as a whole would have served to strengthen their bonds with each other. Unlike the contemporary church, which reads the Bible in fragments with the result that members pick up dif-ferent elements of it and lack the whole picture, the early church, whose members were experienced in listening, read Paul's letters in their entirety. Consequently they started from a much more unified basis in their appreciation of what it meant to have a shared experience in Christ. Modern communication theory has taught us that the medium of communication is never a neutral factor in conveying a message but has implications for the way a message is heard, interpreted and understood. So 'reading', in the sense of a collective exercise in hearing rather than a private act of seeing, strengthened the collectivist understanding of the faith and underscored that being a Christian was not primarily a matter of entering an individual life choice, but of joining a com-munity, becoming a member of a body and entering into an ongo-ing tradition.

Conclusion

There are other aspects of the culture of the Mediterranean world of the early church to which the scholars associated with the Social Context Group have given attention, such as the 'evil eye' and witchcraft. But the core values of honour and shame, purity and impurity, the way in which attitudes and beliefs about the body served as a microcosm of beliefs and attitudes about the body of society, along with the arrangements found in terms of patrons and clients and for reading seem those which are most relevant to our understanding of Colossians and serve to help us read/hear the letter more as its original recipients would have done.

9

Concluding Comments

The Christian faith is an incarnational faith. A central tenet of Christian belief is that in Jesus Christ God lived as a human being, and lived at a particular time, in a particular country, inhabited a particular culture, and spoke a particular language. God chose to make himself known in the flesh and blood of the real world. Given this, it is not surprising that God should also operate in and through the normal sociological dynamics that were at work, even if he is not confined to them, any more that Jesus Christ was confined to the unyielding physical laws of the earth. To investigate the sociological factors involved in the New Testament is, then, perfectly consistent with Christianity as an incarnate faith.

The particularity of time and space, culture and language has been the foundation for historical critics and biblical scholars as they have sought to understand the text. But, too often, the sociological factors have been ignored, perhaps because they are less tangible or less visible than matters of history, art, geography or language. They are, though, no less real. As is often said, if you want a definition of water, don't ask a goldfish. They are immersed in this see-through liquid, have no distance from it, and would find it hard to explain, even if they had the brain-power to do so! So it is with us. Being immersed in a set of sociological dynamics means they are often taken for granted and therefore left unexpressed, even if they could be understood correctly.

In spite of the difficulty, sociological dynamics are real and we cannot truly understand human behaviour without giving consideration to them. People are members of a social body, have a place in a social system,[1] and link to a network of social relation-ships. All these exercise a formative influence on the individual since in a very real sense 'no man is an island'. In this respect, sociological enquiry is not about adding yet another dimension of explanation to others, or illuminating particular aspects of life, but seeks to shed light on the whole of life.

In approaching the New Testament sociologically, the sociolo-gist has to begin with the raw data of social history and social context, which is why we began by asking about the city of Colossae and its citizens. While it would only be honest to admit that sociologists can get lost in their own theories, just like other academics, their commitment is to seek to understand actual people and their relationships. Having understood something of the historical and social context, we then looked at the religious context. Religion is, now as then, an extremely potent force in the world, even if contemporary sociologists are curiously myopic about it. But even if sociologists can pretend it is insignificant now, it would be impossible to understand people's lives in the ancient world without it.

Given that Colossae was alive with gods, spirits and powers, most of which were embedded in the ethnic, family and social networks people inhabited, the question of why some would break out of their inherited positions and become disciples of Jesus Christ suggests itself. Theologically, *the* explanation lies in the regenerating work of the Holy Spirit and the preaching of the gospel. But, consistent with belief in an incarnate God, it would be surprising if the way people were converted did not follow a recognizable pattern like that which has become familiar through recent studies of conversions. What we know of the situation of the Colossian converts and what we can learn from the language used in the letter suggests that such a path was probably taken there too.

Having been converted to Christ, the next question that sug-gests itself concerns their self-identity. Who did they perceive themselves to be? Here recent studies in social identity were deployed and shed light on the way in which they categorized themselves above all as being 'in the Lord'. More customary social and ethnic identity markers, although not abolished, were neutralized by the greater fact of being brothers and sisters in

Christ, and God's 'chosen . . . holy and beloved' people. The challenge to water down their identity came from the insidious incursion of syncretistic teaching into the church, which suggested that they were wiser to hedge their bets and add other religious practices to their worship of Christ. But the message of Colossians is that any degree of compromise to their faith in Christ is not to improve it but to fatally corrupt it. Again, the mechanisms which aid the formation of social identity in our world were also apparent in the letter to the Colossians.

All New Testament Christians would share the identity of being in Christ, so why was Colossians written? The answer to this question leads us to understand how our beliefs are socially constructed. It should be understood that this does not imply beliefs are made up and have no basis, or that they are nothing but the product of social forces at work. Indeed, Peter Berger, who with Thomas Luckmann is chiefly responsible for this perspective, has recently denied this is what they meant and lamented the way in which people have misunderstood their proposal that reality is 'socially constructed'. What they meant, he confessed, 'was that all reality is subject to socially derived interpretations' and no more.[2] In Colossians the 'reality' of the apostolic gospel is interpreted so that it relates to the needs of believers living in Colossae with their view that the unseen world housed powers which were malevolent towards them and who constantly needed to be placated. So the gospel, making use of the normal social mechanisms which composed a plausibility structure, is presented in a new light and Christ is presented on the widest canvas of all as Creator and Re-Creator, Lord over everything and every being.

The faith of the believers is equally interpreted so as to match their need. Their desperate need is for their confidence in the gospel to grow, so they are taught that just as Christ is already raised and is at the right hand of God so, too, they are seated already with Christ, even while they live out the implications of his victory on earth. They do not need to fear how they might ascend to heaven for, the truth is, they are already there! In this way, the one and same gospel declared throughout the New Testament is 'tweaked' to answer the needs thrown up by their social situation.

Once the church comes into being, it is subject to the forces of change. Social groups 'age' just as individual human beings age, and freely formed and creative communities settle down and become institutions which are less nimble and more rigid in their thinking and operation. While scholars may disagree as to whether Colossians was written by Paul or not, all would agree that it does not belong to the early part of his ministry. Since it is a later writing and addressed to a second-generation church it makes a happy hunting ground for those who want to detect the onset of institutionalization. Indeed, some not only stress the advantages of stability that institutionalization brings but advocate it in order to justify patterns of ministry and worship that developed after the New Testament era. If that's where the New Testament is heading, they argue, we should follow where it leads and not seek to reconstitute the church as it was in its immaturity. Although a great deal of discussion has taken place about this issue, I remain cautious that Colossians shows much evidence of institutionalization, even though the odd hint may be present. The topic remains one of immense relevance for the contemporary church.

Sociologists are naturally concerned with the way societies organize themselves and how the various bricks fit together to form a coherent building. In the world of Colossians the basic building brick was that of the household, and its impact on the way the early church functioned is crucial. It influenced their evangelistic mission, shaped their leadership and fashioned their approach to ethics. Colossians has much to say implicitly about the relationship between the household and the church's mission and organization. But its special interest lies in the fact that it includes the earliest use of the household ethical code being applied to Christians; although whether the code is merely conventional or radically Christian is much debated. No sociological understanding of the early church can ignore the way in which people's lives and morals are shaped by the external social institutions around them.

Societies are equally shaped by their value systems and, in the final chapter, a number of issues were reviewed that have been put high on the agenda by the Social Context Group. These included the pivotal value of honour and shame, attitudes to the physical and social body, questions of purity and impurity, the role of patrons, brokers and clients, and the sense that 'good' was considered to be limited in supply in the ancient world. Lastly, mention was made of the fact that the Colossian culture was an oral one in which literacy was low and in which even those who did read, read in a different way from ours today. Since Paul tells them to swap this letter with the one he sent to Laodicea once they had read it, this is no incidental fact.

Paul writes the final greeting with his own hand, suggesting, typically, that he had orally dictated the letter to an amanuensis. Then he pleads 'Remember my chains'. The request is heavy with sociological freight. In a society that made much of honour, asking people to identify with him and remember him in that condition is remarkable. As their apostle, even if his 'truth' was mediated through Epaphras; as their 'patron', in at least a partial sense; and as their 'significant other', to use a sociological term, drawing attention to the dishonour he suffers as a prisoner is remarkable. He does not, of course, say how they are to remember him. In prayer, that he might be released? In pity, so that he might be sent support? In anger, so they might cry against the injustice of it? No, more likely, he is asking them to remember him with thanksgiving, since he has the honour of sharing in the suffering of the crucified Messiah he proclaimed and making up in his own body 'what is lacking in Christ's afflictions' (1:24). In the social context of the day, the request is not only remarkable, but a testimony to the radical nature and the transforming power of the gospel he preached; however much it may have been disseminated through the sociological channels that can be identified as already formed in the Colossian world.

Colossians was not written to intellectuals who lived in a bubble of ideas but to ordinary men and women wrestling with the harsh realities of their lives, so much of which were socially determined. Reading Colossians sociologically hopefully rescues it from ideational captivity and releases it to be a letter that continues to speak to ordinary 'lay' believers today.

Bibliography

Ancient works

Eusebius, *Chronicles*.
Heroditus, *History*.
Josephus, *Against Apion*.
Josephus, *Antiquities*.
Pliny the Elder, *Natural History*.
Strabo, *Geography*.
Tacitus, *Annals*.
Xenophon, *Anabasis*.

Modern works

Abrams, D. and M.A. Hogg, eds. *Social Identity Theory: Constructive and Critical Advances* (New York: Harvester Wheatsheaf, 1990).
Achtemeier, P. '*Omne verbum sonat*: The New Testament and the Oral Environment of Late Western Antiquity'. *Journal of Biblical Literature* 109 (1990): pp. 3–27.
Arnold, C.E. 'Colossae.' Pages 1089–90 in vol. 1 of *Anchor Bible Dictionary* (ed. D.N. Freeman; New York: Doubleday, 1992).
— *The Colossian Syncretism: The Interface Between Christianity and Folk Belief at Colossae* (Tubingen: J.C.B. Mohr, 1995).
Balch, D. 'Household Codes'. Pages 25–48 in *Greco-Roman Literature and the New Testament* (ed. D.E. Aune; Atlanta: Scholars Press, 1988).

— *Let Wives be Submissive: The Domestic Code in 1 Peter*, SBLMS 26 (Chico: Scholars, 1981).

Banks, R. *Paul's Idea of Community: The Early House Churches in the Historical Setting* (Exeter: Paternoster Press, 1980).

Barclay, J. *Colossians and Philemon*, New Testament Guides (Sheffield: Sheffield Academic Press, 1987).

Barker, E. *The Making of a Moonie* (Oxford: Blackwells, 1984).

Bartchy, S.S. *Mallōn Chrēsai: First Century Slavery and the Interpretation of 1 Corinthians 7:21*, Society for Biblical Literature Dissertation Series 11 (Missoula: Scholars Press, 1973).

— 'Undermining Ancient Patriarchy: The Apostle Paul's Vision of a Society of Siblings'. *Biblical Theology Bulletin* 29 (1999): pp. 68–78.

Barton, S.C. 'Paul and the Cross: A Sociological Approach'. *Theology* 85 (1982): pp. 13–19.

— 'Social-Scientific Approaches to Paul'. Pages 892–900 in *Dictionary of Paul and his Letters* (eds. Gerald F. Hawthorne, Ralph P. Martin and Daniel G. Reid; Downers Grove: IVP, 1993).

Batten, A. 'Brokerage: Jesus as Social Entrepreneur'. Pages 167–77 in *Understanding the Social World of the New Testament* (ed. D. Neufeld and R.E. DeMaris; London: Routledge, 2010).

— 'God in the Letter of James: Patron or Benefactor?' Pages 49–64 in *The Social World of the New Testament: Insights and Models* (ed. J.H. Neyrey and E.C. Stewart; Peabody: Hendrickson, 2008).

Bauman, Z. *Community: Seeking Safety in an Insecure World* (Cambridge: Polity, 2001).

Bendix, R. *Max Weber: An Intellectual Portrait* (London: Methuen, 1966).

Berger, P.L. *A Rumour of Angels* (New York: Doubleday, 1969. Repr. New York: An Anchor Book, 1990).

— 'Charisma and Religious Innovation: The Social Location of Israelite Prophecy', *American Sociological Review* 28 (1963): pp. 940–50.

— *The Social Reality of Religion* (New York: Doubleday, 1967. Harmondsworth: Penguin University Books, 1973). US title: *The Sacred Canopy: Elements of a Sociological Theory of Religion*.

Berger, P.L. and T. Luckmann. *The Social Construction of Reality: A Treatise in the Sociology of Knowledge* (Harmondsworth: Penguin University Books, 1971).

Berger, P.L. and A. Zijderveld. *In Praise of Doubt: Having Convictions Without Becoming a Fanatic* (New York: HarperOne, 2009).

Blasi, A.J. *Making Charisma: The Social Construction of Paul's Public Image* (New Brunswick: Transaction Publishers, 1991).

Bruce, F.F. *Commentary on Galatians*. New International Greek Testament Commentary (Exeter: Paternoster, 1982).

— *Commentary on the Epistles to the Ephesians and Colossians*. New International Commentary on the New Testament (Grand Rapids: Eerdmans, 1957).

Bruce, S. *Choice and Religion: A Critique of Rational Choice* (Oxford: Oxford University Press, 1999).

Carr, W. *Angels and Principalities: The Background, Meaning and Development of the Pauline Phrase hai archai kai hai exousiai*. Society of New Testament Studies: Monograph Series, 42 (Cambridge: Cambridge University Press, 1981).

Campbell, D. 'The Scythian Perspective in Col. 3:11: A Response to Troy Martin'. *Novum Testamentum* XXXIX (1997): pp. 81–4.

— 'Unravelling Col. 3:11b'. *New Testament Studies* 42 (1996): pp. 120–32.

Cannon, G.E. *The Use of Traditional Materials in Colossians* (Macon: Mercer University Press, 1983).

Chadwick, H. 'All Things to All Men'. *New Testament Studies* 1 (1954/5): pp. 261–75.

Chester, S. *Conversion at Corinth: Perspectives on Conversion in Paul's Theology and the Corinthian Church*. Studies of the New Testament and its World (Edinburgh: Continuum, 2003).

Chow, J.K. *Patronage in Corinth: A Study of Social Networks in Corinth*. Journal for the Study of the New Testament: Supplement Series 75 (Sheffield: Journal for the Study of the Old Testament Press, 1992).

Clark, D. *Between Pulpit and Pew: Folk Religion in a North Yorkshire Fishing Village* (Cambridge: Cambridge University Press, 1982).

Clarke, A.D. *Serve the Community of the Church: Christians as Leaders and Ministers* (Grand Rapids: Eerdmans, 2000).

Cohn, N. *The Pursuit of the Millennium* (London: Paladin, 1970).

Crouch, J.E. *The Origin and Intention of the Colossians Haustafel* (Gottenberg: Vandenhoeck, 1972).

DeMaris, R.E. *The Colossian Controversy*. Journal for the Study of the New Testament: Supplement Series 96 (Sheffield: Journal for the Study of the Old Testament Press, 1994).

DeSilva, D.A. *Honor, Patronage, Kinship and Purity: Unlocking New Testament Culture* (Downers Grove: Inter-Varsity Press, 2000).

Douglas, M. *Natural Symbols: Explorations in Cosmology* (Harmondsworth: Penguin Books, 1970).

— *Purity and Danger: An Analysis of Concept of Pollution and Taboo* (London: Routledge, 1966).

Duling, D.C. 'Ethnicity and Paul's Letter to the Romans'. Pages 68–89 in *Understanding the Social World of the New Testament* (ed. D. Neufeld and R.E. DeMaris; London: Routledge, 2010).

Durkheim, E. *The Elementary Forms of Religious Life* (Formes élémentaires de la vie religieuse, 1912, trans. Karen Fields; New York: The Free Press, 1995).

Dunn, J.D.G. *The Epistle to the Colossians and to Philemon*. New International Greek Testament Commentary (Grand Rapids: Eerdmans, and Carlisle: Paternoster, 1996).

— *The Epistle to the Galatians*. Black's New Testament Commentaries (London: A&C Black, 1993).

— *The Theology of Paul the Apostle* (Edinburgh: T&T Clark, 1998).

— *Unity and Diversity in the New Testament: An Inquiry into the Character of Earliest Christianity* (Philadelphia: Westminster Press, and London: SCM, 1977).

Einsenstadt, S.N. ed. *Max Weber on Charisma and Institution Building* (Chicago: University of Chicago Press, 1968).

Elliott, J.H. 'Patronage and Clientage'. Pages 144–56 in *The Social Sciences and New Testament Interpretation* (ed. R. Rohrbaugh; Peabody: Hendrickson, 1996).

— 'Paul, Galatians and the Evil Eye'. Pages 223–34 in *The Social World of the New Testament* (ed. J.H. Neyrey and E.C. Stewart; Peabody: Hendrickson, 2008).

— 'The Jesus Movement was not Egalitarian but Family-Orientated'. *Biblical Interpretation* 32 (2002): pp. 173–210.

Esler, P.E. *Community and Gospel in Luke-Acts: The Social and Political Motivations of Lucan Theology*. Society of New

Testament Studies: Monograph Series 57 (Cambridge: Cambridge University Press, 1987).

— *Conflict and Identity in Romans: The Social Setting of Paul's Letter* (Minneapolis: Fortress Press, 2003).

— *Galatians*. New Testament Readings (London: Routledge, 1998).

— 'Jesus and the Reduction of Intergroup Conflict: The Parable of the Good Samaritan in the Light of Social Identity Theory'. *Biblical Interpretation* 8 (2000): pp. 325–57.

— *New Testament Theology: Communion and Community* (London: SPCK, 2005).

— ed. *Modelling Early Christianity: Social-Scientific Studies of the New Testament in its Context* (London: Routledge, 1995).

Esler, P.E. and R.A. Piper. *Lazarus, Mary and Martha: A Social-Scientific and Theological Reading of John* (London: SCM, 2006).

Filson, F.V. 'The Significance of the Early House Churches'. *Journal of Biblical Literature* 58 (1939): pp. 105–12.

Fox, R.L. *Pagans and Christians* (New York: Alfred A Knopf, 1987).

Francis, F.O. and W. Meeks, eds. *Conflict at Colossae*. Sources for Biblical Study, 4 (Missolua: Society for Biblical Literature and Scholars Press, 1975).

Gager, J. *Kingdom and Community: The Social World of Early Christianity* (Englewood Cliffs: Prentice-Hall, 1975).

Garrett, W. 'Sociology and New Testament Studies: A Critical Evaluation of Rodney Stark's Contribution'. *Journal for the Scientific Study of Religion* 29 (1990): pp. 377–84.

Gehring, R.W. *House Church and Mission: The Importance of Household Structures in Early Christianity* (Peabody: Hendrickson, 2004).

Gerth, H.H. and C. Wright Mills, eds. *From Max Weber: Essays in Sociology* (London: Routledge, 1948).

Giddens, A. *The Constitution of Society: Outline of the Theory of Structuration* (Cambridge: Polity Press, 1984).

Hafemann, S.J. *Suffering and Ministry in the Spirit: Paul's Defence of His Ministry in 2 Corinthians 2:14–3:3* (Carlisle: Paternoster, 2000).

Harris, M.J. *Colossians and Philemon: Exegetical Guide to the Greek New Testament* (Grand Rapids: Eerdmans, 1995).

Harris, W. *Ancient Literacy* (Cambridge: Harvard University Press, 1989).

Hezser, C. *Jewish Literacy in Roman Palestine* (Tubingen: Mohr/Siebeck, 2001).

Hock, R.F. *The Social Context of Paul's Ministry* (Philadelphia: Fortress Press, 1980).

Hogg, M.A. and D. Abrams. *Social Identifications: A Social Psychology of Intergroup Relations and Group Processes* (London: Routledge, 1988).

Holmberg, B. *Paul and Power: The Structure of Authority in the Primitive Church as Reflected in the Pauline Epistles* (Philadelphia: Fortress Press, 1978).

— *Sociology and the New Testament* (Philadelphia: Fortress Press, 1990).

Hooker, M.D. 'Were there False Teachers in Colossae?' Pages 315–31 in *Christ and the Spirit: Studies in Honour of C.F.D. Moule* (ed. B. Lindars and S.S. Smalley; Cambridge: Cambridge University Press, 1973).

Horrell, D. 'The Development of Theological Ideology in Pauline Christianity: A Structuration Theory Perspective.' Pages 224–36 in *Modelling Early Christianity: Social-Scientific Studies of the New Testament in Its Context* (ed. Philip F. Esler; London and New York: Routledge, 1995).

Horrell, D.G. *The Social Ethos of the Corinthians Correspondence: Interest and Ideology from 1 Corinthians to 1 Clement.* Studies of the New Testament and its World (Edinburgh: T&T Clark, 1996).

— ed. *Social-Scientific Approaches to New Testament Interpretation* (Edinburgh: T&T Clark, 1999).

Johnson, E.E. 'Review of Margaret MacDonald's *The Pauline Churches*'. *Interpretation* 45 (1991): p. 91.

Johnson, L.T. 'Review of Margaret MacDonald's *The Pauline Churches*'. *Journal of the American Academy of Religion* 58 (1990): p. 719.

Johnson, S.E. 'Asia Minor and Early Christianity'. Pages 77–145 in *Christianity, Judaism and other Greco-Roman Cults II* FS M. Smith (Studies in Judaism in Late Antiquity 12, ed. Jacob Neusner; Leiden: E.J. Brill, 1975).

Judge, E.A. 'St Paul as a Radical Critic of Society'. Pages 99–115 in *Social Distinctives of the Christians in the First Century: Pivotal Essays by E.A. Judge* (ed. D. M. Scholer; Peabody: Hendrickson, 2008).

— 'The impact of Paul's Gospel on Ancient Society'. Pages 297–308 in *The Gospel to the Nations: Perspectives on Paul's Ministry* (ed. P. Bolt and M. Thompson; Downers Grove: Inter-Varsity Press, and Leicester: Apollos, 2000).

— 'The Social Patterns of the Christian Groups in the First Century'. Pages 1–56 in *Social Distinctives of the Christians in the First Century: Pivotal Essays by E.A. Judge* (ed. D.M. Scholer; Peabody: Hendrickson, 2008).

Kanter, R. *Commitment and Community* (Cambridge: Harvard University Press, 1972).

Käsemann, E. *Essays on New Testament Themes* (trans. W.J.Montague; London: SCM, 1964).

— *New Testament Questions for Today* (trans. W.J. Montague; London: SCM, 1969).

Kee, H.C. *Christian Origins in Sociological Perspective* (London: SCM, 1980).

Knox, J. *Philemon among the Letters of Paul* (London: Collins, 1960).

Lightfoot, J.B. *Saint Paul's Epistles to the Colossians and Philemon* (New York: MacMillan, rev. edn, 1879. Grand Rapids: Zondervan, repr. 1959).

Lincoln, A. 'Liberation from the Powers: Supernatural Spirit or Societal Structures?' Pages 335–54 in *The Bible in Human Society: Essays in Honour of John Rogerson*. Journal for the Study of Old Testament: Supplement 200 (eds. M.D. Carroll, D.J.A. Clines and P.R. Davies; Sheffield: Sheffield Academic Press, 1995).

— *Paradise Now and Not Yet*. Society of New Testament Studies: Monograph Series 43 (Cambridge: Cambridge University Press, 1981).

— 'The Household Code and Wisdom Mode of Colossians'. *Journal for the Study of the New Testament* 74 (1999): pp. 93–112.

— 'The Letter to the Colossians', Pages 551–669 in *New Interpreters' Bible* XI (Nashville: Abingdon, 2000).

Lincoln, A. and A.J.M. Wedderburn. *The Theology of the Later Pauline Letters* (Cambridge: Cambridge University Press, 1993).

Lofland, J. *Doomsday Cult: A Study of Conversion, Proselytization and Maintenance of Faith* (New York: Irvington, rev. and enl. edn, 1977).

Lohse, E. *Colossians and Philemon*. Hermenia (Philadelphia: Fortress Press, 1971).

MacDonald, M.Y. *Colossians and Ephesians*. Sacred Pagina Commentary Series (Collegeville: Liturgical Press, 2000).

— *The Pauline Churches: A Socio-Historical Study of Institutionalization in the Pauline and Deutero-Pauline Writings*. Society of New Testament Studies: Monograph Studies 60 (Cambridge: Cambridge University Press, 1988).

MacMullen, R. *Christianizing the Roman Empire* (AD 100–400) (New Haven: Yale University Press, 1984).

Malherbe, A.J. *Paul and the Thessalonians* (Philadelphia: Fortress Press, 1987).

— *Social Aspects of Early Christianity* (Baton Rouge: Louisiana State University Press, 1977).

Malina, B. 'Collectivism in Mediterranean Culture'. Pages 17–28 in *Understanding the Social World of the New Testament* (ed. D. Neufeld and R.E. DeMaris; London: Routledge, 2010).

— 'Patron and Client: The Analogy behind the Synoptic Theology'. *Forum* 4 (1988): pp. 2–32.

— 'Reading Theory Perspective: Reading Luke-Acts'. Pages 3–23 in *The Social World of Luke-Acts: Models for Interpretation* (ed. J.H. Neyrey; Peabody: Hendrickson, 1991).

— *The New Testament World: Insights from Cultural Anthropology* (Louisville: Westminster John Knox Press, rev. edn, 2001).

— *The Social World of Jesus and the Gospels* (London: Routledge, 1996).

— 'Understanding New Testament Persons'. Pages 41–61 in *The Social Sciences and New Testament Interpretation* (ed. R. Rohrbaugh; Peabody: Hendrickson, 1996).

Malina, B. and J.H. Neyrey. 'Ancient Mediterranean Persons in Cultural Perspective'. Pages 257–75 in *The Social World of the New Testament* (ed. J.H. Neyrey and E.C. Stewart; Peabody: Hendrickson, 2008).

Malina, B. and R.L. Rohrbaugh. *Social-Science Commentary on the Synoptic Gospels* (Minneapolis: Fortress, 1992).

Martin, B. 'The Pentecostal Gender Paradox: A Cautionary Tale for the Sociology of Religion'. Pages 53–66 in *The Blackwell Companion to Sociology of Religion* (ed. Richard K. Fenn; Oxford: Blackwell, 2003).

Martin, D.B. *The Corinthian Body* (New Haven: Yale UP, 1995).

Martin, T.W. *By Philosophy and Empty Deceit: Colossians as Response to a Cynic Critique*. Journal for the Study of the New Testament: Supplement Series 118 (Sheffield: Sheffield Academic Press, 1996).

— 'The Scythian Perspective in Col. 3:11'. *Novum Testamentum* XXXVII (1995): pp. 249–61.

Meeks, W. 'In One Body: The Unity of Humankind in Colossians and Ephesians'. Pages 209–21 in *God's Christ and His People: Studies in Honour of Nils Alstrop Dahl* (ed. Wayne Meeks and Jacob Jervell: Oslo: Uniiversitetsforlaget, 1977).

— *The First Urban Christians: The Social World of the Apostle Paul* (New Haven: Yale University Press, 2nd edn, 2003).

Meggitt, J. *Paul, Poverty and Survival. Studies of the New Testament and its World* (Edinburgh: T&T Clark, 1998).

Moo, D.J. *The Letters to the Colossians and to Philemon*. Pillar New Testament Commentary (Grand Rapids: Eerdmans, and Apollos: Nottingham, 2008).

Moxnes, H. 'Parent-Client Relations and the New Community in Luke-Acts'. Pages 241–68 in *The Social World of Luke-Acts: Models for Interpretation* (ed. J.H. Neyrey; Peabody: Hendrickson, 1991).

— 'What is a Family? Problems in Constructing Early Christian Families'. Pages 13–42 in *Constructing Early Christian Families: Family as Social Reality and Metaphor* (ed. H. Moxnes; London: Routledge, 1997).

Murphy-O'Connor, J. *St Paul's Corinth: Texts and Archaeology* (Wilmington: Michael Glazer, 1983).

Neufeld, D. and R.E. DeMaris, eds. *Understanding the Social World of the New Testament* (London: Routledge, 2010).

Neyrey, J.H. 'Clean/Unclean, Pure/Polluted and Holy/Profane: The Idea and System of Purity'. Pages 80–104 in *The Social Sciences and New Testament Interpretation* (ed. R. Rohrbaugh; Peabody: Hendrickson, 1996).

— *Paul in Other Words: A Cultural Reading of His Letters* (Louisville: Westminster John Knox Press, 1990).

Neyrey, J.H. and R.L. Rohrbaugh. ' "He Must Increase, I Must Decrease" (John 3:10): A Cultural and Social Interpretation'. Pages 237–51 in *The Social World of the New Testament: Insights and Models* (ed. J.H. Neyrey and E.C. Stewart; Peabody: Henrickson, 2008).

Neyrey, J.H. and E.C. Stewart, eds. *The Social World of the New Testament: Insights and Models* (Peabody: Hendrickson, 2008).

Nock, A.D. *Conversion: The Old and the New in Religion from Alexander the Great to Augustine of Hippo* (Oxford: Oxford University Press, 1933).

O'Brien, P.T. *Colossians, Philemon*. World Biblical Commentary (Waco: Word, 1982).

O'Dea, T.F. 'Five Dilemmas in the Institutionalization of Religion'. *Journal for the Scientific Study of Religion* 1 (1961): pp. 30–39.

— *The Sociology of Religion* (Englewood Cliffs: Prentice–Hall, 1966).

Oakes, P. 'Remapping the Universe: Paul and the Emperor in 1 Thessalonians and Philippians'. *Journal for the Study of the New Testament* 27 (2005): pp. 301–22.

Osiek, C. and D.L. Balch. *Families in the New Testament World: Households and House Churches* (Louisville: Westminster John Knox, 1997).

Petersen, N. *Rediscovering Paul: Philemon and the Sociology of Paul's Narrative World* (Philadelphia: Fortress Press, 1985).

Poloma, M.M. *The Assemblies of God at the Crossroads: Charisma and Institutional Dilemmas* (Knoxville: University of Tennessee Press, 1989).

Putnam, R. *Bowling Alone* (New York: Touchstone, 2000).

Rambo, L. *Understanding Religious Conversion* (New Haven: Yale University Press, 1993).

Roberts, K. *Religion in Sociological Perspective* (Belmont: Wadsworth, 1990).

Rohrbaugh, R. ed. *The Social Sciences and New Testament Interpretation* (Peabody: Hendrickson, 1996).

Rohrbaugh, R.L. 'Honor: Core Value in the Biblical World'. Pages 109–25 in *Understanding the Social World of the New Testament* (ed. D. Neufeld and R.E. DeMaris; London: Routledge, 2010).

— 'The Pre-Industrial City in Luke-Acts'. Pages 107–25 in *The Social Sciences and New Testament Interpretation* (ed. R. Rohrbaugh; Peabody: Hendrickson, 1996).

Roth, G. and C. Wittich, eds. *Sociology of Religion* (New York: Bedminister Press, 1968).

Roth, G. and C. Wittich, eds. *Theory of Social and Economic Organisation* (New York: Bedminister Press, 1968).

Saller, R. *Personal Patronage under the Early Empire* (Cambridge: Cambridge University Press, 1982).

Sanders, J.T. *Charisma, Converts, Competitors: Societal and Sociological Factors in the Success of Early Christianity* (London: SCM, 2000).

Sandes, K.O. 'Equality Within Patriarchal Structures'. Pages 150–65 in *Constructing Early Christian Families: Family as Social Reality and Metaphor* (ed. H. Moxnes; London: Routledge, 1997).

Shkul, M. *Reading Ephesians: Exploring Social Entrepreneurship in the Text*. Library of New Testament Studies 408 (London and New York: T&T Clark, 2009).

Schnabel, E.J. *Early Christian Mission,* vol. 2, Paul and the Early Church (Downers Grove: Inter-Varsity Press, and Leicester: Apollos, 2004).

— *Paul the Missionary: Realities, Strategies and Methods* (Downers Grove: Inter-Varsity Press, and Nottingham: Apollos, 2008).

Scholer, D.M. ed. *Social Distinctives of the Christians in the First Century: Pivotal Essays by E.A. Judge* (Peabody: Hendrickson, 2008).

Schüssler Fiorenza, E. *In Memory of Her: A Feminist Reconstruction of Christian Origins* (London: SCM, 1983).

Schweizer, E. *The Letter to the Colossians: A Commentary* (trans. Andrew Chester; London: SPCK, 1982).

Smith, C. *American Evangelicalism: Embattled and Thriving* (Chicago: Chicago University Press, 1998).

Stambaugh, J. and D. Balch. *The Social World of the First Christians* (London: SPCK, 1986).

Stark, R. *The Rise of Christianity: A Sociologist Reconsiders History* (Princeton: Princeton University Press, 1996).

Stark, R. and R. Finke. *Acts of Faith, Explaining the Human Side of Religion* (Berkeley: University of California Press, 2000).

Stewart, E. 'Social Stratification and Patronage in Ancient Mediterranean Societies'. Pages 156–77 in *Understanding the Social World of the New Testament* (ed. D. Neufeld and R.E. DeMaris; London: Routledge, 2010).

Tajfel, H. ed. *Differentiation between Social Groups: Studies in the Social Psychology of Intergroup Relations* (London: Academic Press, 1978).

Theissen, G. *The Social Setting of Pauline Christianity. Studies of the New Testament World* (ed. and trans. J.H. Schütz; Edinburgh: T&T Clark, 1982).

Thiselton, A.C. *The Living Paul: An Introduction to the Apostle and His Thought* (London: SPCK, 2009).

Tidball, D. *Ministry by the Book: New Testament Patterns for Pastoral Leadership* (Nottingham: Apollos, and Downers Grove: Inter-Varsity Press, 2009).

Trainor, M. *Epaphras: Paul's Educator at Colossae.* Paul's Social Network (Collegeville: Liturgical Press, 2008).

— 'Unearthing Ancient Colossae in Southern Turkey: Theology and Archaeology in Dialogue.' http://www.compassreview .org/summer02/8.html.

Trebilco, P.R. 'Jewish Communities in Asia Minor'. Pages 562–9 in *Dictionary of New Testament Background* (ed. C.A. Evans and S.E. Porter; Downers Grove: Inter-Varsity Press, 2000.

Trebilco, P.R. and C.A. Evans. 'Diaspora Judaism'. Pages 281–96 in *Dictionary of New Testament Background* (ed. C.A. Evans and S.E. Porter; Downers Grove: Inter-Varsity Press, 2000).

Troeltsch, E. *The Social Teaching of the Christian Church* (2 vols; trans. Olive Wyon; London: George Allen & Unwin, 1931).

Turner, J.C. et al. *Rediscovering the Social Group: A Self-Categorization Theory* (Oxford: Blackwell, 1987).

Turner, V. *The Ritual Process* (Chicago: Aldine, 1969).

Van Broekhoven, H. 'The Social Profiles on the Colossians Debate'. *Journal for the Study of the New Testament* 66 (1997): pp. 73–90.

Van Gennep, A. *The Rites of Passage* (Chicago: University of Chicago Press, 1908; repr. 1960).

Verner, D.C. *The Household of God: The Social World of the Pastoral Epistles.* Society for Biblical Literature Dissertation Series 71 (Chico: Scholars Press, 1983).

Walsh, B. and S.C. Keesmaat. *Colossians Remixed: Subverting the Empire* (Downers Grove: Inter-Varsity Press, 2004).

Weber, M. *Economy and Society: An Outline of Interpretive Sociology* (ed. Guenther Roth and Claus Wittich; New York: Bedminster Press, 1968).

Wedderburn, A.J.M. *Baptism and Resurrection: Studies in Pauline Theology against Its Graeco-Roman Background* (Tubingen: J.C.B. Mohr, 1987).

Wilson, B. *Magic and the Millennium* (London: Heinemann, 1973).

— *The Noble Savages: The Primitive Origins of Charisma and its Contemporary Survival* (Berkeley: University of California Press, 1975).

Wilson, R.McL. *Colossians and Philemon*. International Critical Commentary (Edinburgh: T&T Clark, 2005).

Wilson, W.T. *The Hope of Glory: Education and Exploration in the Epistle of Colossians* (Leiden: Brill, 1997).

Winter, B. *After Paul Left Corinth: The Influence of Secular Ethics and Social Change* (Grand Rapids: Eerdmans, 2001).

— *Seek the Welfare of the City: Early Christians as Benefactors and Citizens* (Grand Rapids: Eerdmans, and Carlisle: Paternoster, 1994).

Witherington III, B. *The Letters of Philemon, the Colossians and the Ephesians: A Socio-Rhetorical Commentary on the Captivity Epistles* (Grand Rapids: Eerdmans, 2007).

Wright, N.T. *Colossians and Philemon*. Tyndale New Testament Commentaries (Leicester: Inter-Varsity Press, and Grand Rapids: Eerdmans, 1986).

Yaghjian, L.B. 'Ancient Reading'. Pages 206–30 in *The Social Sciences and New Testament Interpretation* (ed. R. Rohrbaugh; Peabody: Hendrickson, 1996).

Young, L. ed. *Rational Choice Theory and Religion* (London: Routledge, 1997).

Zeisler, J. *Pauline Christianity*. Oxford Bible Series (Oxford: Oxford University Press, rev. edn, 1990).

Endnotes

1 – Why Sociological Perspectives on Colossians?

[1] James D.G. Dunn, *The Epistle to the Colossians and to Philemon*, NIGTC (Grand Rapids: Eerdmans, and Carlisle: Paternoster, 1996), p. 19.

[2] Eduard Lohse calculates that, although there is much in Colossians which is Pauline, there are thirty–four words which are used only here in the New Testament, a further twenty–eight which, although found elsewhere in the New Testament, are not found in other Pauline letters, ten words which are found only in Colossians and Ephesians, and fifteen words found in Colossians and Ephesians and elsewhere in the New Testament but not in the other letters of Paul. This makes it distinctive enough before one starts considering the differences in style. *Colossians and Philemon*, Hermenia (Philadelphia: Fortress Press, 1971), pp. 84–91.

[3] For details on these issues see Lohse, *Colossians*, pp. 177–83 and Andrew Lincoln, 'The Letter to the Colossians', *New Interpreters' Bible*, XI (Nashville: Abingdon, 2000), pp. 568–83.

[4] For the history of this approach see *Conflict at Colossae*, ed. Fred O. Francis and Wayne Meeks, Sources for Biblical Study 4 (Missolua: SBL and Scholars Press, 1975), pp. 1–12. More generally see Abraham J. Malherbe, *Social Aspects of Early Christianity* (Baton Rouge: Louisiana State University Press, 1977), pp. 1–4. A recent example can be found in T.W. Martin, *By Philosophy and Empty Deceit: Colossians as Response to a Cynic Critique* (Sheffield: Sheffield Academic Press, 1996), who stresses (pp. 58–105, especially p. 63), however, that Cynic philosophy was essentially practical. Margaret Y. MacDonald rightly warns that historical and textual study remains crucial for the sociologist 'who must not contradict or exceed the . . . data', *The Pauline*

Churches: A Socio-Historical Study of Institutionalization in the Pauline and Deutero–Pauline Writings, SNTS MS 60 (Cambridge: CUP, 1988), p. 24.

5 Stephen Barton, 'Paul and the Cross: A Sociological Approach', *Theology* 85 (1982): p. 14.

6 S.C. Barton, 'Social-Scientific approaches to Paul', *DPL*, p. 893. Docetism was the ancient heresy that believed the body of Christ was not real and therefore denied the incarnation.

7 See Justin J. Meggitt, *Paul, Poverty and Survival*, SNTW (Edinburgh: T&T Clark, 1998). Meggitt may overstate his case but he offers a necessary corrective to thinking that survival in Paul's world was as easy as it is in the contemporary Western world.

8 The phrase is ironic in view of the presentation of the cosmic rule of Christ and encouragement to the readers to 'set your minds on things above, not on earthly things' (3:2).

9 Fairly recent surveys can be found in Bent Holmberg, *Sociology and the New Testament* (Philadelphia: Fortress Press, 1990) and D.G. Horrell, ed., *Social-Scientific Approaches to New Testament Interpretation* (Edinburgh: T&T Clark, 1999), especially pp. 3–27.

10 Good introductions to this area can be found in Bruce J. Malina, *The New Testament World: Insights from Cultural Anthropology* (Louisville: Westminster John Knox Press, rev. edn, 2001); D. Neufeld and R.E. DeMaris, eds, *Understanding the Social World of the New Testament* (London: Routledge, 2010); J.H. Neyrey, *Paul in Other Words: A Cultural Reading of His Letters* (Louisville: Westminster John Knox Press, 1990); J.H. Neyrey and E.C. Stewart, eds, *The Social World of the New Testament: Insights and Models* (Peabody: Hendrickson, 2008); and Richard Rohrbaugh, ed., *The Social Sciences and New Testament Interpretation* (Peabody: Hendrickson, 1996).

11 Reinhard Bendix, *Max Weber: An Intellectual Portrait* (London: Methuen, 1966), p. 6.

12 Gerd Theissen, *The Social Setting of Pauline Christianity*, SNTW (ed. and trans. John H. Schütz; Edinburgh: T&T Clark, 1982). The essays that compose it were originally published in German in 1974–5.

13 David G. Horrell, *The Social Ethos of the Corinthians Correspondence: Interest and Ideology from 1 Corinthians to 1 Clement*, SNTW (Edinburgh: T&T Clark, 1996).

14 Five volumes are currently available covering the synoptic gospels, John, Acts, the letters of Paul and Revelation, published by Fortress

Press from 1992 to 2008 and written by either Bruce Malina and Richard Rohrbaugh or Bruce Malina and John Pilch.

[15] See further p. 15.

[16] MacDonald, *Pauline Churches*, pp. 2, 8.

[17] Peter L. Berger and Thomas Luckmann, *The Social Construction of Reality: A Treatise in the Sociology of Knowledge* (Harmondsworth: Penguin University Books, 1971), pp. 65–109; and S.N. Einsenstadt, ed., *Max Weber on Charisma and Institution Building* (Chicago: University of Chicago Press, 1968).

[18] Margaret Y. MacDonald, *Colossians and Ephesians*, SP (Collegeville: Liturgical Press, 2000), p. 3.

[19] Ben Witherington III, *The Letters of Philemon, the Colossians and the Ephesians: A Socio-Rhetorical Commentary on the Captivity Epistles* (Grand Rapids: Eerdmans, 2007) p. 38.

[20] Clinton E. Arnold, *The Colossian Syncretism: The Interface Between Christianity and Folk Belief at Colossae* (Tubingen: J.C.B. Mohr, 1995), p. 3. The work was republished by Baker Books in 1996. Page references in this book refer to the Mohr edition.

[21] *Paredroi* is an assistant or attendant and is used of supernatural beings.

[22] Arnold, *Colossian Syncretism*, p. 33.

[23] He refers to 'Christian "Angel" Texts' in Arnold, *Colossian Syncretism*, pp. 83–7.

[24] He recognises this difficulty, Arnold, *Colossian Syncretism*, p. 107.

[25] Arnold, *Colossian Syncretism*, p. 87.

[26] Arnold, *Colossian Syncretism*, p. 227.

[27] For a modern study, which deserves to be better known, see David Clark, *Between Pulpit and Pew: Folk Religion in a North Yorkshire Fishing Village* (Cambridge: CUP, 1982, 2009).

[28] Witherington, *Letters of Philemon*, p. 109. See also his critique on p. 161, n. 42.

[29] Witherington, *Letters of Philemon*, p. 110.

[30] R.E. DeMaris, *The Colossian Controversy*, JSNTSup 96 (Sheffield: JSOT Press, 1994), pp. 38–9, cited in Martin, *Philosophy and Empty Deceit*, p. 11. Martin's 'Introduction', pp. 10–17, provides a very succinct summary of the discussion.

[31] Brian J. Walsh and Sylvia C. Keesmaat, *Colossians Remixed: Subverting the Empire* (Downers Grove: IVP, 2004).

[32] To give one example, Walsh and Keesmaat speak of the gospel 'bearing fruit and growing in the whole world' as not only echoing Israel's

story but as an allusion which 'deepen(s) the critique of the empire' because Rome claimed to be 'the source of fruitful abundance'. Such abundance, they point out, was only possible because Rome operated as an oppressive military and economic regime, *Colossians Remixed*, pp. 71–2. Schweizer sees it rather as taking 'over eschatological promises like Ps. 98:2f and Isa. 66:20' in Eduard Schweizer, *The Letter to the Colossians: A Commentary* (trans. Andrew Chester; London: SPCK, 1982), p. 36. See also Dunn, *Colossians and Philemon*, p. 61.

33 Whether the terminology refers to supernatural beings or institutionalized evil has, of course, been a subject of major discussion in recent years. For a very sane assessment of the debate see Andrew Lincoln, 'Liberations from the Powers: Supernatural Spirit or Societal Structures?' in *The Bible in Human Society: Essays in Honour of John Rogerson*, ed. M. Daniel Carroll, David J.A. Clines and Philip R. Davies, JSOT Supp. Series 200 (Sheffield: Sheffield Academic Press, 1995), pp. 335–54.

34 No reference is made to MacDonald's work and only very brief reference is made to Arnold or Berger. The only significant sociologist of the New Testament they reference is Richard Horsley. More significant for these authors is a post–modern philosopher such as Michael Foucault.

35 Lincoln, 'Letter to the Colossians', p. 583.

2 – Colossae: Its History, People and Church

1 Eckhard J. Schnabel, *Early Christian Mission*, vol. 2, Paul and the Early Church (Downers Grove: IVP and Leicester: Apollos, 2004), p. 1220.
2 The name Epaphroditus occurs in Phil. 2:25 and 4:18 and refers to a different person than Epaphras.
3 Michael Trainor, *Epaphras: Paul's Educator at Colossae*, Paul's Social Network (Collegeville: Liturgical Press, 2008), pp. 6–10.
4 J.B. Lightfoot, *Saint Paul's Epistles to the Colossians and Philemon* (1879; repr. Grand Rapids: Zondervan, 1959), p. 4.
5 Lightfoot, *Saint Paul's Epistles*, pp. 4–5.
6 Pliny the Elder, *Natural History*, 25.9.67, cited by Schnabel, *Early Christian Mission*, p. 1244.
7 Xenophon, *Anabasis*, 1.2.6, cited by R.McL. Wilson, *Colossians and Philemon*, ICC (Edinburgh: T&T Clark, 2005), p. 4; P.T. O'Brien,

Colossians, Philemon, WBC (Waco: Word, 1982) and many other commentators. The quotations from ancient sources are commonly found
in scholarly commentaries.

[8] Michael Trainor, 'Unearthing Ancient Colossae in Southern Turkey:
Theology and Archaeology in Dialogue'. www.compassreview.org/
summer02/8.html, accessed 1 Oct. 2009.

[9] Heroditus, *History*, 7.30.1.

[10] Xenophon, *Anabasis*, 1.2.6.

[11] Pliny the Elder, *Natural History*, 25.9.67.

[12] The date of Strabo's *Geography* is uncertain but usually placed
somewhere between 7 and 20 AD. The reference to Colossae is in
12.8.13.

[13] Pliny the Elder, *Natural History*, 5.105.

[14] Strabo, *Geography*, 12.8.16.

[15] Tacitus, *Annals*, 14.27.1.

[16] Eusebius, *Chronicles*, 1:21–2.

[17] O'Brien, *Colossians, Philemon*, p. xxvi.

[18] Lightfoot, *Saint Paul's Epistles*, p. 17.

[19] Based on Richard L. Rohrbaugh, 'The Pre–Industrial City' in Richard
Rohrbaugh, ed. *The Social Sciences and New Testament Interpretation*
(Peabody: Hendrickson. 1996), pp. 107–25. See also Wayne Meeks,
The First Urban Christians: The Social World of the Apostle Paul (New
Haven: Yale University Press, 2nd edn, 2003), pp. 9–50.

[20] Philip E. Esler, *New Testament Theology: Communion and Community*
(London: SPCK, 2005), p. 175. Esler cites the work of William Harris,
Ancient Literacy (Cambridge: Harvard University Press, 1989), and
Catherine Hezser, *Jewish Literacy in Roman Palestine* (Tubingen:
Mohr/Siebeck, 2001) as his authority.

[21] For a good summary of the social composition of the Greco–Roman
world in the New Testament era, see Carolyn Osiek and David L.
Balch, *Families in the New Testament World: Households and House
Churches* (Louisville: Westminster John Knox 1997), pp. 91–102.

[22] Dunn, *Colossians and Philemon*, p. 226.

[23] The debate is well summarized in Holmberg, *Sociology*, pp.
21–76.

[24] Osiek and Balch, *Families*, p. 97.

[25] It is not germane to our subject but Meggitt argues that although Paul
is distinguished from other artisans because he and his writings
have left such a mark on history, in most other respects he shared the

material existence of other artisans and 'it was nothing less than the arduous and bitter experience of the urban poor', *Paul*, p. 97.

[26] This paragraph is based on Meggitt, *Paul*, pp. 41–73.

[27] Meggitt, *Paul*, p. 50.

[28] Meggitt, *Paul*, p. 54.

[29] Meggitt, *Paul*, p. 73.

[30] Meggitt, *Paul*, p. 179.

[31] Josephus, *Antiquities*, 12.3.4.

[32] Lightfoot, *Saint Paul's Epistles*, p. 20.

[33] Most commentators, following Lightfoot (*Saint Paul's Epistles*, p. 20), mention 11,000 but Dunn (*Colossians and Philemon*, p. 21) says 'that could represent as many as fourteen thousand males'. Since the calculation depends on how one calculates the tax, Dunn rightly points out the actual numbers are very uncertain.

[34] Dunn, *Colossians and Philemon*, p. 22. R.McL. Wilson, *Colossians*, pp. 5–6, esp. n. 9, is more cautious.

[35] P.R. Trebilco, 'Jewish Communities in Asia Minor', *DNTB*, p. 569. See also P.R. Trebilco and C.A. Evans, 'Diaspora Judaism', *DNTB*, pp. 281–96.

[36] Josephus, cited in Trebilco and Evans, 'Diaspora Judaism', p. 565.

[37] Trainor, *Epaphras*, p. 8.

[38] Trainor, *Epaphras*, p. 9.

[39] Aristarchus is mentioned as a 'fellow–prisoner' in Col. 4:10 but Epaphras is not. This may mean that they changed places during Paul's imprisonment. See Dunn, *Colossians and Philemon*, p. 348; and Douglas J. Moo, *The Letters to the Colossians and to Philemon*, Pillar NTC (Grand Rapids: Eerdmans and Apollos: Nottingham, 2008), pp. 439–40.

[40] Dunn, *Colossians and Philemon*, p. 276.

[41] Trainor, *Epaphras*, p. 95.

[42] The Pauline authenticity of Philemon is not in dispute.

[43] The close personal connection he had with Paul would suggest this and his ability to travel on business makes it likely that he might have encountered Paul away from Colossae. But it is not beyond possibility that he became a disciple of Christ through Epaphras and then came directly in touch with Paul because he was in a position to support Paul's mission generously.

[44] If both letters were sent together, it is curious that Tychicus is mentioned in Col. 4:7–8 as the messenger but is not mentioned in

Philemon. Furthermore, Philemon includes Archippus in its address and he is personally addressed in Colossians. This is more easily resolved, however, in that the greeting sent to Archippus in Col. 4:17 was a personal word about his responsibilities in the church which would have been out of place in the letter to Philemon.

[45] John Knox, *Philemon among the Letters of Paul* (London: Collins, 1960).

[46] See discussion in O'Brien, *Colossians, Philemon*, pp. 257–8 and R.McL. Wilson, *Colossians*, p. 321, who describes Knox's ideas as building 'on too many dubious assumptions'.

[47] The female Nympha was in a similar position in Laodicea (4:15). Her role will be considered in Chapter 7.

[48] Roger W. Gehring, *House Church and Mission: The Importance of Household Structures in Early Christianity* (Peabody: Hendrickson, 2004), p. 152.

[49] Lightfoot, *Saint Paul's Epistles*, p. 309. MacDonald, *Colossians*, p. 39, speaks of it as a revered title for a leader but not yet an established office.

[50] MacDonald, *Colossians*, p. 39.

[51] Schweizer, *Colossians*, p. 199.

[52] Josephus, *Against Apion*, 2.269. The meaning of barbarian and Scythian has been much debated. Troy Martin, 'The Scythian Perspective in Col. 3:11', *NovT* XXXVII (1995): pp. 249–61, proposed that the writer is not using the terms from a Greek perspective but from a Scythian perspective whereby anyone who did not speak Scythian was considered by them to be a barbarian. To the Greeks, this was the great dividing line among people. This is supported by the identification of the Scythians with Cynic philosophy since both are influenced by Heracles or his son, *Skythēs*. Douglas Campbell, 'The Scythian Perspective in Col. 3:11: A Response to Troy Martin', *NovT* XXXIX (1997): pp. 81–4, rightly finds 'the presence of an indigenous Scythian perspective within a Greek letter addressed to an Asian Christian community' puzzling and 'rather implausible'.

[53] Douglas A. Campbell, 'Unravelling Col. 3:11b', NTS 42 (1996): pp. 120–32 and R.McL. Wilson, *Colossians*, p. 255.

[54] R.McL. Wilson, *Colossians*, p. 255.

[55] Schweizer, *Colossians*, p. 200.

[56] Dunn, *Colossians and Philemon*, p. 142.

[57] Murray J. Harris, *Colossians and Philemon: Exegetical Guide to the Greek New Testament* (Grand Rapids: Eerdmans, 1995), p. 107.

[58] Meeks, *First Urban Christians*, p. 67.

[59] Lincoln, 'Letter to the Colossians', p. 656.

[60] James E. Crouch, *The Origin and Intention of the Colossians Haustafel* (Gottenberg: Vandenhoeck & Ruprecht, 1972). For the opposite view see S. Scott Bartchy, *Mallōn Chrēsai: First Century Slavery and the Interpretation of 1 Corinthians 7:21*, SBL Diss. Series 11 (Missoula: Scholars Press, 1973). Also see discussion in MacDonald, *Pauline Churches*, pp. 111–4.

[61] Rom. 16:6,23 and 1 Cor. 1:11–15; 5:3; 14:23; 16:15,19 strongly suggest this and probably assume it and therefore do not need to state it explicitly. See Meeks, *First Urban Christians*, p. 76. Meeks states, without supporting evidence but nonetheless probably correctly, 'The household assembly in Philemon's house was apparently not the whole of the Colossian church, nor that in Nympha's household the only one in Laodicea (Col. 4:15).' See also Robert Banks, *Paul's Idea of Community: The Early House Churches in the Historical Setting* (Exeter: Paternoster Press, 1980), pp. 37–9; and Gehring, *House Church*, pp. 24–6, 130–65. See further pp. 119–21.

[62] Wesley Carr, *Angels and Principalities: The Background, Meaning and Development of the Pauline Phrase hai archai kai hai exousiai*, SNTS MS 42 (Cambridge: CUP, 1981), p. 43. His view is a minority one.

3 – Conversion: How and Why People Became Christians in Colossae

[1] John Stambaugh and David Balch, *The Social World of the First Christians* (London: SPCK, 1986), pp. 41–52 gives a succinct introduction to religion in the Greco–Roman world.

[2] Carr, *Angels and Principalities*, pp. 12, 15.

[3] One of the criticisms of Arnold's *Colossian Syncretism*, on which we shall rely below, is that much of his archaeological evidence comes from the second century. But (a) his argument rests on a broader base than that and (b) any developments or novelty in the second century were almost certainly the outworking of antecedent beliefs and practices. See his discussion, pp. 17–20.

[4] Arnold, *Colossian Syncretism, passim*.

[5] Sherman E. Johnson, 'Asia Minor and Early Christianity' in *Christianity, Judaism and other Greco–Roman Cults* (ed. Jacob Neusner; Leiden: E. J. Brill, 1975), p. 93.

[6] Peter Oakes, 'Remapping the Universe: Paul and the Emperor in 1 Thessalonians and Philippians', *JSNT* 27 (2005): p. 312.

[7] Eckhard Schnabel, *Paul the Missionary: Realities, Strategies and Methods* (Downers Grove: IVP Academic and Nottingham: Apollos, 2008), pp. 186–7.

[8] Arnold, *Colossian Syncretism*, pp. 369–70.

[9] Clinton Arnold, 'Colossae', *ABD*, pp. 1089–90.

[10] The fuller list is in *Colossian Syncretism*, pp. 107–8.

[11] Carr, *Angels and Principalities*, pp. 15–18.

[12] Arnold, *Colossian Syncretism*, p. 142, writes, 'In popular belief, the intersection of roads was commonly believed to be dangerous and haunted by evil spirits. Her statue – usually a three–sided figure (*triformis*) – was erected at crossroads throughout Asia Minor where she was believed to function as an averter of evil.' Hekate is not mentioned on the coins of Colossae but her co–conspirators from the underworld, Artemis and Selene, are.

[13] A good survey is found in relation to Corinth in Stephen Chester, *Conversion at Corinth: Perspectives on Conversion in Paul's Theology and the Corinthian Church*, SNTW (Edinburgh: Continuum, 2003), pp. 267–80.

[14] Dunn, *Colossians and Philemon*, pp. 159–60.

[15] Dunn, *Colossians and Philemon*, p. 271.

[16] Stambaugh and Balch, *Social World*, pp. 44–5.

[17] Commenting on the accuracy of Luke's portrait of the religious milieu of Paul's mission in Acts, Carr, *Angels and Principalities*, p. 21, says, 'The ideas that are missing, however, are even more intriguing. There are no hints of mystery religion, nor of astrology, nor of men bound by decrees of Fate. The conclusion must be that they were of little or no significance in Asia and Greece in the mid–first century.' But more recent evidence calls this into question.

[18] Andrew T. Lincoln and A.J.M. Wedderburn, *The Theology of the Later Pauline Letters* (Cambridge: Cambridge University Press, 1993), pp. 17–18, a section written by Wedderburn.

[19] Lincoln and Wedderburn, *Theology*, p. 18.

[20] Lightfoot, *Saint Paul's Epistles*, p. 97. 'The Colossian Heresy' is reproduced in Francis and Meeks, *Conflict*, pp. 13–59.

21 This interpretation relies on Arnold, *Colossian Syncretism*, whose interpretation, as previously indicated, I am aware is not universally accepted. Regardless of the accuracy of details, the cumulative picture Arnold presents is, I believe, persuasive and sufficient at this stage to enable us to draw an accurate picture of the general religious milieu, which is the interest of the sociologist.

22 Lewis Rambo, *Understanding Religious Conversion* (New Haven: Yale University Press, 1993) serves as the best introduction to the discussion.

23 Rambo, *Understanding Ibid*. The charting of the stages is the substance of Rambo's book. It is similar to 'the value added process' outlined previously by John Lofland as a result of his research into the Moonies. He spoke of there being (1) a tension; (2) a religious problem–solving perspective; (3) religious seekership; (4) a turning point in life; (5) the growth of close affective bonds; (6) the weakening of extra–cult affective bonds; and (7) intensive interaction. John Lofland, *Doomsday Cult: A Study of Conversion, Proselytization and Maintenance of Faith* (New York: Irvington, enlarged edn, 1977), *passim*.

24 Eileen Barker's research into the Moonies showed that only 10 per cent of those who attended a two–day workshop joined the movement and only 3.5 per cent remained after three years. *The Making of a Moonie* (Oxford: Blackwells, 1984), p. 146.

25 Berger and Luckmann, *Social Construction of Reality*, p. 177.

26 Rosabeth Kanter, *Commitment and Community* (Cambridge: Harvard University Press, 1972).

27 Functionalism views society as a body and sees change as occurring in response to a need. It focuses on the 'function' of the change that may have intended or unintended consequences. It is criticized for fostering a largely static view of society and for offering an insufficient causal explanation of change. Wayne Meeks, *First Urban Christians*, and Gerd Theissen, *Social Setting*, employ it in reference to the New Testament church.

28 Sociology of knowledge approaches stem from Peter Berger and Thomas Luckmann in their work, *Social Construction of Reality*. They argue that humans are engaged in a constant attempt to construct meaning out of their precarious lives. This theory, critics argue, like functionalism, gives insufficient attention to the causes of change in society.

[29] Antony Giddens, *The Constitution of Society: Outline of the Theory of Structuration* (Cambridge: Polity Press, 1984).

[30] Horrell, *Social Ethos*, and Chester, *Conversion at Corinth*. A brief introduction may be found in David Horrell, 'The Development of Theological Ideology in Pauline Christianity: A Structuration Theory Perspective' in Philip F. Esler (ed.) *Modelling Early Christianity: Social-Scientific Studies of the New Testament in Its Context* (London and New York: Routledge, 1995), pp. 224–36.

[31] Giddens, cited by Horrell, *Social Ethos*, p. 49.

[32] Horrell, *Social Ethos*, p. 54.

[33] Chester, *Conversion at Corinth*, p. 213.

[34] Recent works, to which Chester refers, by Rodney Stark and Jack T. Sanders, in the tradition of Nock and MacMullen, will be considered in the final section of this chapter.

[35] Chester, *Conversion at Corinth*, p. 33.

[36] Chester, *Conversion at Corinth*, discusses 1 Cor. 14:20–25 on pp. 114–25.

[37] Chester, *Conversion at Corinth*, p. 125. The passage is discussed on pp. 125–46.

[38] Chester, *Conversion at Corinth*, p. 147.

[39] Chester, *Conversion at Corinth*, pp. 149–204.

[40] Chester, *Conversion at Corinth*, p. 202.

[41] *Emathete* is the 2nd plural, aorist, active, indicative of *manthano*, 'to learn'.

[42] *Edidachthete* is the 2nd plural, passive, indicative of *didascho*.

[43] Dunn, *Colossians and Philemon*, p. 64.

[44] O'Brien, *Colossians, Philemon*, p. 15.

[45] Lincoln and Wedderburn, *Theology*, pp. 48–53. Ernst Käsemann proposed that *Colossians* was 'A Primitive Christian Baptismal Liturgy', *Essays on New Testament Themes* (trans. W.J. Montague; London: SCM, 1964), pp. 149–68.

[46] Lightfoot, *Saint Paul's Epistles*, pp. 141–2.

[47] R.McL. Wilson, *Colossians*, p. 117.

[48] The exact meaning of 'the record that stood against us with its legal demands' is much debated, as the standard commentaries show.

[49] Meeks, *First Urban Christians*, pp. 22–3, 53–5.

[50] For a critique see Holmberg, *Sociology*, pp. 128–34.

[51] Popular evangelicalism used to speak until recently of 'receiving Christ into one's heart'. N.T. Wright comments 'today the phrase "to

receive Christ" often expresses the conception of becoming a Christian which focuses on the new believer's invitation to Jesus Christ to enter his or her heart and life.' *Colossians and Philemon*, TNTC (Leicester: IVP and Grand Rapids: Eerdmans, 1986), p. 98.

[52] Dunn, *Colossians and Philemon*, p. 138. Dunn points out Paul uses *paralambanō* in this way in 1 Cor. 11:23; 15:1,3; Gal. 1:9,12; Phil. 4:9; 1 Thess. 2:13; 4:1; 2 Thess. 3:6).

[53] O'Brien, *Colossians, Philemon*, p. 104.

[54] Acts 2:36.

[55] Rom. 10:9; 1 Cor. 12:3; Phil. 2:11.

[56] M.J. Harris, *Colossians and Philemon*, p. 88.

[57] The command 'see to it that no one takes you captive through philosophy and empty deceit' (2:8) suggests Paul believed the new believers were active agents of what they believed rather than helpless victims.

[58] The phrases 'in Christ' and 'Christ in' are rich phrases which are used in a variety of ways and are incapable of precise definition (Moo, *Colossians and Philemon*, p. 77). The phrase is chiefly used in an objective way but refers on occasions to a subjective, spiritual experience, so some sense of spiritual, existential 'experience' cannot be completely ruled out in the references in Colossians. See James D.G. Dunn, *The Theology of Paul the Apostle* (Edinburgh: T&T Clark, 1998), pp. 396–401, who writes 'at the heart of the motif is not merely a belief about Christ, but an experience understood as that of the risen and living Christ' (p. 400).

[59] David Balch, 'Household Codes' in *Greco–Roman Literature and the New Testament* (ed. D.E. Aune; Atlanta: Scholars Press, 1988), pp. 25–50; *Let Wives be Submissive: The Domestic Code in 1 Peter*, SBLMS 26 (Chico: Scholars, 1981); and Dunn, *Colossians and Philemon*, pp. 242–6.

[60] 3:18,20,23,24 (x 2); 4:1 (Master).

[61] Eckhard Schnabel is critical of such approaches and as a theologian explains the growth of the church as due to the power of God, *Paul the Missionary*, pp. 356–73, esp. pp. 370–71. But, alongside this, there is a legitimate place for sociological and historical explanation.

[62] A.D. Nock, *Conversion: The Old and the New in Religion from Alexander the Great to Augustine of Hippo* (Oxford: OUP, 1933), p. 7. The first modern study in the area was Adolf von Harnack, *The Mission and Expansion of Christianity in the First Three Centuries*, first published in German in 1904–5.

[63] Nock, *Conversion*, p. 156.

[64] Nock, *Conversion*, p. 192.

[65] Nock, *Conversion*, pp. 210–11.

[66] Nock, *Conversion*, pp. 218, 220.

[67] Nock, *Conversion*, pp. 212, 251.

[68] Ramsey MacMullen, *Christianizing the Roman Empire* (AD 100–400) (New Haven: Yale University Press, 1984), p. 5. On the question of strategy see Schnabel, *Paul the Missionary*, pp. 256–87 where Schnabel argues that Paul had a general strategy but was flexible and not controlled by a 'grand strategy' as missiologists often claim.

[69] MacMullen, *Christianizing*, pp. 30–39.

[70] MacMullen, *Christianizing*, pp. 26–30.

[71] Subtitled *A Sociologist Reconsiders History* (Princeton: Princeton University Press, 1996).

[72] Stark, *Rise of Christianity*, p. xii.

[73] Stark, *Rise of Christianity*, pp. 3–27.

[74] Stark, *Rise of Christianity*, pp. 29–47.

[75] Stark, *Rise of Christianity*, pp. 49–71.

[76] Stark, *Rise of Christianity*, pp. 73–94.

[77] Stark, *Rise of Christianity*, pp. 95–128.

[78] Stark, *Rise of Christianity*, pp. 163–89.

[79] A recent explanation of the theory is found in Rodney Stark and Roger Finke, *Acts of Faith, Explaining the Human Side of Religion* (Berkeley: University of California Press, 2000). For a critique, see Steve Bruce, *Choice and Religion: A Critique of Rational Choice* (Oxford: OUP, 1999) or, more convincingly, L. Young (ed.), *Rational Choice Theory and Religion* (London: Routledge, 1997).

[80] William Garrett, 'Sociology and New Testament Studies: A Critical Evaluation of Rodney Stark's Contribution', *JSSR* 29 (1990): pp. 377–84, esp. p. 381.

[81] Jack Sanders, *Charisma, Converts, Competitors: Societal and Sociological Factors in the Success of Early Christianity* (London: SCM Press, 2000).

[82] Sanders, *Charisma*, p. 150.The comment particularly relates to Stark's chapter on Antioch which has not been mentioned here.

[83] Sanders, *Charisma*, pp. 142–3.

[84] Sanders, *Charisma*, p. 159.

[85] Sanders, *Charisma*, p. 172. He discusses the evidence for this conclusion on pp. 163–70.

[86] See Sanders, *Charisma*, p. 160, where Sanders comments on Blasi's view of the value of the diffuse form of Christianity.

[87] Much of Paul's instruction indirectly strengthens the internal cohesion of the Colossian church but the subject of unity (or disunity) is not as evident as it is in, for example, Rom. 14:1–23, 1 Cor. 1:10 – 3:22; 8:1–13; Eph. 4:1–16; Phil. 4:2–3.

4 – Identity: The Construction of Personal and Social Identity

[1] Robert Putnam, *Bowling Alone* (New York: Touchstone, 2000).

[2] See Zygmunt Bauman, *Community: Seeking Safety in an Insecure World* (Cambridge: Polity, 2001).

[3] Berger and Luckmann, *Social Construction of Reality*, p. 195.

[4] Berger and Luckmann, *Social Construction of Reality*, p. 195.

[5] Berger and Luckmann, *Social Construction of Reality*, p. 195. In the discussion that follows, on the adequacy of psychological theories, Berger and Luckmann use the illustration of how psychoanalysis proves an adequate interpretation of the identity problems of middle-class, Jewish intellectuals in New York City, whereas theories of demon possession would not make sense. In rural Haiti, however, the reverse would be the case.

[6] Michael A. Hogg and Dominic Abrams, *Social Identifications: A Social Psychology of Intergroup Relations and Group Processes* (London: Routledge, 1988), p. 24. Further discussion is found in Dominic Abrams and Michael A. Hogg, eds, *Social Identity Theory: Constructive and Critical Advances* (New York: Harvester Wheatsheaf, 1990).

[7] Hogg and Abrams, *Social Identifications*, p. 18.

[8] The summary can be found on Hogg and Abrams, *Social Identifications*, p. 23.

[9] Peter Berger has explored this in his discussion of plausibility structures. See Peter Berger, *A Rumour of Angels* (New York: Doubleday, 1969. Repr. New York: An Anchor Book, 1990), pp. 38–53. We explore it in great depth in Chapter 5.

[10] Cited by Philip F. Esler and Ronald A. Piper, *Lazarus, Mary and Martha: A Social–Scientific and Theological Reading of John* (London: SCM, 2006), p. 26.

[11] Cited by Philip F. Esler, *Galatians*, New Testament Readings (London: Routledge, 1998), p. 42, from Henri Tajfel, ed., *Differentiation between*

Social groups: Studies in the Social Psychology of Intergroup Relations (London: Academic Press, 1978), p. 28.

[12] John C. Turner et al., *Rediscovering the Social Group: A Self-Categorization Theory* (Oxford: Blackwell, 1987).

[13] Christian Smith, *American Evangelicalism: Embattled and Thriving* (Chicago: Chicago University Press, 1998).

[14] See note 10.

[15] Philip F. Esler, *Conflict and Identity in Romans: The Social Setting of Paul's Letter* (Minneapolis: Fortress Press, 2003).

[16] See note 11.

[17] Esler, *Conflict and Identity*, p. 12. See also Dennis C. Duling, 'Ethnicity and Paul's Letter to the Romans', in *Understanding the Social World of the New Testament* (ed. Dietman Neufeld and Richard E. DeMaris; London: Routledge, 2010), pp. 68–89.

[18] Esler, *Conflict and Identity*, p. 26.

[19] Esler, *Conflict and Identity*, pp. 29–30.

[20] Philip F. Esler, 'Jesus and the Reduction of Intergroup Conflict: The Parable of the Good Samaritan in the Light of Social Identity Theory', *BibInt* 8 (2000): pp. 325–57.

[21] Minna Shkul has recently offered an interpretation of Ephesians in which this phrase is taken as the interpretive key. See *Reading Ephesians: Exploring Social Entrepreneurship in the Text*, LNTS 408 (London: T&T Clark, 2009).

[22] Esler, *Conflict and Identity*, p. 38.

[23] Esler, *Conflict and Identity*, p. 31.

[24] Esler, *Galatians*, p. 50.

[25] Esler, *Galatians*, pp. 49–55.

[26] Esler, *Galatians*, p. 53.

[27] Esler, *Galatians*, pp. 53–7.

[28] To what extent Paul caricatures his opponents is a moot point. The only picture we have of them is drawn by Paul and so we have no way of checking. But, while it is clear that Paul feels passionately about those who are spreading heresy, it serves no purpose if he overstates his case and presents a portrait of them which is so distorted that it cannot be recognized by his readers. On this point, see Harold van Broekhoven, 'The Social Profiles on the Colossians Debate', *JSNT* 66 (1997): p. 80.

[29] Jerome H. Neyrey believes that in using this language Paul is making a formal accusation of witchcraft against rival preachers. The

argument is based on 'bewitched' being a technical term for 'the evil eye' and from an anthropological perspective this indicates witch-craft. *Paul in Other Words*, pp. 182, 203. See further John H. Elliott, 'Paul, Galatians and the Evil Eye', in *The Social World of the New Testament* (ed. Jerome H. Neyrey and Eric C. Stewart; Peabody: Hendrickson, 2008), pp. 223–34.

30 Neyrey, *Paul in Other Words*, p. 204.

31 See Malina, *New Testament World*, pp. 58–80; Bruce J. Malina, 'Understanding New Testament Persons', in *The Social Sciences and New Testament Interpretation* (ed. Richard Rohbaugh; Peabody: Hendrickson), pp. 41–61; Bruce J. Malina and Jerome H. Neyrey, 'Ancient Mediterranean Persons in Cultural Perspective', in *Social World of the New Testament* (ed. J.H. Neyrey and E.C. Stewart; Peabody: Hendrickson), pp. 257–75; and, most recently, Bruce J. Malina, 'Collectivism in Mediterranean Culture', in *Understanding the Social World* (ed. D. Neufeld and R.E. DeMaris; London: Routledge), pp. 17–28.

32 Malina accepts that 'at a lower level of abstraction, at the level of sub-cultures in the area, there were notable differences.' *New Testament World*, p. 68.

33 Malina, *New Testament World*, p. 75.

34 Malina, *New Testament World*, p. 75.

35 Malina, *New Testament World*, p. 62.

36 This is mostly based on Malina, *New Testament World*, pp. 76–9.

37 Based on Malina, *New Testament World*, p. 78.

38 The balance has shifted from society to the individual dramatically in Britain since the Second World War. Immediately post-war, individ-uals knew and accepted their place; lower orders were deferential to superiors; authority figures were unquestioned and institutions and customs sacrosanct. The 1960s saw a moral revolution which brought the individual to the fore aided and abetted by, as well as manifest in, the rise of consumer choice.

39 See Chapter 5.

40 This becomes even more obvious in the expanded parallel passage in Eph. 5:21–33.

41 See further pp. 133-34.

42 The issue is covered in most standard commentaries. See also Francis and Meeks, *Conflict*. Particular theories are advanced, *inter alia*, in Arnold, *Colossian Syncretism*; DeMaris, *Colossian Controversy*; Morna

D. Hooker, 'Were there False Teachers in Colossae?' in *Christ and the Spirit: Studies in Honour of C.F.D. Moule* (ed. B. Lindars and S.S. Smalley; Cambridge: CUP, 1973), pp. 315–31; T.W. Martin, *Philosophy;* and Van Broekhoven, 'Social Profiles'. The author favours Arnold's explanation that the problem lay in the incursions of syncretistic folk religion.

[43] Hooker, 'False Teachers', p. 315, *contra* John Barclay, *Colossians and Philemon*, NTG (Sheffield: Sheffield Academic Press, 1987), p. 38.

[44] Hooker, 'False Teachers', p. 315.

[45] Lincoln, 'Letter to the Colossians', p. 567.

[46] Hooker, 'False Teachers', pp. 316, 318.

[47] These two terms come from Walter T. Wilson, *The Hope of Glory: Education and Exploration in the Epistle of Colossians* (Leiden: Brill, 1997), p. 181.

[48] W.T. Wilson, *Hope of Glory*, p. 171.

[49] 1:2,4,14,16,17,19,28; 2:3,5,6,7,10,11.

[50] 2:12; 3:1,3,4.

[51] 3:18,20, 4:7,17.

[52] John Ziesler explains 'Generally, believers exist in Christ, but Christ is active in believers, so the two notions are not exactly parallel.' *Pauline Christianity*, Oxford Bible Series (Oxford: OUP, rev. edn, 1990), p. 50.

[53] Dunn, *Theology of Paul*, p. 399.

[54] Anthony C. Thiselton, *The Living Paul: An Introduction to the Apostle and His Thought* (London: SPCK, 2009), p. 89, perhaps more helpfully terms this 'a representative use'.

[55] Thiselton, *Living Paul*, pp. 64, 65.

[56] Schweizer, *Colossians*, p. 39.

[57] In Rom. 6:5 Paul sees believers as anticipating sharing in Christ's risen life. In Col. 2.12 and 3:1 the anticipation has already been realized and what is now awaited is the revelation of Christ's glory in which believers will share. How is the 'development' to be explained? It is best explained in terms of the circumstances in Colossae causing a development in Paul's thought. It is unnecessary to assume a conflict between Colossians and Romans or that this is evidence of non-Pauline authorship. See A.J.M Wedderburn, *Baptism and Resurrection: Studies in Pauline Theology against Its Graeco-Roman Background* (Tubingen: J.C.B. Mohr, 1987), pp. 70–84, esp. p. 83.

[58] Dunn, *Colossians and Philemon*, p. 203.

[59] Mary Douglas, *Natural Symbols: Explorations in Cosmology* (Harmondsworth: Penguin Books, 1970), esp. pp. 77–92.

[60] Van Broekhoven, 'Social Profiles', pp. 73–90.

[61] For details, see Van Broekhoven, 'Social Profiles', pp. 76–80.

[62] Van Broekhoven, 'Social Profiles', p. 76.

[63] Van Broekhoven, 'Social Profiles', p. 81.

[64] Van Broekhoven, 'Social Profiles', p. 89.

[65] Van Broekhoven, 'Social Profiles', p. 84.

[66] Van Broekhoven, 'Social Profiles', p. 87.

[67] Hooker, 'False Teachers', p. 323.

[68] Shkul, *Reading Ephesians, passim*, demonstrates a parallel process in Ephesians which legitimates and sharpens the identity of the vulnerable Christian community by remembering and reshaping the 'reputation' of Christ in relation to his Jewish heritage and law. It does this essentially by positive exposition of the work of Christ, although at later points the letter (e.g. 4:17–19) resorts to the use of stereotypes in distinguishing Christians from others.

5 – Theology: The Social Construction of Belief

[1] Berger, *Rumour of Angels*, p. 50.

[2] See Berger, *Rumour of Angels*, pp. 31–53.

[3] This in itself is a very difficult thing to establish since particular cultures create a context in which some interpretations make more sense than others. See p. 49 and p. 185, esp. note 5.

[4] Berger, *Rumour of Angels*, pp. 38–53. For a fuller exposition see Berger and Luckmann, *Social Construction of Reality*, pp. 166–76. Significant others, conversation, rites, rituals and, to a lesser extent, sanctions are key components of a 'plausibility structure'.

[5] Berger and Luckmann, *Social Construction of Reality*, p. 13.

[6] Peter Berger, *The Social Reality of Religion* (1967; Harmondsworth: Penguin University Books, 1973). It was first published in America under the title of *The Sacred Canopy: Elements of a Sociological Theory of Religion.*

[7] Berger and Luckmann, *Social Construction of Reality*, p. 149.

[8] Berger and Luckmann, *Social Construction of Reality*, p. 79. Italics theirs.

[9] Other levels are detailed in Berger and Luckmann, *Social Construction of Reality*, pp. 112–13.

10 Berger and Luckmann, *Social Construction of Reality*, p. 113.

11 Berger and Luckmann, *Social Construction of Reality*, p. 114.

12 Norman Petersen, *Rediscovering Paul: Philemon and the Sociology of Paul's Narrative World* (Philadelphia: Fortress Press, 1985), p. 59.

13 Berger and Luckmann, *Social Construction of Reality*, p. 115.

14 Berger and Luckmann, *Social Construction of Reality*, p. 116.

15 Berger and Luckmann, *Social Construction of Reality*, p. 118.

16 Berger and Luckmann, *Social Construction of Reality*, p. 120.

17 Berger and Luckmann, *Social Construction of Reality*, p. 121.

18 This was, of course, most famously expounded in 1912 by Emile Durkheim in *The Elementary Forms of Religious Life* (trans. Karen Fields; New York: The Free Press, rev. edn, 1995). For all the faults of Durkheim's work, his perception of the revitalizing effect of rituals, of their importance in reintegrating individuals into the collective body, and of what he calls the 'moral remaking' of a society and 'reaffirming itself' is powerfully persuasive and hard to refute.

19 Berger and Luckmann, *Social Construction of Reality*, p. 125.

20 He never got to the cross and resurrection at Lystra because he was not given the opportunity to get beyond his introduction!

21 Schnabel, *Paul the Missionary*, p. 183. For his whole argument, see pp. 183–9.

22 Rom. 5:6–11; 6:1–11; 8:31–4; 1 Cor. 1:17 – 2:5; 15:3; Gal. 6:14; Eph. 2:11–22; Phil. 2:5–11; 3:10–11; Col 1:20; 2:13–15; Heb. 10:1–18; 1 Pet. 1:17–21; 2:21–5; 3:18; 1 John 3:16; 4:7–14; Rev. 5:6.

23 Deut. 21:23, which Paul reconstructs in Gal. 3:13.

24 Barton, 'Social-Scientific Approaches', p. 895. See also Barton, 'Paul and the Cross', pp. 13–19.

25 Berger and Luckmann, *Social Construction of Reality*, p. 170.

26 Trainor, *Epaphras*, p. 95.

27 The self–presentation of Paul in Colossians is consistent with the practice of other moral teachers in the ancient world. See W.T. Wilson, *Hope of Glory*, pp. 50–82. Those who believe that the author is not Paul argue that the author has constructed 'a credible persona' as if he were Paul (W.T. Wilson, *Hope of Glory*, p. 64). It would lend support of Blasi's argument that Paul's charisma develops over time through his followers socially constructing and augmenting it, rather than the more usual argument that charisma 'evaporates' as time goes on: Anthony J. Blasi, *Making Charisma: The Social Construction of Paul's Public Image* (New Brunswick: Transaction Publishers, 1991).

[28] W.T. Wilson, *Hope of Glory*, p. 73.

[29] Berger and Luckmann, *Social Construction of Reality*, p. 172.

[30] It is true that conversation and particular language can sometimes become so common that it loses its force in maintaining reality and becomes taken for granted. Berger and Luckmann are wise to write, '*On the whole*, frequency of conversation enhances its reality-generating potency' (italics mine, *Social Construction of Reality*, p. 174; see also pp. 170–74).

[31] Heb. 10:24–5 shows an awareness of the significance of this.

[32] Berger and Luckmann, *Social Construction of Reality*, p. 173.

[33] W.T. Wilson, *Hope of Glory*, pp. 47–50.

[34] Petersen, *Rediscovering Paul*, p. 55.

[35] Bruce Malina, 'Reading Theory Perspective: Reading Luke-Acts' in *The Social World of Luke-Acts: Models for Interpretation* (ed. Jerome H. Neyrey; Peabody: Hendrickson, 1991), p. 20.

[36] Rituals are rites that are undertaken irregularly as needed. They look to the future and have a transforming purpose. By contrast, ceremonies are regular and predictable rites that look to the past and have a confirmatory purpose: Neyrey, *Paul in Other Words*, p. 76.

[37] Meeks, *First Urban Christians*, p. 157.

[38] See Meeks, *First Urban Christians*, pp. 150–57.

[39] See further Chapter 6.

[40] John H. Elliott, 'The Jesus Movement was not Egalitarian but Family–Orientated', *BibInt* 32 (2002): pp. 173–210.

[41] Col. 1:9,28; 2:3,23.

[42] Col. 1:12; 2:7; 3:15,17; 4:2.

[43] Lincoln, 'Letter to the Colossians', p. 593.

[44] See pp. 113 and 143.

[45] Barclay, *Colossians and Philemon*, pp. 75–6. He argues that the commentary form militates against seeing the theology of the whole; that its perceived pseudonymous nature has downgraded it in comparison with the so-called genuine letters of Paul; that it is often viewed merely as polemical; and that it has suffered from reductionism whereby interest has focused on the preformed traditions the letter uses. To this we should add a preoccupation with questions of authorship, dating, and the nature of the Colossian 'error'.

[46] Barclay, *Colossians and Philemon*, p. 78.

[47] Barclay, *Colossians and Philemon*, pp. 79–80.

[48] Barclay, *Colossians and Philemon*, pp. 80–92.

⁴⁹ Many scholars consider the 'hymn' to have been amended, with 'the church' and the phrase 'making peace through the blood of his cross' being added later. Others think the elaboration of the 'invisible' things in terms of 'thrones or dominions or rules or powers', which interrupts the flow is also a later addition (See Dunn's comment, *Colossians and Philemon*, p. 92). Debate as to what constituted the original 'hymn' has produced 'a certain weariness' since no original sources have been discovered and therefore whatever is proposed is unprovable: Barclay, *Colossians and Philemon*, pp. 62–3. If it were true, however, that a pre-existing creed has been supplemented to suit the purpose of the letter it would underline the point that its theology is socially constructed to deal with a particular situation.

⁵⁰ Paul does not mention that his words are directed towards Gentile converts but a comparison of 1:21 with Eph. 2:11–22 and 4:17–19 which are specifically about Gentiles suggests it is so. Gentiles were the predominant group in the church at Colossae.

⁵¹ The use of the four terms upsets the flow of the 'hymn' and has been regarded by some as an insertion. See Dunn, *Colossians and Philemon*, p. 92.

⁵² F.F. Bruce, *Commentary on the Epistles to the Ephesians and Colossians*, NICNT (Grand Rapids: Eerdmans, 1957), p. 198; also Arnold, *Colossian Syncretism*, pp. 252–5.

⁵³ F.F. Bruce, *Ephesians and Colossians*, p. 198. See further the discussion in Lightfoot, *Saint Paul's Epistles*, pp. 152–4.

⁵⁴ Wright, *Colossians*, p. 72.

⁵⁵ Undoubtedly the original reference was to 'beings' rather than impersonal power structures. See Lincoln, 'Liberation', pp. 335–54.

⁵⁶ For a full, if inconclusive, discussion about whether these powers were hostile or not see R.McL. Wilson, *Colossians*, pp. 139–43. A contrary, but minority and unpersuasive case, is set out by Carr, *Angels and Principalities*, p. 40.

⁵⁷ Lincoln, 'Letter to the Colossians', p. 565.

⁵⁸ Lincoln, 'Letter to the Colossians', *passim*.

⁵⁹ W.T. Wilson, *Hope of Glory*, p. 3.

⁶⁰ W.T. Wilson, *Hope of Glory*, p. 3.

⁶¹ Robin Lane Fox, *Pagans and Christians* (New York: Alfred A Knopf, 1987).

⁶² See Lincoln, 'Letter to the Colossians', pp. 575–7, 605.

⁶³ The theology of the 'hymn' is very similar to John 1 and Hebrews 1, but probably predates them and is, in any case, new in the Pauline corpus.

⁶⁴ Acts 28:31; Rom. 10:9; 1 Cor. 1:7,8; 12:3; 2 Cor. 4:5; 8:9; Phil. 2:9–11; 3:20; 1 Thess. 5:9.

⁶⁵ Rom. 9:5; 2 Cor. 5:19; Phil. 2:6.

⁶⁶ Rom. 5:10; 2 Cor. 5:18–20.

⁶⁷ Rom. 8:29; 1 Cor. 15:20,23.

⁶⁸ Rom. 5:1; Phil. 4:7; 1 Thess. 5:23; 2 Thess. 3:16.

⁶⁹ Lohse, *Colossians*, p. 48.

⁷⁰ Lohse, *Colossians*, p. 48.

⁷¹ Arnold points out that there is a close affinity here between what is claimed of Christ and what is claimed of God himself in 1 Cor. 8:6: *Colossian Syncretism*, p. 257.

⁷² While the gospels record the resurrection of Jairus' daughter, the widow of Nain's son and Lazarus, they, unlike what is implicit in the resurrection of Jesus Christ, were destined to die again. His resurrection is of a different order to theirs but not a different order to that to which believers look forward.

⁷³ W.T. Wilson, *Hope of Glory*, p. 146.

⁷⁴ F.F. Bruce says, 'The peace effected by the death of Christ may be freely accepted or it may be compulsorily imposed', *Ephesians and Colossians*, p. 210. Barclay comments similarly, 'If one were to spell out the force of this image, it looks less like a *reconciliation* of the powers and more like a *defeat*', *Colossians and Philemon*, p. 85.

⁷⁵ George E. Cannon, *The Use of Traditional Materials in Colossians* (Macon: Mercer University Press, 1983), stresses the importance of the eschatological perspective and its coherence with what is regarded as authentic Pauline theology. Yet it is 'redacted' to convince the readers that they need not appease the 'powers' either through cultic or ascetic practices.

⁷⁶ Lohse, *Colossians*, p. 108.

⁷⁷ Schweizer, *Colossians*, p. 148, believes it to be a personal IOU, as found in Phlm. 19, rather than a bond attested by a notary.

⁷⁸ So Dunn, *Colossians and Philemon*, p. 164. Schweizer, *Colossians*, p. 148, rightly states 'The idea that man has put himself under obligation to the devil or evil powers, and cannot discharge himself of this debt, lies completely beyond the compass of this passage.'

⁷⁹ See R.McL. Wilson, *Colossians*, p. 208.

⁸⁰ Lohse, *Colossians*, pp. 109–11.

⁸¹ The 'worship of angels' could be subjective or objective. That is to say, it could mean either participating in the worship offered by angels or offering prayer to the angels. The evidence persuasively stacks up in favour of it meaning invoking angels in order to gain their protection and assistance. See, *inter alia*, Arnold, *Colossian Syncretism*, pp. 90–102.

⁸² RSV translates *apekdusamenos* 'disarmed', a translation favoured by many commentators because it is an aorist participle in the middle voice which has 'the rulers and authorities' as its object (accusative). It generally means to 'strip off' or 'divest oneself' and is used in that sense in 2:11 and 3:9.

⁸³ One of the problems in 2:14 and 15 is who the 'he' refers to. The last referent is in v. 13 and refers to God.

⁸⁴ For a discussion of the background and development of the Roman triumphal procession, see Scott J. Hafemann, *Suffering and Ministry in the Spirit: Paul's Defence of his Ministry in 2 Corinthians 2:14–3:3* (Carlisle: Paternoster, 2000), pp. 12–34.

⁸⁵ See, for example, Lohse, *Colossians*, pp. 180–81.

⁸⁶ Henry Chadwick, 'All Things to All Men', *NTS* 1 (1955): p. 272, cited in Andrew Lincoln, *Paradise Now and Not Yet*, SNTS MS 43 (Cambridge: CUP, 1981), p. 127.

⁸⁷ Lincoln, *Paradise*, p. 127.

⁸⁸ Lincoln, *Paradise*, p. 125.

⁸⁹ Lincoln, *Paradise*, p. 130.

⁹⁰ Lincoln, *Paradise*, pp. 122–3.

⁹¹ Wedderburn, *Baptism and Resurrection*, p. 72.

6 – Institutionalization: From Charisma to Institution

¹ Weber was building on the work of Rudolf Sohm: Eisenstadt, *Max Weber*, p. 246. Eisenstadt has collected Weber's relevant writings from a variety of sources, but chiefly from Guenther Roth and Claus Wittich, eds, *Theory of Social and Economic Organisation and Sociology of Religion* (New York: Bedminister Press, 1968) and H.H. Gerth and C. Wright Mills, eds. *From Max Weber: Essays in Sociology* (London: Routledge, 1948). The references and quotations that follow are taken from Eisenstadt for convenience.

2 Eisenstadt, *Max Weber*, pp. 46–7.

3 Eisenstadt, *Max Weber*, p. 48.

4 Bengt Holmberg, *Paul and Power: The Structure of Authority in the Primitive Church as Reflected in the Pauline Epistles* (Philadelphia: Fortress Press, 1978), p. 139. In fact, as Holmberg acknowledges, Weber's concept of charisma is fairly general and involves some lack of clarity, such as, the importance of the psychological aspect in the sociological concept. Holmberg provides a good critique of Weber's concept, pp. 140–48.

5 Eisenstadt, *Max Weber*, pp. 253–68. See, further, Peter Berger, 'Charisma and Religious Innovation: The Social Location of Israelite Prophecy', *ASR*, 28 (1963): pp. 940–50.

6 Greater recognition has been given subsequently to the place of charismatic leadership in non-crisis times.

7 Eisenstadt, *Max Weber*, p. 51.

8 Eisenstadt, *Max Weber*, p. 51.

9 Eisenstadt, *Max Weber*, p. 52.

10 Eisenstadt, *Max Weber*, p. xx.

11 Max Weber, *Economy and Society: An Outline of Interpretive Sociology* (ed. Guenther Roth and Claus Wittich; New York: Bedminster Press, 1968), p. 1121.

12 Eisenstadt, *Max Weber*, p. 54.

13 *Ibid.*

14 Holmberg legitimately criticizes Weber for 'a fundamental vagueness in defining the nature of routinization, as is manifest in his inability to decide when the process begins and what the leader's role is', *Paul and Power*, p. 163. For his full critique see pp. 163–5.

15 Eisenstadt, *Max Weber*, pp. 55–7.

16 Eisenstadt, *Max Weber*, p. 57.

17 Eisenstadt, *Max Weber*, pp. 60–61.

18 Holmberg, *Paul and Power*, p. 140.

19 E.g. Norman Cohn, *The Pursuit of the Millennium* (London: Paladin, 1970); Bryan Wilson, *The Noble Savages: The Primitive Origins of Charisma and its Contemporary Survival* (Berkeley: University of California Press, 1975); and more recently, Margaret M. Poloma, *The Assemblies of God at the Crossroads: Charisma and Institutional Dilemmas* (Knoxville: University of Tennessee Press, 1989).

20 Many have adopted this line and we shall explore its implications for Colossians later in the chapter. Theologically the most important

work is by Ernst Käsemann, 'Ministry and Community in the New Testament', in *Essays on New Testament Themes*, and 'Paul and Early Catholicism' in *New Testament Questions for Today* (London: SCM, 1969). See also James D.G. Dunn, *Unity and Diversity in the New Testament: An Inquiry into the Character of Earliest Christianity* (Philadelphia: Westminster Press and London: SCM, 1977). Sociologically, see John Gager, *Kingdom and Community: The Social World of Early Christianity* (Englewood Cliffs: Prentice–Hall, 1975); Bruce J. Malina, *The Social World of Jesus and the Gospels* (London: Routledge, 1996); and Sanders, *Charisma*. The key work combining both disciplines is MacDonald, *Pauline Churches*.

21 Berger and Luckmann, *Social Construction of Reality*, pp. 70–71.

22 Berger and Luckmann, *Social Construction of Reality*, p. 71.

23 Berger and Luckmann, *Social Construction of Reality*, p. 72, write 'Institutionalization occurs whenever there is a reciprocal typification of habitualized actions by types of actors. Put differently, any such typification is an institution.'

24 Berger and Luckmann, *Social Construction of Reality*, p. 72.

25 Berger and Luckmann, *Social Construction of Reality*, pp. 73–7.

26 Berger and Luckmann, *Social Construction of Reality*, p. 77.

27 Berger and Luckmann, *Social Construction of Reality*, p. 77.

28 Berger and Luckmann, *Social Construction of Reality*, p. 78.

29 T.F. O'Dea, 'Five Dilemmas in the Institutionalization of Religion', *JSSR* 1 (1961): pp. 30–39.

30 T.F. O'Dea, *Sociology of Religion* (Englewood Cliffs: Prentice–Hall, 1966), p. 91.

31 O'Dea, *Sociology of Religion*, p. 92.

32 O'Dea, *Sociology of Religion*, p. 92.

33 Keith Roberts, *Religion in Sociological Perspective* (Belmont: Wadsworth, 1990), pp. 160–62.

34 Roberts, *Religion*, p. 160.

35 See, further, Roberts, *Religion*, pp. 162–4.

36 Roberts, *Religion*, p. 163.

37 Holmberg, *Paul and Power*, p. 162.

38 Holmberg, *Paul and Power*, p. 165.

39 Holmberg, *Paul and Power*, p. 170.

40 Holmberg, *Paul and Power*, pp. 176, 172.

41 Holmberg, Paul and Power, pp. 177–9.

42 Blasi, *Making Charisma*.

[43] Holmberg, *Paul and Power*, p. 177.

[44] Holmberg, *Paul and Power*, p. 177.

[45] Holmberg, *Paul and Power*, p. 177.

[46] Holmberg, *Paul and Power*, pp. 177–8.

[47] Holmberg, *Paul and Power*, 179.

[48] See Holmberg, *Paul and Power*, pp. 180–83.

[49] Holmberg, *Paul and Power*, p. 182.

[50] Holmberg, *Paul and Power*, p. 184.

[51] Holmberg, *Paul and Power*, pp. 185–8.

[52] Holmberg, *Paul and Power*, p. 185.

[53] Holmberg, *Paul and Power*, p. 186.

[54] Holmberg, *Paul and Power*, p. 187.

[55] Holmberg, *Paul and Power*, p. 188.

[56] Holmberg, *Paul and Power*, p. 190.

[57] Holmberg, *Paul and Power*, p. 192.

[58] MacDonald, *Pauline Churches*, p. 23.

[59] 2 Thessalonians only rates two mentions in the context of the deutero-Pauline letters, MacDonald, *Pauline Churches*, pp. 100–01, although she is unsure of its date.

[60] MacDonald, *Pauline Churches*, p. 84. The rest of this paragraph is dependent on pp. 32–45.

[61] Bryan Wilson identified seven types of sect, distinguished by their attitude to evil in the wider world: namely, conversionist (saved out of but still in the world), introversionist (withdrawal from the world), gnostic or manipulationist (reinterpretation of evil), adventist (re-creation from outside), reformist (re-creation through human and political reform), thaumaturgical (salvation by miracle), utopian (creation of heaven on earth). See B. Wilson, *Magic and the Millennium* (London: Heinemann, 1973).

[62] MacDonald has derived the concept of love-patriarchy from Theissen, *Social Setting*, p. 164, in which he claims the early church softened the hard edge of ancient patriarchy and social stratification by mixing it with love. The position is disputed by S. Scott Bartchy, 'Undermining Ancient Patriarchy: The Apostle Paul's Vision of a Society of Siblings', *BTB* 29 (1999), who finds it not radical enough.

[63] See MacDonald, *Pauline Churches*, pp. 46–61.

[64] MacDonald, *Pauline Churches*, p. 62. The topic of ritual is explored on pp. 61–71.

[65] MacDonald, *Pauline Churches*, p. 65.

66 MacDonald, *Pauline Churches*, p. 64.

67 See MacDonald, *Pauline Churches*, pp. 72–83.

68 MacDonald, *Pauline Churches*, p. 83.

69 MacDonald, *Pauline Churches*, pp. 86–122.

70 MacDonald, *Pauline Churches*, p. 121.

71 MacDonald, *Pauline Churches*, pp. 123–38.

72 MacDonald, *Pauline Churches*, p. 130.

73 MacDonald, *Pauline Churches*, pp. 139–46.

74 MacDonald, *Pauline Churches*, pp. 147–56.

75 MacDonald, *Pauline Churches*, p. 156.

76 MacDonald, *Pauline Churches*, p. 164.

77 See MacDonald, *Pauline Churches*, pp. 160–202.

78 See further below. The sect-church dichotomy was introduced by Ernst Troeltsch in his *The Social Teaching of the Christian Church*, vol. 1 (trans. Olive Wyon; London: George Allen & Unwin, 1931), pp. 331–43.

79 MacDonald, *Pauline Churches*, p. 166, admits Tit. 3:3–8 is an exception to this.

80 MacDonald, *Pauline Churches*, p. 201.

81 MacDonald, *Pauline Churches*, p. 202, citing Bultmann.

82 MacDonald, *Pauline Churches*, p. 220.

83 The topic is examined in MacDonald, *Pauline Churches*, pp. 221–4.

84 Review of Margaret MacDonald's *Pauline Churches* by Luke T. Johnson, *JAAR* 58 (1990), p. 719.

85 Derek Tidball, *Ministry by the Book: New Testament Patterns for Pastoral Leadership* (Nottingham: Apollos and Downers Grove: IVP, 2009), pp. 157–60.

86 L.T. Johnson, 'Review', p. 718.

87 Review of Margaret MacDonald's *Pauline Churches* by E. Elizabeth Johnson, *Interpretation* 45 (1991), p. 91.

88 MacDonald, *Colossians*, p. 3.

89 MacDonald, *Colossians*, p. 69.

90 MacDonald, *Colossians*, p. 43.

91 MacDonald, *Colossians*, p. 39.

92 MacDonald, *Colossians*, p. 40.

93 MacDonald, *Colossians*, p. 90.

94 MacDonald, *Colossians*, pp. 6–9.

95 MacDonald, *Colossians*, p. 31.

96 Troeltsch, *Social Teaching*, p. 331.

97 Troeltsch, *Social Teaching*, p. 329.

98 See, for example, Philip F. Esler, *Community and Gospel in Luke-Acts: The Social and Political Motivations of Lucan Theology*, SNTS Monograph, 57 (Cambridge: CUP, 1987).

99 MacDonald, *Pauline Churches*, p. 99, comments in the light of this that it is still appropriate to speak of the Colossian community as a conversionist sect.

100 See Neyrey, *Paul in Other Words*, pp. 75–101.

101 Neyrey, *Paul in Other Words*, p. 125.

102 MacDonald, *Colossians*, p. 54.

103 For example, she mentions that 1:12–14 'recall baptism [and] may in fact constitute a doxology that was once part of a baptism liturgy', *Colossians*, p. 56. And see comments on the use of the word 'image' in 1:15 as connecting with the renewal of the image of God in humans 'in the description of baptism in 3:10', MacDonald, *Colossians*, p. 58.

104 MacDonald, *Colossians*, p.106.

105 MacDonald, *Colossians*, p. 107.

106 Victor Turner, *The Ritual Process* (Chicago: Aldine, 1969). His work develops that of Arnold Van Gennep, *The Rites of Passage* (1908, Chicago: University of Chicago Press, 1960). See MacDonald, *Colossians*, p. 125.

107 MacDonald, *Colossians*, p. 107.

108 MacDonald, *Colossians*, p. 132.

109 According to Turner, as cited by MacDonald, *Colossians*, p. 107, the liminal stage often involves some forms of humiliation and the 'stripping of the signs and insignia of preliminal status'. This was captured in early Christian baptism as candidates stripped off their clothes and reclothed themselves after baptism, language which is reflected in Col. 3:9–10,12–14.

110 Her statement, 'In Col. 2:8–15 Paul argues that baptism alone is what transforms the individual creating identity in Christ. Psalms and hymns celebrate that identity and teaching brings it to maturity (Col. 3:16–17), but the new life shared by believers ultimately depends on baptism' (MacDonald, *Colossians*, p. 108) certainly overemphasizes the place of baptism.

111 MacDonald, *Colossians*, pp. 142–4.

112 E.g. MacDonald, *Colossians*, pp. 67, 68, 108, 143.

113 In this she is drawing on the work of Wayne Meeks, 'In One Body: The Unity of Humankind in Colossians', in *God's Christ and His*

People: Studies in Honour of Nils Alstrop Dahl FS (ed. Wayne Meeks and
Jacob Jervell; Oslo: Uniiversitetsforlaget, 1977), pp. 209–21. On the
sociological significance of the body generally, see Neyrey, *Paul in
Other Words*, pp. 102–46.

[114] MacDonald, *Colossians*, pp. 67, 69.

[115] There is no need to assume that the opponents were advocating
circumcision. Traditional use of this image and their ascetic attitude alone is sufficient to explain why Paul speaks of circumcision
here.

[116] On the complexities of interpretation, see Dunn, *Colossians and
Philemon*, pp.153–8. Here, particularly, p. 157.

[117] Moo, *Colossians and Philemon*, p. 199. Some interpret Christ as 'divest-
ing himself' of 'rulers and authorities' in Col. 2:15 as opposed to 'dis-
arming them'. If this interpretation is adopted, though there are good
grounds against it, it could indicate a further aspect of the 'stripping
off' implicit in the circumcision image. See discussion in Moo,
Colossians and Philemon, pp. 212–13.

[118] MacDonald, *Pauline Churches*, p. 98. See also Meeks, 'In One Body', p.
212.

[119] MacDonald, *Colossians*, p. 131.

[120] MacDonald, *Colossians*, p. 166.

[121] MacDonald, *Colossians*, p. 166.

[122] Cf. 1 Pet. 3:1.

[123] MacDonald, *Colossians*, p. 168.

[124] For a discussion of this in relation to a contemporary movement, see
Bernice Martin, 'The Pentecostal Gender Paradox: A Cautionary Tale
for the Sociology of Religion', in *The Blackwell Companion to Sociology
of Religion* (ed. Richard K. Fenn; Oxford: Blackwell, 2003), pp. 53–66.

7 – Household: Its Significance for Ethics, Mission and Organization

[1] On the history and variations see D.C. Verner, *The Household of God:
The Social World of the Pastoral Epistles*, SBLDS, 71 (Chico: Scholars
Press, 1983), pp. 27–81. Verner argues that by the time of the Pastoral
Letters, social changes had minimized differences between Roman,
Greek and even Jewish households, p. 80.

[2] Meeks, *First Urban Christians*, p. 75.

3 Halvor Moxnes, 'What is a Family? Problems in Constructing Early Christian Families', in *Constructing Early Christian Families: Family as Social Reality and Metaphor* (ed. Halvor Moxnes; London: Routledge, 1997), p. 17.

4 David M. Scholer, ed., *Social Distinctives of the Christians in the First Century: Pivotal Essays by E.A. Judge* (Peabody: Hendrickson, 2008), p. 24.

5 Verner, *Household of God*, p. 79.

6 The power of religion to generate social solidarity in this way was the central thesis of Emile Durkheim's classic *Elementary Forms of Religious Life*.

7 Meeks, *First Urban Christians*, pp. 75–6.

8 On the importance of Filson's article, see Gehring, *House Church*, pp. 1–5. Gehring continues his work by outlining the course of the scholarly discussion from Filson to the present, pp. 5–27.

9 Floyd V. Filson, 'The Significance of the Early House Churches', *JBL* 58 (1939): p. 110.

10 Meeks, *First Urban Christians*, p. 76.

11 J. Murphy-O'Connor, *St Paul's Corinth: Text and Archaeology* (Wilmington: Michael Glazer, 1983), p. 158; Dunn, *Colossians and Philemon*, p. 285.

12 Gehring, *House Church*, p. 258.

13 Gehring, *House Church*, p. 27.

14 Verner, *Household of God*, p. 81. Note this concern in 1 Tim. 2:2 where Christians are encouraged to pray 'for kings and all who are in high positions, so that we may lead a quiet and peaceable life'.

15 Elizabeth Schüssler Fiorenza, *In Memory of Her: A Feminist Reconstruction of Christian Origins* (London: SCM, 1983), p. 253. Later examples are found in Eph. 5:21 – 6:9; 1 Pet. 2:18 – 3:7.

16 A good survey of the debate is found in Witherington, *Letters of Philemon*, pp. 183–97.

17 See discussion in Balch, 'Household Codes', pp. 25 and 35. Stoic guidance listed duties that were addressed to individuals rather than, as in Aristotle and Colossians, classes of people arranged in pairs. Furthermore, the Stoic philosophy advocated self-sufficiency rather than mutual subordination, as here.

18 Dunn, *Colossians and Philemon*, p. 243; and Osiek and Balch, *Families*, pp. 118–19, both of which refer to Aristotle's *Politica I* 1253b. 1–14, as do others.

[19] Balch, 'Household Codes,' p. 39; and Andrew T. Lincoln, 'The Household Code and Wisdom Mode of Colossians,' *JSNT* 74 (1999): pp. 93–112, esp. pp. 100–01.

[20] On Paul's use of tradition, see Cannon, *Use of Traditional Materials*.

[21] Dunn, *Colossians and Philemon*, pp. 243–4.

[22] Cannon, *Use of Traditional Materials*, pp. 125–8.

[23] Gehring, *House Church*, p. 258.

[24] Crouch, *Origin and Intention*, pp. 120–27.

[25] Balch, 'Household Codes', p. 29.

[26] The first two points of objection are found in MacDonald, *Colossians*, p. 163.

[27] Schüssler Fiorenza, *In Memory*, p. 251.

[28] Gehring, *House Church*, p. 230.

[29] Schüssler Fiorenza, *In Memory*, pp. 208–9.

[30] See discussion in F.F. Bruce, *Commentary on Galatians*, NIGTC (Exeter: Paternoster, 1982), pp. 187–91. Bruce applies the removal of the distinctions to church leadership. Referring to the possibility that Onesimus became Bishop of Ephesus, Bruce argues that restriction on slaves and women becoming leaders in the church had been removed but adds this qualification: 'In other spheres, indeed, the distinctions which ceased to be relevant in church fellowship might continue to be observed' (p. 190). See also James D.G. Dunn, *The Epistle to the Galatians*, BNTC (London: A&C Black, 1993), pp. 205–8.

[31] Gehring, *House Church*, p. 233.

[32] Dunn, *Colossians and Philemon*, p. 247.

[33] Lincoln, 'Letter to the Colossians', p. 655.

[34] E.A. Judge, 'The Social Patterns of the Christian Groups in the First Century', in *Social Distinctives* (ed. D.M. Scholer), p. 43. Judge makes the comment of 1 Cor. 7:20–24 but it equally applies here.

[35] Theissen, *Social Setting*, p. 164. The concept of 'love-patriarchy' was originally developed in relation to 1 Cor. 11:17–34 but was immediately applied by Theissen to Col. 3:18 – 4:1 as representing the ethos of the NT social ethic.

[36] Balch, 'Household Codes', p. 33. See also p. 47.

[37] Lincoln, 'Letter to the Colossians', p. 655.

[38] Lincoln, 'Letter to the Colossians', p.656. Lincoln points out that *teknon* (child) highlights their relationship rather than their age and may refer to children who were old enough to have a faith of their own rather than to small children.

[39] Gehring, *House Church*, p. 239.

[40] Balch, 'Household Codes', pp. 33–4.

[41] Gehring, *House Church*, p. 236.

[42] E.A. Judge, 'The Impact of Paul's Gospel on Ancient Society' in *The Gospel to the Nations: Perspectives on Paul's Ministry* (ed. P. Bolt and M. Thompson; Downers Grove: IVP and Leicester: Apollos, 2000), pp. 297–308.

[43] E.A. Judge, 'St Paul as a Radical Critic of Society' in *Social Distinctives* ed. D.M. Scholer), p. 115. The whole of this carefully argued and finely researched historical article is worth reading. It demonstrates how radical Paul was but not in any straightforward way.

[44] Abraham J. Malherbe, *Paul and the Thessalonians* (Philadelphia: Fortress Press, 1987), p. 11. For a contra position see Ronald F. Hock, *The Social Context of Paul's Ministry* (Philadelphia: Fortress Press, 1980), p. 29, who assumes Paul would have stayed in inns, at least during his shorter stays.

[45] Malherbe, *Social Aspects*, p. 66.

[46] Hock, *Social Context*, p. 30.

[47] Hock, *Social Context*, pp. 37–42.

[48] Schüssler Fiorenza, *In Memory*, p. 177.

[49] See further, Karl Olave Sandes, 'Equality Within Patriarchal Structures', in Moxnes, *Early Christian Families*, pp. 151–56.

[50] Meeks, *First Urban Christians*, p. 77.

[51] Meeks, *First Urban Christians*, p. 77.

[52] Meeks, *First Urban Christians*, pp. 30–31.

[53] Meeks, *First Urban Christians*, p. 76.

[54] On other significant forms of association see Meeks, *First Urban Christians*, pp. 77–84; and Judge, 'Social Pattern', pp. 27–34.

[55] Osiek and Balch, *Families*, pp. 40–41.

[56] Meeks, *First Urban Christians*, p. 79; Malina, *New Testament World*, p. 215; and Schüssler Fiorenza, *In Memory*, p. 180.

[57] E.g. 1 Cor. 16:15–16.

[58] See discussion on pp. 23–24.

[59] On the radical nature of this change see Andrew D. Clarke, *Serve the Community of the Church: Christians as Leaders and Ministers* (Grand Rapids: Eerdmans, 2000).

[60] K.O. Sandnes, quoted by Clarke, *Serve the Community*, p. 204. The position adopted in this paragraph owes much to Clarke's work. He deals with Philemon on pp. 202–07 but is more concerned with Paul's approach to persuading Philemon to take Onesimus back than with

Philemon's role in the church as such. The word 'equality' is perhaps not ideal since a family is not an egalitarian group but the gospel, and its eschatological focus as demonstrated in Col. 4:1, certainly had a levelling effect and undermined rigid conventional hierarchies. On the supposed egalitarianism, see Elliot, 'Jesus Movement'.

61 *Contra* Meeks, *First Urban Christians*, p. 219, n. 80.

62 Eph. 4:11–12; see also 1 Cor. 12:27–31.

63 MacDonald, *Colossians*, p. 188.

64 Details may be found in Osiek and Balch, *Families*, pp. 27–8 and further evidence from elsewhere in Schüssler Fiorenza, *In Memory*, pp. 176–82.

65 Schüssler Fiorenza, *In Memory*, p. 176.

66 On the textual evidence that the female form *Nympha*, rather than the male *Nymphas* is correct, see MacDonald, *Colossians*, p. 183 and O'Brien, *Colossians, Philemon*, p. 260.

67 MacDonald, *Colossians*, p. 188.

68 Robert Banks, *Paul's Idea of Community* (Exeter: Paternoster, 1980), pp. 127.

8 – Culture: Values and Arrangements

1 See earlier discussions on p.3 and p. 56. Key publications of this group are listed in Chapter 1, note 10, p. 173.

2 Horrell, *Social-Scientific Approaches*, pp. 12–15.

3 Colossians is mentioned in the writings of the various Social Context Group members but the focus of their attention has often been on the gospels or the authentic letters of Paul, especially 1 Corinthians, which stimulates a good deal of sociological interest.

4 Richard L. Rohrbaugh, 'Honor: Core Value in the Biblical World' in *Understanding the Social World* (ed. D. Neufeld and R.E. DeMaris), p. 109.

5 An extensive introduction to the subject is found in 'Honor and Shame: Pivotal Values in the First-Century Mediterranean World', pp. 27–57 in Malina, *New Testament World*. (For a complimentary and wider perspective see David A. deSilva, *Honor, Patronage, Kinship and Purity: Unlocking New Testament Culture* (Downers Grove: IVP, 2000), pp. 22–93.

6 MacDonald, *Colossians*, p. 76.

7 MacDonald, *Colossians*, p. 76. The concept is most explicit in 2 Cor. 11:2, where Paul applies it to himself.

8 DeSilva, *Honor, Patronage*, p. 74.

9 MacDonald, *Colossians*, p. 33.

10 Trainor, *Epaphras*, p. 95.

11 MacDonald, *Colossians*, p. 40.

12 See pp. 131–34.

13 I owe this to DeSilva, *Honor, Patronage*, p. 95. Pages 95–156 give an excellent overview of historical data and its relevance for the New Testament, especially to the concept of grace. Other introductions are found in: John Elliott, 'Patronage and Clientage' in *Social Sciences* (ed. R. Rohrbaugh), pp. 144–56; Bruce J. Malina, 'Patron and Client: The Analogy behind the Synoptic Theology', *Forum* 4 (1988), pp. 2–32; and Eric Stewart, 'Social Stratification and Patronage in Ancient Mediterranean Societies,' in *Understanding the Social World* (ed. Neufeld and DeMaris), pp. 156–77.

14 Richard Saller, *Personal Patronage under the Early Empire* (Cambridge: CUP, 1982), p. 1, as cited by Alicia Batten, 'God in the Letter of James: Patron or Benefactor?' in *Social World* (ed. Neyrey and Stewart), p. 50. Batten distinguished between patronage and benefaction on the basis that patrons were powerful and in a position to exploit their clients whereas benefactors lacked self-interest, p. 51.

15 Batten, 'God in the Letter of James', p. 50; and DeSilva, *Honor, Patronage*, p. 99.

16 DeSilva, *Honor, Patronage*, pp. 113–16.

17 See Halvor Moxnes, 'Parent-Client Relations and the New Community in Luke-Acts', in *The Social World of Luke-Acts: Models for Interpretation* (ed. Jerome H. Neyrey; Peabody: Hendrickson, 1991), pp. 248–9.

18 E.g. Alicia Batten, 'Brokerage: Jesus as Social Entrepreneur', in *Understanding the Social World* (ed. Neufeld and DeMaris), pp. 167–77; Bruce J. Malina and Richard L. Rohrbaugh, *Social-Science Commentary on the Synoptic Gospels* (Minneapolis: Fortress, 1992); and Moxnes, 'Parent-Client Relations', *Social World of Luke-Acts* (ed. Neyrey), pp. 241–68.

19 J.K. Chow, *Patronage in Corinth: A Study of Social Networks in Corinth* JNTSSup 75 (Sheffield: JSOT Press, 1992); and Bruce Winter, *Seek the Welfare of the City: Early Christians as Benefactors and Citizens* (Grand Rapids and Carlisle: Eerdmans and Paternoster, 1994).

20 Batten, 'God in the Letter of James'.

21 deSilva, *Honor, Patronage*, pp. 126–7.

22 The only reference to the Holy Spirit is in Col. 1:8 but that reference may suggest the Spirit is the one who provides the love which members of the church have for one another.

23 Bruce Winter, *After Paul Left Corinth: The Influence of Secular Ethics and Social Change* (Grand Rapids: Eerdmans, 2001), pp. 203–5.

24 Winter, *After Paul Left Corinth*, p. 203.

25 MacDonald, *Colossians*, pp. 44–5.

26 MacDonald, *Colossians*, pp. 142 and 151.

27 The best introduction is found in Neyrey, *Paul in Other Words*, pp. 102–46, on which this paragraph is based.

28 Mary Douglas, *Purity and Danger: An Analysis of Concept of Pollution and Taboo* (London: Routledge, 1966) and *Natural Symbols*.

29 1 Cor. 12:23.

30 For a review see Neyrey, *Paul in Other Words*, pp. 128–44.

31 1 Cor. 5:5; 6:12–20; 7:1–4; 9:24–7; 11:4–12; 12:12–27; 14:13–25; 15:35–57.

32 Some viewed it traditionally also as a microcosm of the universe, which is significant for the way it is used in *Colossians*. Dale B. Martin, *The Corinthian Body* (New Haven: Yale UP, 1995) p. 16.

33 Paul uses *sarx* here instead of the more natural *soma*. He may be responding to those who held a docetic view of Christ that belittled Christ's humanity, so O'Brien, *Colossians, Philemon*, p. 68, or, more likely, to distinguish it from his use of *soma* in 1:18, so Dunn, *Colossians and Philemon*, p.108.

34 On 2:23, MacDonald, *Colossians*, p. 124, notes 'The conflict between the Paul of Colossians and his opponents has to do with rival understandings of the physical body. For Paul the body is no longer an obstacle to be overcome; it has been transformed to such an extent that believers have already been exalted (Col. 2:12–13; 3:1–4)'.

35 Meeks, 'In One Body', pp. 209–221, argues that Colossians explores the reconciliation theme in the present-day church through the baptism motif.

36 Ephesians develops the same perspective, but our concern here is with Colossians.

37 MacDonald, *Colossians*, p. 42.

38 See note 28 for references to Mary Douglas' seminal works in this area.

39 On the importance of the biblical theme from an anthropological viewpoint, see DeSilva, *Honor, Patronage*, pp. 241–315; Malina, *New*

Testament World, pp 161–97; Jerome H. Neyrey, 'Clean/Unclean. Pure/Polluted and Holy/Profane: The Idea and System of Purity', in *Social Sciences* (ed. Rohrbaugh), pp. 80–104; and Neyrey, *Paul in Other Words*, pp. 21–55.

40 Neyrey, *Paul in Other Words*, pp. 54–5.

41 The language is both sacrificial language, although Paul does not develop that idea in the context, and legal language referring to a person being formally arraigned in a court with the hope of their being declared irreproachable, Dunn, *Colossians and Philemon*, p. 109; and MacDonald, *Colossians*, p. 72.

42 MacDonald, *Pauline Churches*, p. 144.

43 Neyrey, *Paul in Other Words*, pp. 41–2.

44 See, further, Malina, *New Testament World*, p. 192.

45 For an introduction to this theme see Malina, *New Testament World*, pp. 81–107; and Jerome H. Neyrey and Richard L. Rohrbaugh, '"He Must Increase, I Must Decrease" (John 3:10): A Cultural and Social Interpretation', in *Social World* (ed. Neyrey and Stewart), pp. 237–51. Neyrey and Rohrbaugh admit that 'the notion of limited good was formulated by a modern scholar studying modern peasant societies' rather then being a notion which is explicitly found in the first-century world. Even so, they argue it helps to interpret a host of ancient writings, including the Bible, and produce evidence of the perception in a variety of ancient texts.

46 Neyrey and Rohrbaugh, 'He must increase', p. 237.

47 For examples of its application to various Scriptures, see Rohrbaugh, 'Pre-Industrial City', pp. 125–49; and Neyrey and Rohrbaugh, 'He Must Increase', *Social World* (ed. Neyrey and Stewart).

48 The position is reminiscent of Isa. 42:8, 'I am the LORD, that is my name; my glory I give to no other, nor my praise to idols.'

49 See O'Brien, Colossians, *Philemon*, pp. 257–9; and Moo, *Colossians*, p. 351.

50 W.T. Wilson, *Hope of Glory*, p. 81; and Howard Kee, *Christian Origins in Sociological Perspective* (London: SCM, 1980), pp. 129–33.

51 Esler, *New Testament Theology*, p. 176. Kee, *Christian Origins*, pp. 131–2, writes of there being 'an exact correspondence between his [Paul's] apostolic presence in the flesh and in his letters' citing 2 Cor. 10:10–11 as his authority.

52 Esler, *New Testament Theology*, p. 177.

53 See p. 78.

54 See p. 16.
55 The NT notes some exceptions to this general rule, such as when the Ethiopian eunuch was reading to himself in his chariot from Isa. 53 (Acts 7:27–31). Even here the most natural interpretation is that he was reading aloud rather than silently for Stephen to be able to engage him in conversation about it.
56 Lucretia B. Yaghjian, 'Ancient Reading', in *Social Sciences* (ed. Rohrbaugh), p. 207. Yaghjian provides a masterly survey of the literature in this increasingly complex area.
57 Paul Achtemeier, '*Omne verbum sonat*: The New Testament and the Oral Environment of Late Western Antiquity', *JBL* 109 (1990): p. 19.
58 Malina, 'Reading Theory', in *Social World* (ed. Neyrey), pp. 3–23.
59 Malina, 'Reading Theory', p. 15.
60 See Kee, *Christian Origins*, pp. 126–70.

9 – Concluding Comments

1 In some respects the idea of a 'social system' is an unsatisfactory one since it implies a mechanistic, even inflexible, view of the social world. Nonetheless it is convenient shorthand for a pattern of social relationships.
2 Peter Berger and Anton Zijderveld, *In Praise of Doubt: Having Convictions Without Becoming a Fanatic* (New York: HarperOne, 2009), p. 66.